Alden W

ARTIFICIAL INTELLIGENCE:

A Personal, Commonsense Journey

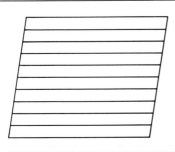

ARTIFICIAL INTELLIGENCE:
A Personal, Commonsense Journey

William R. Arnold
John S. Bowie

Prentice-Hall, Inc.
Englewood Cliffs, N.J. 07632

Library of Congress Cataloging in Publication Data

Arnold, William R. (William Robert)
  Artificial intelligence.

  Includes index.
  1. Artificial intelligence.   I. Bowie,
John S.   II. Title.
Q335.A76   1986   001.53′5   85-9472
ISBN 0-13-048877-1

Editorial/production supervison: Tracey Orbine
Cover design: Bruce Kenselaar
Manufacturing buyer: Gordon Osbourne
Cover photo courtesy of Hewlett-Packard

Printed in the United States of America

10   9   8   7   6   5   4   3   2   1

ISBN 0-13-048877-1 01

Prentice-Hall International (UK) Limited, *London*
Prentice-Hall of Australia Pty. Limited, *Sydney*
Prentice-Hall Canada Inc., *Toronto*
Prentice-Hall Hispanoamericana, S. A., *Mexico*
Prentice-Hall of India Private Limited, *New Delhi*
Prentice-Hall of Japan, Inc., *Tokyo*
Prentice-Hall of Southeast Asia Pte. Ltd., *Singapore*
Editora Prentice-Hall do Brasil, Ltda., *Rio de Janeiro*
Whitehall Books Limited, *Wellington, New Zealand*

This book is dedicated to the people who, like Theodore Roosevelt's men in the arena, will discover the nature and value of artificial intelligence and then use it day-by-day to make the world a better place in which to live. May they succeed!

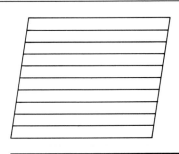

CONTENTS

3 DIGITAL DIALECTICS   46

4 LISP: A VEHICLE FOR ARTIFICIAL INTELLIGENCE   69

5 EXPERT SYSTEMS   82

6 TOOLS FOR INTELLIGENCE DESIGN   114

B EXISTING EXPERT SYSTEMS   202

C AI TRAINING AND INFORMATION   205

D PRINCIPLE INFLUENCES OF AI   211

INDEX   213

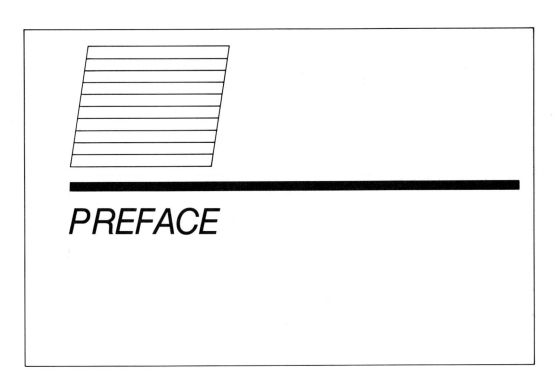

PREFACE

This book was written for people who want an introduction to artificial intelligence, otherwise known as AI. The book should appeal to professional people who want fundamental information about AI, university students who are not computer science majors, and citizens who are concerned about happenings in the current world scene.

The book discusses a range of topics at a down-to-earth level:

- Certain historical events are traced and certain themes are developed that provide a perspective for examining artificial intelligence (AI).
- Artificial intelligence is explained at a fundamental level so you can understand what it is and how it works. The various ''camps'' into which AI people have aligned themselves are discussed so you know how the experts relate, or do not relate, to each other. From this base, you could go on to explore AI according to your needs.
- A broad range of information about AI is included at an easy-to-read level. This information provides a base for examining AI and making intelligent decisions about how it can help you.
- Artificial intelligence is discussed in relation to languages such as Lisp and Prolog and in relation to applications such as expert systems. This gives you a picture of how AI fits into our emerging high-tech society.
- The above information is consolidated by discussing a variety of ways you can make use of AI in business, education, and other areas. Existing systems (hardware and software) are examined in relation to what they do. Evolving developments are also discussed. Overall, you get a clear picture of how to use AI.

- Types of AI systems are discussed, and for people who want an AI system, practical and general step-by-step procedures explain how to obtain and use an AI system.

The discussion is kept simple at all times so you can learn about AI without being a computer expert. Happy reading!

ACKNOWLEDGMENTS

We appreciate the support, encouragement, and criticism given to us by our wives, Janie and Judy. They are true examples of people who did not initially understand artificial intelligence, but who are extremely gifted in their areas and contribute much to the people of the world.

We also appreciate the permission and support given to us by Hewlett-Packard, a company that truly does let people shine by their lights.

Finally, we acknowledge the known and anonymous people who reviewed the book. Without their help, we could not have written adequately to the intended audience in an appropriate yet accurate manner.

ABOUT THE AUTHORS

William (Bill) Arnold received his Ph.D. in mathematics education from the University of Oregon in 1968. He then taught mathematics and mathematics education courses for several years at the University of Northern Colorado in Greeley, Colorado.

During this time, he conducted research designed to fathom relationships between the content of mathematics and how people could learn it most effectively in addition to regular teaching duties. This work led to publishing a mathematics methods textbook for teachers and numerous articles.

In 1977, when the microcomputer became readily available, Bill examined computer-aided instruction, looking for ways to use the microcomputer to help people become computer literate and then use the microcomputer to learn mathematics.

Bill left the University of Northern Colorado in 1979 to develop computer labs in Fort Collins, Colorado, and other places. He then wrote a user's guide for the COMPAQ portable computer before going to work for Hewlett-Packard in the Technical Documentation Department as a senior technical writer, where he has frequent opportunities to examine artificial intelligence and use the latest AI products.

John Bowie received his Bachelor of Arts degree in English and computer science from the University of Indiana in 1978. An honors student, John demonstrated his range of interests by researching the iconography of the American Civil War.

John returned to Indiana University in 1980 to study computer science and complete a bachelor's degree in biology, graduating in 1981. He then entered the University of Indiana, Graduate School of Computer Science to study operating systems and computability theory.

In 1982, John moved to Fort Collins, Colorado, to work for Hewlett-Packard in the Quality Assurance Department of the Engineering Systems Division. Later, he transferred to the Technical Documentation Department, where he now works as a senior technical writer. Among other things, John was recognized within Hewlett-Packard as an innovative writer and won an award for his users' guides.

Besides studying Lisp at the University of Indiana, John has numerous opportunities at Hewlett-Packard to investigate AI and use the latest AI products.

Both authors look forward to simplifying and demystifying the apparently complex field of artificial intelligence and making it understandable to lay people.

William R. Arnold
John S. Bowie

ARTIFICIAL INTELLIGENCE:

*A Personal,
Commonsense Journey*

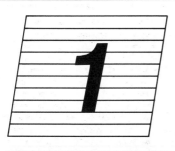

THE ROAD TO ARTIFICIAL INTELLIGENCE

A SETTING

Do you have anything in common with this person? Leslie had an excellent job, but like many people in today's society, there were times when Leslie had too many responsibilities, too many problems to solve, and too many people to deal with. Still, most of the time Leslie was happy, intellectually alive, and able to cope with the world.

Leslie began reading about a thing called AI. At parties, lunch breaks, or dinners people talked about expert systems, robotics, and fifth-generation computers. It all sounded interesting, perhaps a little space-agey. If you are like Leslie, a bright person who has heard about AI, but knows little, read on. The next several paragraphs mention assorted things and give you an initial impression about how and why AI was invented, what it can do, and where it is headed. Subsequent chapters discuss particular aspects of AI.

AI refers to Artificial Intelligence. AI is available today as a new tool for solving problems because a few intellectuals combined modern technology, computer science, and concepts about reasoning from several disciplines. Intellectuals spent years developing the disciplines; the technology was developed in a few years, after inventors had spent many years developing an adequate knowledge and machine base.

You might be witnessing a milestone event. The Romans effected immense change in the known world, but the rate of change was slow; no individual got to see much of the whole picture. The slaves who rowed boats around the Mediterranean Sea probably did not appreciate the scope of what the Roman Empire was doing. On the other hand, AI could effect drastic change in your world at a very rapid rate. The next two or three decades should be interesting. You might witness unparalleled change, or you might witness a return to simpler ways of doing things. Mathematicians, philosophers, and logicians have attempted to formalize and automate reasoning processes for at least 3000 years. The pioneers made rapid progress. Euclidean geometry, still the basis for most people's knowledge of geometry, was invented about 2400 years ago. Formal algebra is at least 800 years old, depending on your point of view. Through the years, intellectuals developed rather specific systems of reasoning, but they sought a universal system of reasoning as if it were the Holy Grail of intellectual achievement.

By 1600, many intellectuals believed that universal systems could be developed. For example, in 1677, G. W. Leibnitz advanced the idea that a calculus of reasoning was feasible. He also said that a calculus of reasoning could be applied to all inquiry: grammar, mathematics, physiology, theology, politics, philosophy, and discovery in general. In this context, calculus does not refer to the subject in mathematics that some people love to hate. Instead, calculus refers to a method of analysis.

Leibnitz suggested that a calculus of reasoning was feasible, but it took intellectuals about 200 more years to convince themselves that a universal formal logic could work in mathematics, the queen of sciences. Most of them had concluded that formal logic would never work in politics. Soon, however, mathematicians such as Russell, Whitehead, and Hardy showed that an across-the-board type of formal logic could not work even in mathematics. For example, the parallel postulate in Euclidean geometry fell apart in Lobachevski's system of geometry.

Facing this obstacle, mathematicians stopped trying to develop a universal system of mathematics and focused on smaller systems in which practitioners do not encounter exceptions as long as they stay inside accepted definitions, axioms, and assumptions. The development of rather limited but carefully defined systems became the basis for advancing mathematics. Intellectuals in some other areas continued to search for a universal formal system of logics.

By 1940, A.M. Turing, A. Church, K. Godel, S.C. Kleene, and others showed that developing a universal calculus of reasoning was not feasible. They also showed that their conclusion related to humans and to machines, but they left the door ajar for continued research by suggesting that some machines could use some human reasoning processes in a limited context. In particular, Turing and Church provided a link between the formalization of reasoning and the computation done by machines by extending the concept of computation to include symbol processing! In addition, Turing invented a simple, universal, and nonnumerical model of computation and indicated how machines that did computation could perform intelligently. This advancement in thinking made the prospect of using AI viable, and that prospect was soon realized when AI became a branch of computer science. Under the umbrella of computer science, intellectuals created powerful computer languages, operating systems, tools, and environments to help them advance AI in several areas.

This is a brief look at AI via the development of formal reasoning. Our point, in discussing the long-standing preoccupation of intellectuals with reasoning and showing how that preoccupation led to AI, is that AI may have arrived only recently on the world scene, but it had a long development period. That is, AI is emerging now, but it had a long history whether it was called AI or not. Like making a good soup, the ingredients had to simmer for a long time before the final condiments could be added.

To people who are discovering AI, knowing that it did not just appear on the world scene like a bolt of lightning is important. People who market AI products often use a bandwagon approach. They overwhelm you with jargon, fancy graphics, superlatives, and suggestions that an AI system can fulfill all your computer needs. The claims are not correct. Actually, as you will see, the AI systems appearing on the market are mostly commercialized versions of systems that experts have used to conduct research. Most of them are about 5 to 15 years old in the minds of intellectuals, but they are brand new and very exciting to professional people. If you think of an AI system as a significant development in the long study of machines, languages, and reasoning, you will be better equipped to attend conferences, read articles, and converse with people.

Throughout this book, most areas of AI are discussed in several contexts. We often use nontypical vehicles to trace events in the development of AI. We do this to give you a broad look at AI. For example, the road that led to the invention of an AI system is discussed in relation to the development of counting devices and to how people struggled to obtain a better life for two reasons: (1) an AI system is a machine, not a logical construct; and (2) people want AI systems to solve problems in an information era when many people feel that problems cannot be solved by conventional methods.

Notice that we have used the terms AI and AI system and that we used them in about the same context. There are distinctions, but they often get lost in the process of talking about something else. An AI system is a computer system that lets you solve certain types of problems. Artificial intelligence is an area, a discipline, in which people study relationships between how humans behave intelligently and how machines can emulate intelligent human behavior. Lately, many people think of AI as a branch of computer science. The distinctions are probably not very important in the long run although they do account for differences between when AI began and when AI systems were invented.

Three guidelines were used consistently throughout the writing of this book:

- Information is presented in several contexts. The major concepts are developed sequentially and the contexts are varied so that you'll get an overall picture of AI.

- We presented information from an "other" point of view, not from an expert's point of view. We did this because most information about AI has been disseminated by experts in AI. Originally, when AI was in the laboratory, this was natural. But AI is no longer the exclusive domain of researchers who ply their trade in secluded laboratories. AI has gone public; we present a lay person's view of it.

- We do not just describe AI. We often become emotional, because AI does not exist exclusively in a cognitive domain. There is an affective side of AI. People have feelings about AI and about what it will do. The intellectuals who created AI have strong feelings about what is happening to it and how people are handling it. We talked about this, often in relation to unusual examples, attitudes, or orientations.

We hope that reading this book does three things for you: You'll become better informed about AI; you'll become motivated to learn much more about AI; and you'll develop an optimistic, but cautious, attitude toward the use of AI to solve problems.

A REASON FOR INVENTING AI

The construction of the road to AI began when people decided not to exist like animals and decided, instead, to organize societies, invent tools, and communicate via symbolic languages. At first the road to AI was probably just an imagined path. Looking at the stars, wondering about paradise, or dreaming about fulfillment, people apparently imagined that life could be better if they could devise the means and methods. This supposition is suggested by the fact that people have sought a better way of life throughout recorded history. In whatever status people find themselves, they are driven to make it possible for themselves and their offspring to exist on a higher plane. Without this urge, people would not have AI or any of the things that make AI viable today.

It has not mattered through the ages that people often had no clear definition of what constituted a better life. A better life, whatever it might be, was always a drive, a process, and a goal more than a physical entity that a person could hold. Thus, a goal of finding a comfortable cave, once attained, was replaced by the goal of finding a comfortable cave with running water. The goal of inventing a better spear, once attained, was replaced by the goal of inventing a device to throw the spear. Whatever people did through the ages, they always wanted better tools, better living conditions, and a higher plane of existence.

People sought to live on a higher plane in several dimensions. Intellectually, they struggled to invent better means of reasoning. We discussed this earlier. Physically, people invented more and better tools and machines. We'll develop this theme throughout the book. Emotionally and spiritually, people attempted to define the meaning of living and the morals, ethics, values and belief systems that would enable all people to achieve personal and group fulfillment. We'll touch on this often.

In seeking a better way of life, people invented tools. Later, people invented machines. But people did not just invent tools and machines. They were fascinated by them. For example, ancient warriors were obsessed by a desire to obtain the "right" sword. With a sword that felt like a true extension of his arm, a warrior thought he could defeat an army. We mention these things to make this point: People have been driven through the ages to do new and exciting things, to make things better, and to achieve ultimate goals. People focused part of that drive on creating ever more intelligent machines. The need to invent machines, exercised for thousands of years, led people to invent today's AI computer systems.

People are fascinated by machines that have human attributes. It was this drive, as much as any other factor, that kept people on the road to AI. In reading the history of computing machines, we have become convinced that people were destined to invent AI.

Today, the field of AI is about 45 years old. The road that leads beyond the mere invention of AI is beginning to look like a freeway. Some people say the 45 years is really

25 years; it depends on your definition and whom you talk to. On one hand, some people view artificial intelligence as an extension of the general area of logic. In this context, it would be hard to determine just when AI began. We found some references to artificial intelligence that date back 200 years. Many people believe that AI began with Turing's development of symbolic computation. On the other hand, some people view artificial intelligence as a branch of computer science. In this context, AI is about 25 to 35 years old.

We talk about the road to AI because people have not arrived at AI. Perhaps they never will. AI has been invented. Applications are available, mostly as implementations of expert systems that were vehicles for much fundamental research and development of AI during the past 10 years. Today, people from varied walks of life are looking at AI, but like so many aspects of human life, it appears that today's marvel will be replaced by tomorrow's ultramarvel. It is amazing how often the word *ultra* is used today. Ultrafast processors, ultrafast communications, and ultramodern computing devices are so commonplace today that they often don't seem very "ultra."

This replacement process may never end, as people continue to pursue paradise. Today, as AI emerges, there is already discussion of the fifth-generation movement currently underway in Japan. Besides the Japanese effort to create more intelligent computers, hints of things to come appear in the popular and technical media. Throughout the industrial world, intellectuals are tucked away in laboratories inventing new supergenerations of computers and the software to run them.

As you read, take time to think about AI and how it might affect you personally. From our point of view, it is just as important for you to develop an attitude about AI and get an overall feel for it as it is for you to acquire information about AI.

SOME OFTEN-ASKED QUESTIONS

What is AI, anyway? How did it start? How long has it been around? Does anyone really need AI? Do you need AI? Can real people understand it, or is AI just for geniuses who work in labs? What are the facts about AI? Can AI be used now for practical things, or is it necessary to await development of more technology? What's the fifth-generation stuff that's in the news? What is an expert system? How much does an AI system cost? Will AI robots replace people in every job?

Read on to find answers to these and other questions. Here are a few scenarios to focus your attention.

The Last Minute Crisis Scenario

Envision yourself as a top-level manager. You've had a hectic day. It's getting late. Picking up the phone to return calls, you are interrupted by a distressed foreman who says "We have big trouble, boss. The number 36 Well in Alaska just blew and caught on fire. We're losing millions. What should we do?"

Top-level managers must often make decisions quickly in crisis situations. It's easy to panic and make illogical or improper decisions when you have no quick access to appropriate information. Managers need AI.

The Data Sifting Scenario

You are a pro football coach. It's draft day. Each coach eagerly awaits an opportunity to draft the best available players. Scouts have fed information into computers for months, presumably so you and your assistants can select the best players. But drafting a player is a dynamic process. Coaches who draft ahead of you often do not draft according to predictions. You cringe because your top two choices have been taken. You must adjust, but how can you assimilate the information about remaining players in a few critical minutes? You need AI.

The Critical Process Scenario

A critically mutilated patient is wheeled into an operating room. A team of world-famous surgeons is ready to operate. Each surgeon on the team helped diagnose the situation and conceptualize an operation that would correct the patient's injuries.

The operation begins. Gradually, the surgeons discover hidden problems. They regroup and try to remember all the world's knowledge related to similar operations. A new plan is formulated, but certain details are overlooked. The patient's condition worsens, but the surgeons recall essential details just in time to save the patient.

Does this scenario really happen? Could surgeons have benefited from access to all the world's knowledge about similar operations? Could they have used AI, or is it not possible for a computer to emulate the Captain Kirk type of intuition that actually saved the patient's life?

The Complexity of Information Scenario

A group of farm experts meet to fathom recent cuts in crop productivity. They attempt to formulate a plan for dealing with the myriad variables that affect crop production: soil type, available moisture, pesticide applications, seed selection, crop selection, rotation, and such. The list of variables is staggering. The information about the rules for dealing with each variable is even more staggering. Finally, one expert says, "There's just no way to get a handle on all this information. We'll just have to stick with what we already do and hope for luck." They need AI.

These scenarios illustrate the nature of human problems and imply ways that AI could be used.

Given these scenarios, you may suppose that AI deals with these things:

- Existing knowledge is the base for AI. You store the knowledge and access it according to how it works.

- AI is used when you're in trouble and must make critical decisions quickly, but need time to think and assimilate information.
- AI uses information to help you make decisions; maybe it even makes the decisions for you.
- If you use AI, the system could get out of hand and use the knowledge for evil purposes.

If the scenarios gave you these impressions, you are beginning to understand AI, but some of the impressions just mentioned are not correct.

Let's look more closely at artificial intelligence and determine its real nature. We'll sort myths from facts and discover what you can do with AI.

To begin our journey into the world of AI, we'll trace how people invented better ways to collect and organize data (numbers or labels). We'll see how people used the data to create information which, in turn, was used to help them make better decisions. By tracing this progress, we can learn the ancestry, so to speak, of AI. From this, we should be able to define AI and see how it might help us today.

THE INITIAL PATH TO AI

A thighbone of an antelope, carbon dated to 30,000 B.C., contains tallies like those kids use to keep track of who has how much of what things. This thighbone suggests that people probably always had a need to gather data and use the information it could generate. A tribal chief may have used tallies to keep track of which hunters contributed the most antelope to the tribe's larder. Perhaps the tallies were analyzed to see who was least productive. Then the loser had to entice the mastodons to stampede over a cliff.

The tally system was primitive, but it was a giant mental leap forward. It separated people from animals because making tallies on an object was an abstract, not concrete, method of numbering. Without knowing it, people had invented the concept of mapping, a one-to-one correspondence between things or events and marks on a bone. Today, students in mathematics know how professors can make a mapping into a very abstract concept.

Perhaps the tallies were the first data collected by people. In any event, there was room for improvement. After all, thighbones are hard to come by. You have to catch an antelope first. Thus people continued to invent new, but not always better, tallying or counting devices.

The abacus is, perhaps, the best tallying (counting) device ever invented. An abacus is a frame that contains parallel wires. Each wire contains beads which are used to tally amounts. The Chinese, Greeks, and Romans, among other civilizations, used the abacus extensively. It is still used by many people.

To operate an abacus, you slide beads along wires to indicate an amount (a number). Any of the digits from 0 to 9 can be represented on a single wire. Besides repre-

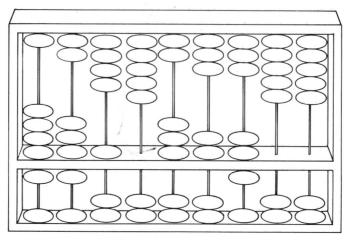

Figure 1.1 An abacus.

senting a number, the beads on a given wire have a certain place value in the decimal number system. Starting on the right and proceeding to the left, the beads show ones, then tens, then hundreds, and so on. Operations such as addition and subtraction are performed by sliding the beads according to definite rules.

The major limitation in using an abacus was that no permanent data could be collected. It was, and is, a device used for immediate calculation. A person gets answers, but there is no way to store them. Figure 1.1 shows an abacus. At this point along the road to AI, people had created four great ideas: (1) numbering or tallying amounts; (2) arithmetic operations that are performed on numbers (amounts); (3) the decimal number system; and (4) a set of abstract symbols called digits which could be used to represent numbers. People had elevated themselves far above animals with regard to looking at the world and formulating goal-oriented behavior. It had taken people at least 30,000 years to get this far in their development. The year was about 1,000 A.D.

THE MIDDLE PART OF THE ROAD TO AI

Time marched on, but people stopped inventing better information-processing machines for about 600 years while they were going through the Dark Ages. Then, due in part to the Renaissance, a Scotsman named John Napier invented Napier's bones in the 1600s.

Napier's bones consisted of ten sticks on which digits (0, 1, 2, 3, 4, 5, 6, 7, 8, and 9) were marked according to a multiplication pattern. A person could arrange the sticks according to rules and get answers to multiplication or division problems.

The bones worked very well once a person learned to arrange and interpret them. Again, however, the bones were a device that had to be physically manipulated to do calculations. It was not easy to do large calculations because it was difficult to interpret the arrangement of the bones. Again, data storage was not available. There had to be

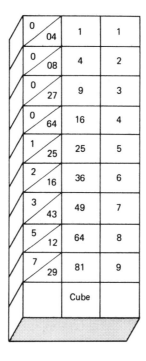

0 / 04	1	1
0 / 08	4	2
0 / 27	9	3
0 / 64	16	4
1 / 25	25	5
2 / 16	36	6
3 / 43	49	7
5 / 12	64	8
7 / 29	81	9
	Cube	

Figure 1.2 Napier's bones.

better ways to make intelligent computing devices. Figure 1.2 shows a set of Napier's Bones.

People continued to invent counting machines, but other people busied themselves with inventing paper, pencils, and printing presses. It does not matter that the original pencil was a finger or a stylus. The important thing was that people envisioned how to collect data and create information without using physical devices; they invented *calculation algorithms*.

Essentially, a calculation algorithm is a procedure used to do a pencil-and-paper calculation. Given any two numbers (data), you calculate an answer (information) by using a certain procedure for writing the numbers and calculations. The table shows two algorithms for multiplying whole numbers.

TWO MULTIPLICATION ALGORITHMS

Traditional algorithm	Modern math algorithm
4	
36	36
× 7	× 7
252	42
	210
	252

Calculation algorithms were well received by people. The algorithms made it easy to organize numbers (data), do calculations quickly (create information), and use the information immediately to solve problems. It was easy to use the algorithms. A person did not have to be a mathematician. Another plus was that both data (numbers) and the information (calculated answers) could be stored in a ledger.

The invention of algorithms for numerical calculation was a milestone event along the road to AI. An algorithm is a memorized procedure which people can use to solve a problem. Admittedly, the problems in computation are very simple, but the simplicity is unimportant. It's the concept that is important. A computation algorithm let anyone, not just a mathematician, perform operations on assorted numbers.

This capability (i.e., that everyone could do computation) was revolutionary. Computation was no longer the exclusive domain of expert mathematicians. This meant that clerks and accountants could keep track of payrolls, production schedules, and profits. Accumulated written records could be shown to investors. It was possible to have a white-collar class of people. Industry and business could flourish. Good grief, the people could create an Industrial Revolution—and they did! The obstacles to having such a revolution had been cleared away by people whose inventive minds created the necessary intellectual basis for engineering machines, organizations, logistics, and such.

Notice the pattern in how people traveled the road to AI. Not having original ideas is a major obstacle to progress. But societies create a continuous minority that is never satisfied with the status quo. Such people seek out their kind and use existing knowledge as a basis for study that invents new ideas. When a new concept is invented, it is added to the knowledge and then used in new studies.

To illustrate the creation and use of original ideas, examine this sequence:

- People collected things and wanted to know how many they had, so they invented tallies, marks for things.
- People used tallies and then invented digits, the symbols 1, 2, 3, . . . , 9, which represent amounts.
- People used digits and then invented number systems that had a set of digits, the concept of zero as a place holder, the concept of place value, one or more operations defined on a set of numbers, and a scheme for writing numbers.
- People used number systems. To deal with calculations within a number system, people invented algorithms.
- People used algorithms and then invented heuristics.

The last term in the list, *heuristics,* deserves special attention. An heuristic is a trick, rule of thumb, or strategy people can use to solve a problem. A particular heuristic may not work, but it can guide problem solving so a person can obtain a solution; better yet, it can lead people to invent more effective heuristics. People invented heuristics when they got to a point where there were so many algorithms they needed ways to know when to use which algorithm. Later, as you will see, heuristics became a fundamental concept in AI.

Z. P. Dienes, a mathematician who studied cognition with Jerome Bruner at the

Harvard Institute for Cognitive Studies, gave an interesting name to the process in which people use existing knowledge to create new knowledge, and then use the new knowledge to create newer knowledge: predicating and subjecting. *Predicating* is the process of inventing new concepts. *Subjecting* is the process of accommodating new ideas, thus expanding the existing knowledge base. People do not necessarily predicate and then subject. Predicating and subjecting is a total process that goes on in the mind in assorted ways, depending on how a particular person thinks.

Some people in every generation are driven to predicate and subject. It was this drive, exercised for thousands of years, that fueled people along the road to AI. At times, however, people hit upon an idea that became fundamental. The masses assimilated the concept and incorporated it into their value systems. Then they resisted all attempts to change the concept. Let's look at this for the particular case of computation.

Learning how to use computation algorithms became *the* basis for school math. A rigid sequence of acquiring skill in the use of calculation algorithms became the elementary school mathematics curriculum. First graders learn addition and subtraction facts and rudimentary elements of using the decimal system. Third graders learn the multiplication and division facts. Sixth graders learn to add, subtract, multiply, and divide the large whole numbers, complex fractions, and decimals.

Today, educators feel the wrath of the people whenever they advocate changing this basic curriculum. For example, the new math, which taught children algorithms different from those their parents knew, was soundly criticized. Educators quickly returned to traditional, highly valued ways of doing calculations despite evidence which showed that the new math, when taught via improved methods, enabled children to understand mathematics, solve word problems, and retain a high level of skill in computation.

Bear with us if this seems to be a diversion. Algorithms for computation were discussed because they are *the* basis for most manipulation of data today, some 1000 years after they were invented. The algorithms are highly valued. They are used by most people despite myriad shortcomings. Many more people use computation algorithms than use computers. Even in electronically automated offices, people ''back up'' nearly everything with pencil-and-paper calculations and information stored on standardized forms. It's axiomatic that the paperwork must be done before an action can occur.

We digressed to discuss computation algorithms and related issues because there are several mental constructs in this situation that relate to the invention of AI and to how or whether you use AI:

- The fact that most people use calculation algorithms and believe they should be taught to children illustrates how something can be highly valued in spite of its shortcomings. Calculation algorithms served people well for many years. Today, many people do not care that times have changed and that better means of processing information are available. As popular as microcomputers may be, most homes do not have them and many businesses do not use them.

- On the other hand, AI was invented and is now available; but it is not well known, not well understood, and not well accepted. It has not served people faithfully for years. Though times have changed and AI can probably be very beneficial, most people still believe that AI is best left in the closets of a few universities where brilliant, but weird, people play strategy games.

We believe this dichotomy is important because there is a high probability that people will become polarized over the issues created by using AI.

As you study AI, be acutely aware that what people do is partly rational, partly emotional, and partly due to how they perceive the world. Be aware that AI, like all its predecessors, was developed and nurtured by a few driven people who like to predicate and subject. It is vital for you to understand these phenomena and relationships; otherwise, you could get on the AI bandwagon and lack sufficient perspective to adequately evaluate your personal situation and attitude.

We digressed to discuss algorithms to let you see that there was a major branch in the road to AI during its middle period. Most people accepted the algorithms as the best route. However, the fact that most people did paper-and-pencil calculation, with attendant record keeping, had little effect on a minority who continued to invent counting and calculating machines. As we said, people who invented calculating machines were a driven few. Here are some highlights:

- Blaise Pascal, a Frenchman, invented a mechanical adding machine in 1642, when he was a teenager. Pascal's machine could also do subtraction. Later, a German named Gottfried Wilhelm von Leibnitz invented a machine that could multiply and divide. These machines were not popular, or very practical, but they illustrated the fascination people have with complex machines that perform human tasks.

- Joseph Marie Jacquard, a Frenchman, invented a weaving loom in the 1800s that punched holes in paper according to a pattern. He had no interest in computing, but later, people used his ideas while inventing a computer. This illustrates another dimension of how people search for new ideas—namely, any existing knowledge can be used.

- An Englishman, Charles Babbage, invented a difference machine in 1832. The machine was supposed to allow entry of numbers, calculate answers, and print the answers! The machine never worked, but Babbage is regarded as the father of modern computing.

- Politics works in strange ways. Our founding fathers decreed that a census be taken every 10 years. By 1870, the populations of the United States had grown to a point where the census could not be completed in 10 years. Herman Hollerith, an American, was hired to do the 1890 census. He invented an electronic counting and calculating machine that processed punched cards (remember the weaver who was not working on computers). The census was done in a few years! A merger joined Hollerith's company and another. The new company was called International Business Machines (IBM). Could our founding fathers foresee that they would create a computer giant? Probably not, but events often lead to unusual outcomes.

- World War II caused the development of new electronic technology. After the war, some intellectuals wanted to develop computers; most people wanted to get a job, a house, and a car. Earlier we discussed ways in which this dichotomy always existed, but it became pronounced after World War II. The Mark I computer was invented at Harvard University in 1944. IBM provided the initial resources. Another milestone computer, call ENIAC, was invented in 1946 at the Moore School of Electrical Engineering at the University of Pennsylvania. EDVAC was developed at the Aberdeen Proving Grounds. UNIVAC was invented by the Sperry-Rand Corporation. It was a flood tide.

History shows that circumstances converge in mysterious ways. In 1948, circumstances converged to create an intense focus on computing.

The United States shifted its attention from war to domestic development and applied its industrial might to building highways, supermarkets, tract housing, automobiles, television sets, and nuclear arms. These activities created enormous wealth. Some of that wealth was used to support intellectuals who invented transistors, integrated circuits, and other ever-smaller electronic gadgets. This driven minority had the tools, the time, and the resources to travel the last leg of the road to AI. Best of all, they were hidden away in think tanks and universities where no one bothered them. They were free to explore ideas and invent new ideas to an extent no people had ever experienced. They could do pure predicating and subjecting. So they did.

THE FINAL TRIP TO AI

After ENIAC, people invented new technology at an astounding rate. The modern computer, a term used for electronic computers (contrast with mechanical computers), went through four generations in 40 years!

Think about this for a few moments. Too often we do not take time to think about the marvelous happenings in our lives. Presumably, it took people thousands of years to invent spoken language and go from talking about numbers to making tallies on a bone. It took 30,000 years to go from tallies to computation. It took 1000 years to go from computing with pencil and paper to computing with computers. It took about 10 years to use computers to invent AI.

So far, we have focused on computing and on the invention of computing devices. We will return to this focus shortly when we describe the development of true computers.

We need to digress briefly to show you that the road to AI was not necessarily linear. There were branches from the main road that led to development of other areas. In some cases, branches from other areas, which had been invented and developed, merged with the main road. Be aware that AI was invented about 25 years ago. It had many precursors, and the people who invented it came from several disciplines. Besides computing, here are the major areas that provided the knowledge base for the development of AI:

- Mathematical logic was developed in the 1930s and 1940s. In this area, mathematicians took a fresh look at computation by examining ways to do computation with symbols, not with numbers. This was revolutionary! After all, how does one do computation with names, addresses, zip codes, sentences, and such? Mathematical logic provided the basics that enabled the inventors of AI to create advanced ways to process symbols.

- Psychologists examined macroscopic behavior. In this area of psychology, people examine behavior that does not require special instrumentation, as was the case with Pavlov's dog. Looking at macroscopic behavior, people examined many dimensions of thinking and behaving intelligently. In particular, people invented several models of thinking that were used by the inventors and developers of AI.

- Cybernetics is an area in which people study the control processes in electronic, mechanical, and biological systems. In particular, people examine the flow of information within a system and the schemas people use to control the flow of information within a system. A schema is an outline or representation of something.

- The predicate calculus provided a way of organizing thinking and a method of examining information that helped people envision ways to treat data in AI. Predicate calculus is a branch of mathematics in which primitives (undefined terms), assumptions, and axioms are used to prove propositions. From this basis, people invented several concepts that are used in AI (e.g., blind search algorithms, search spaces, heuristic algorithms, forward chaining, backward chaining, and means-ends analysis).

- Vision was examined in excruciating detail to determine how people identify things. For example, a human can recognize thousands of faces with apparently subconscious ease. No one is sure how a person recognizes a face, but such a task is still too complex for an AI system.

- The semantics, syntax, and lexicon of human languages provided a means of structuring programs in AI. This work occurs within the realm of natural languages, a term for human languages as contrasted with computer languages. The idea is to create a program that lets a computer analyze symbolic statements much as a human analyzes spoken statements. Again, this is complex, and most AI systems are not very capable.

Other areas provided a basis for inventing AI. The ones we mentioned illustrate how people used existing knowledge, but they were selective.

Getting back to computing, here are the four generations of computers developed since the late 1940s:

- The first-generation computers, in the 1940s, used vacuum tubes. They were huge, slow, and generated intense heat. A team of operators ran them. These people were called computer operators because they were the operating system for the computer. They were also the interface that let people interact with the computer.

- Second-generation computers, in the 1950s, used transistors. They were very large and required air-conditioned rooms, but they had an operating system of sorts.

Stacks of punched cards (remember them?) were submitted to the computer in a batch to run a job where certain inputs (data) were manipulated (turned into information). The information was output to a printer.

- Third-generation computers, roughly in the 1960s, used integrated circuits that were put on a piece of material without wires. They were similar to second-generation computers except that they incorporated advances made in languages, operating systems, and programs.

- Fourth-generation computers, the ones we use now, employ silicon chips. Some of these chips are microprocessors which have instruction sets that let them do many tasks. Other chips store data or contain assorted programs that perform routine internal tasks. Many languages, operating systems, programs, and peripherals are available. Today, small computers can have large memories and access data or information stored on disks.

The third-generation computers provided sufficient complexity and capability for people to invent AI, but the fourth-generation computers gave AI its current impetus. The fifth-generation computers, which are discussed later, might spark another revolution.

In any case, pencil-and-paper calculations, done via calculation algorithms, were efficient for many years despite the random manner in which people made mistakes. These methods are not efficient today. The mechanical calculating devices were never very effective, but they were the vehicle for inventing today's computers. Today, a fourth-generation computer can perform billions of calculations in the time required for an able accountant to balance a small ledger sheet. The fourth-generation computers have made artificial intelligence a viable alternative for processing information.

Notice that the road to AI was rocky. If you read more about it, you'll find that people endured the entire human condition. Some were killed for inventing calculating machines. Others were cast into prison. A few were so poor they literally starved while trying to invent better computing machines. These people persevered and gave us the modern mechanical calculator, the forerunner to the modern computer.

The people who developed true computers were not starved or killed; neither were they visible to the public—but they persevered. Finally other people who were not starved but who were driven by the same curiosity as their forebears completed the road by giving all people AI in the 1950s.

Several people did the work, but as in most areas, one person is called the father. Alan M. Turing, who invented ways to process nonnumerical symbols from the 1930s through the 1950s, is regarded by many people as the father of AI. Notice a dual relationship beginning to emerge: (1) the development of ways to process symbols, and (2) the development of computers that do the processing.

So people now have AI. Perhaps a few marketers would say the road is complete. Some might even say they have a final product that will solve all your problems. Do not be misled. AI is now a recognized entity, but it is not complete. Already, several divisions or areas of AI have been identified: gaming strategies, vision, natural languages, expert systems, and robotics. More are being identified.

The paths that could connect AI to the lives of most people have not yet been built. They are being constructed now, before your very eyes. Again, we suggest you take time to reflect on this. If you investigate AI further, be aware that you are examining a new area in which ideas are being exploited as they are developed. Marketing has reached a point in its development where the predicating and subjecting done by lab engineers is mixed with marketing nonexistent products. Be aware that AI systems are being sold that are not yet developed. Now that is marketing!

The inventors of AI are aware that AI is in its infancy, and many are afraid it will be exploited in a manner that could set back research for many years. Some are afraid that premature exploitation of AI systems will destroy the AI movement and plunge people back into times when tallies, mechanical calculators, and computation algorithms prevailed.

We do not know what will happen, but we want you to proceed cautiously. Take time to assess needs, examine alternatives, and think before you take the plunge and purchase a system. We are aware that people can perform mind-boggling feats with AI. We know that the urge to purchase a system and make it work can be powerful. We believe you can find useful applications of AI.

We also want you to be aware of the other side of the coin and remember that immature children can perform simple mental feats that the most complex AI systems cannot fathom.

At this point, let's examine AI, define it, and see how to use it.

A DEFINITION OF ARTIFICIAL INTELLIGENCE

By now you know that people took a long time to invent a computing machine with the power to emulate intelligent human behavior. But we have not yet offered a definition. This was deliberate, because we believe the means by which people invented AI are as important as having AI. We believe this because you live in the era that will exploit AI. You will become a part of the application and development, not the invention. We hope you become a positive part of that process, because we know that the exploitation will contain the same type of pitfalls as the invention.

Many people think AI (artificial intelligence) is false intelligence. After all, it's artificial. Other people think of artificial intelligence as fake intelligence. These people equate "artificial" with "not real" or "not true." This idea, however popular, is not correct.

What about the dictionary? Sorry. Artificial intelligence is not defined in most dictionaries, but definitions are included for artificial and intelligence:

Artificial: Made by man, rather than occurring in nature. Made in imitation of something natural.

Intelligence: The capacity to acquire and apply knowledge. The faculty of thought and reason. The work of gathering information.

If you put these definitions together, you have a working definition of artificial intelligence: man-made capacity to acquire and apply knowledge. Here is another definition, found in several textbooks:

> Artificial intelligence is a part of computer science, concerned with design of computer systems which exhibit human intelligence: understanding language, learning new information, reasoning, and solving problems.

Winston and Prendergast were editors in 1984 of a book entitled *The AI Business*. The book included this simple, but succinct, definition.

> The primary goal of AI is to make machines smarter. The secondary goals of AI are to understand what intelligence is (the Nobel laureate purpose) and to make machines more useful (the entrepreneurial purpose).

By the way, *The AI Business* describes the application of AI in several areas: expert systems, work and play, robotics, and today and tomorrow. The complete entry is:

> WINSTON, PATRICK H., AND KAREN A. PRENDERGAST. *The AI Business*, Cambridge MA: The MIT Press, 1984. ISBN 0-262-23117-4

The articles are readable and not highly technical.

As you read, you encounter other definitions. Study each definition you encounter, because a precise definition of AI has not yet been formulated. The definition is still evolving. As you read assorted definitions, notice how they imply that a computer uses knowledge and models in intelligent ways to solve significant problems, much as a human would use the same knowledge and models for the same purposes.

In AI, data is often something other than numbers. Nonnumerical data such as names, addresses, labels, acronyms, sentences, patterns, and theorems are primary data in AI. At a higher level of abstraction, data can be such things as objects, frames, methods, flavors, rules, and spaces. This type of symbolic data can have many names, depending often on who is examining the data. Using Lisp, a programmer might talk about ids, atoms, elements, structures, or lists. Using an application, a person in industry might talk about objects, rules, or spaces. Numbers are not emphasized in AI; symbols are emphasized.

AI focuses on knowledge engineering. This means that software for artificial intelligence does symbolic manipulation, nonnumerical calculation, and symbolic inference. At a fundamental level, this means the software works with words, sentences, word patterns, phrases within statements, and such. In AI, the term *knowledge* means an area of expertise. The expertise can be a domain of highly technical facts or a domain of heuristic functioning (e.g., knowing rules of practice, possessing judgment, or knowing rules of plausible reasoning). The term *engineering* means using knowledge to solve problems within an identifiable area (e.g., mining gold, cutting diamonds, building crystals, transplanting hearts, or adjudicating criminal trials). By the way, an excellent book about the type of problem solving mentioned above was written by George Polya and is called, simply, *How to Solve It*.

If you study AI for some time, you'll get to a level of abstraction in which you will encounter very sophisticated nonnumerical calculation, calculations or processes performed on symbols. Don't panic. It really is possible to collect symbolic data and then do complex searches, sorts, concatenations, unions, intersections, and such.

By the way, a concatenation is a type of addition done with symbols. For example, the symbols *My, Fair,* and *Lady,* when concatenated, could be written as *My + Fair + Lady* to become *MyFairLady*. Thus, given a set of symbols such as chess moves, imagine the combinations of concatenated moves you could create.

THE INVENTION OF ARTIFICIAL INTELLIGENCE

Recall the Mark I and ENIAC computers. They were two of the first true electronic computers. Ah, but what does it mean to be a true electronic computer?

A true electronic computer has these characteristics:

- The computer uses electricity in a digital manner (i.e., the electricity is in a high or low electrical state). These states are translated into digits (a 1 for a high state and a 0 for a low state). A fixed and designated series of 1s and 0s are used to represent characters such as 1, 2, 9, A, k, *, #, or @. The characters can be collected to form data in the form of numbers or symbols. Data such as 5, 23, 45.67, or 0.009 are *numbers*. Data such as DOG, File #23, Catch-22, and PLUS are *symbols*. Later, in the chapter about Lisp, you'll see that something like (LIST 'FORD 'CHEVY 'DODGE) can be a data object that contains a function named LIST and the symbols FORD, CHEVY, and DODGE, which are arguments for the function. You'll learn that the single quote (') has a special role in Lisp. If you get interested in the language called Lisp, the whole manner in which digital electronics is used to create data objects and structures in AI is exciting.
- Particular 1s or 0s can be stored in specific locations in a computer's memory to act as flags, which cause specific actions when the work being done by the computer is interrupted to check the status of a flag.
- A processor handles all tasks performed by the computer. The processor keeps track of which devices are doing what, sends messages to the right places, and updates the status of all devices as required.
- An arithmetic/control unit handles all processing of data, performs calculations, and interprets and directs execution of instructions.
- A computer allows input of data and can output data to a printer or other device.
- The computer provides data storage in memory or on a tape or disk.

The true modern computer system is not just the physical computing device. A computer system consists of hardware and software. Hardware is the physical devices, the computer, monitor, keyboard, disk drive, and printer. Software is the programs, the operating system, languages, tools, and applications.

The invention of AI was dependent on hardware to a considerable degree, but it was the development of software that enabled John McCarthy to invent AI in 1958. Let's see how this happened.

The first true computers had human operators. This means that a human, literally, operated the computer. Then, computers had physical operating systems. People punched holes in cards (remember them?), and submitted the cards to a card reader (a physical device). The cards were punched and sequenced so the computer could use them to receive operating instructions. Finally, computer experts invented software operating systems and languages. What a step this was! A program operated the computer and provided editors, programming languages, and other things so a person could interact with the computer. The time frame for this was the 1940s and 1950s.

Once operating systems and languages were available as software, computer experts went wild. Seemingly overnight, dozens of operating systems and programming languages were invented. Perhaps you have heard about PL/1, Algol, Snobol, Cobol, FORTRAN, or BASIC. You may not have heard about Jovial, ADA, Simula, or Euclid. Most of these were both an operating system and a programming language. Today you'll hear less about operating systems and languages and more about software environments.

Gradually, people developed programming languages that ran on top of operating systems developed by other people. The important point here is that computer experts, scattered throughout universities, corporations, and agencies, deluged people with languages for about 35 years.

Within this atmosphere, Alan Newell and Herbert Simon of Carnegie-Mellon University and Cliff Show of the Rand Corporation invented a computer language called IPL (Information Processing Language) that used data structures consisting of networks of symbols. IPL was used to prove theorems, among other things. Newell, Simon, and Show discussed IPL at a summer workshop held at Dartmouth University in 1956, a workshop generally regarded as the first workshop on artificial intelligence.

Given this stimulus, an obscure language called Lisp was invented by John McCarthy at the Massachusetts Institute of Technology (M.I.T.) in 1958. Lisp means *list processing*. It provided the base for development of artificial intelligence. You could think of the invention and development of Lisp as the last subjecting and predicating process in the long road that led to a point where AI could be invented. People had discussed artificial intelligence before this time, but they had not done much substantive work. The long road that led to the invention of AI suggested incredible potential, but between successes created by programs that appeared to do human reasoning and pie-in-the-sky speculation about machines that could control people, the advancement of AI suffered from a lack of tools. The invention of Lisp provided a tool. Thus, in one sense, Lisp was a product of the AI movement which further promoted the AI movement. Let's see how this happened.

McCarthy became interested in AI while he attended the IBM-sponsored Dartmouth Summer Research Project on Artificial Intelligence in 1956. The research project stimulated his thinking. Mostly, McCarthy worried about the lack of tangible means to develop

AI. Let's say that the project was a stimulus that elicited a concerted, directed attempt by McCarthy to solve some problems that blocked progress.

The initial development of Lisp was done with an IBM 704 computer that ran FORTRAN. Facing many problems, McCarthy worried about the extent of IBM's commitment to AI, the evolving capability of FORTRAN to handle lists (as contrasted with numbers), and the feasibility of inventing a new language.

McCarthy decided FORTRAN would not work. He invented Lisp instead because, to use AI to solve problems, it is necessary to represent information as lists instead of as numbers. As we mentioned earlier, it is necessary to work with symbols and perform assorted searches, sorts, and concatenations.

McCarthy had other problems. It is difficult to sit down and invent a language that can do work in AI without having a tangible focus for the invention. After all, Edison knew he wanted to invent a light bulb. He had a focus for inventing a new product. The need for a focus led McCarthy to Marvin Minsky.

Marvin Minsky, an M.I.T. assistant professor of mathematics, wanted a program that could prove theorems in plane geometry. McCarthy thought a list-processing language was suited to programming the rules for deducing theorems. IBM supplied the 704 computer. A geometry project was initiated and successfully completed. Then, as an assistant professor of communication sciences, McCarthy and Minsky started the M.I.T. Artificial Intelligence Project in 1958.

There was no written proposal. McCarthy and Minsky had one room, two programmers, one secretary, a keypunch person, and six undergraduate helpers. The implementation of Lisp began. It was completed in 1960.

After Lisp was implemented, McCarthy presented many papers. As had so often been the case for individuals who built milestones along the road to AI, people from the world at large did not beat a path to McCarthy's door. Instead, a few intellectuals who perceived the significance of Lisp took the original implementation and experimented with it. You'll see later that the experimentation was extensive, perhaps even excessive, but it provided the base for today's use of AI. Here are some very limited highlights.

- Marvin Minsky at M.I.T., with the help of several people, developed programs that prove theorems.
- Joel Moses at M.I.T. and Edward Feigenbaum at Stanford developed bases for expert systems. Moses created SIN, which became MACYSMA, an expert system that solves mathematical problems using symbolic processing methods. Feigenbaum developed DENDRAL, an expert system that infers molecular structures from mass spectrograms.
- M.I.T. developed the Lisp Machine, a complex computer system used for research.
- Xerox researched development of hardware and software that became bases for powerful AI systems.
- Several start-up companies appeared on the scene that produced AI hardware, software, or both.

This list is far from complete. You'll learn more later.

Now, about 35 years later, people are at a threshold in processing information where Lisp in general and AI in particular offers much potential benefit.

Will people respond and use AI to help them solve problems? Everything people need to get started is currently available. Better tools are being invented at a rapid rate. The future looks bright, but people will need to keep their use of AI in perspective.

From a humble beginning in 1958 to the present, much development has occurred. About $35 million was spent on AI computer systems in 1984; the projection for 1990 is $2 billion.

Wow! Who would ever think that making marks on the thighbone of an antelope could lead to the invention of AI? We doubt that people who were cast into prison for inventing mechanical calculating devices appreciated the contribution they were making to the eventual invention of AI. It did not matter. They were driven to do their work.

This type of drive is important because, having traced the road that led to the invention of AI, you are about to strike out and see what AI can do in the next 200 odd pages. We provided a little scenario in which we hope to shape your orientation to our description of AI. If you can't wait to get started, go to Chapter 2.

You have much to learn about AI. The learning curve can be very steep at times. Unfortunately, the extremely high level of abstraction of the work done in AI creates pitfalls which make it difficult to interpret what you read. For example, using applications of predicate calculus to build expert systems in which thousands of rules are used to solve problems in a deductive manner is very heady stuff. You can't get a book like this down to the level of writing directions for assembling a child's toy. Thus, this book contains some of the pitfalls we dislike. Here are the most troublesome ones.

- The field of artificial intelligence, only 35 years old, has already been divided into several categories. The pitfalls are that distinctions are nebulous, and many people do not use the categories in a consistent way. Common categories include:

  a. **Perception and Data Acquisition:** This includes visual and sound recognition. Sound recognition includes voice recognition, but is not limited to this. Beeps and other sounds can be important. Some elements of robotics come from this category.

  b. **Understanding and Communication:** This includes knowledge representation, written natural language (e.g., English, Spanish), spoken natural language, and language translation.

  c. **Learning and Induction:** This includes association, inference, reasoning, heuristics, and several other areas. Many elements of building expert systems come from this category.

  d. **Model Building and Problem Solving:** This includes goal analysis, alternative generation, search, selection, games, and several other areas. Actually, this is an immense category in every way you can imagine. Again, many elements of building expert systems come from this category.

  e. **Robotics:** This includes mobility, manipulation, and object recognition.

f. **AI Tools:** This includes computer languages, cognition models, automatic programming, database management, and decisions theory, among other areas. At a lower level of abstraction, software such as compilers, debuggers, editors, and formatters are thought of as tools.

g. **Applications:** This includes several distinct things. One is areas of endeavor, such as medicine, education, and law. Another is types of software such as turnkey expert systems and software used to build expert systems.

- People left assorted disciplines and went into AI. They brought major concepts from those disciplines and applied them to AI. The pitfall is that a particular concept may have several designations, or worse yet, many nuances, depending on the context in which the concept is used.

- There are many dialects of Lisp, the computer language used to do work in AI. There is also much software, such as Prolog, which functions partly as a computer language and partly as a software environment in which you can do AI work in a less direct manner than is required when you use Lisp. When you add the assortment of other software you can use to do work in AI, software such as compilers, editors, translators, emulators, debuggers, human interfaces, and turnkey applications, the whole problem of what is what can be staggering. The pitfall is that you can easily become totally confused when you read assorted materials, not to mention just reading this book.

- AI is being taken from the laboratory to the world at large. Thus, transitions and transformations occur very rapidly. Developments occur rapidly. The context in which you do this or that shifts rapidly. The pitfall is that you might understand something very well in one context and not be able to recognize it in another context.

Whoa! Enough! This is only Chapter 1. No more pitfalls! Sorry, we did not point out some of them to put you off. You are a valuable person whom we respect very much. Although we cannot interface personally, we respect your intelligence and ability.

We just want you to know that everything you read about AI can get fuzzy at times. Writers must put sentences down in a sequence. The sequence that writers use reflects their organization; it might not reflect your needs for information. You'll probably often wish, while reading this book, that we had said something two pages or two chapters earlier so you could understand what is going on. We tried to start from scratch, about 30,000 years ago, and take you into the future. We used a means of organization in which you build up information as you go along. Some terminology that appears to be fuzzy in one chapter will probably become less fuzzy as you move along.

We cannot say anything about how you will perceive what you read in other books and articles. To us, some were dreadful and difficult to understand. Others were delightful and told us exactly what we needed to know. At the risk of offending some readers, let us again say that this book is a straightforward introduction to AI. We do not believe it can appeal to experts in AI.

Experts can probably jump on us in every paragraph and say, ''That's not correct. You should have said this . . . '' The experts are justified in many cases. We took liberties at times because we felt that nonexperts might not have sufficient background.

Students, managers, executives, professionals, and other literate people should find that this book tells them about AI and tickles their curiosity, making them want to read other books and articles. We hope that we can induce you, gentle reader, to become an AI guru.

DISTILLING THE ESSENCE OF THOUGHT

In the last chapter we discussed the advances in computer technology that have brought the dream of artificial intelligence to the brink of reality. It appears that we now possess the hardware and software tools necessary to build intelligent systems. But high technology is only one requirement for the success of AI. Progress in the other essential area—perhaps the most important one—is unfolding with far greater uncertainty.

This last piece of the AI puzzle is by far the most elusive, and it has nothing to do with computers. Were it only as simple as packing more transistors on a silicon chip or designing a more powerful programming language, we could say with reasonable assurance that the age of AI is imminent—that the rapid pace of technological development will soon reach the necessary levels and the puzzle will be solved.

Instead, so uncertain is this last missing piece that there is serious doubt whether AI will come of age in our lifetimes, and some question whether it will ever happen at all. Researchers in the field fear that AI may have reached a plateau which, barring some ground-breaking discoveries, it may never rise above.

What is this missing component that threatens to stall the progress and possibly thwart the fruition of AI technology? The answer is found in the very definition of AI itself.

Artificial intelligence, after all, is a simulation of various aspects of *human* intelligence. Yet we cannot simply walk up to a terminal and command a computer to "act intelligent." Like any other program, we must give it painstakingly explicit instructions on how to behave. There can be no gaps in our logic, no holes in our understanding, no terms left undefined, no missing steps in our process.

The intelligence we load into our computers must come from us, and therein lies the challenge: *Before we can impart intelligence to machines, we must first understand the nature of our own.*

A MODEL OF THE MIND

What is intelligence? German psychologist William Stern called it "a general capacity of an individual consciously to adjust his thinking to new requirements: It is general mental adaptability to new problems and conditions." Alfred Binet, father of the modern intelligence test, likened intelligence to "comprehension, invention, direction and criticism," all of which, he felt, were elements of the more general quality of "judgment."

No matter how erudite these insights into the mind, we are left with only words—mere symptoms of intelligence, not the essence of it. Intelligence is not something that can be neatly captured in a carefully coined phrase. It is not something that can be dissected into its constituent parts, for even if we dismantled the brain neuron by neuron and examined every synaptic connection, we would be no closer to pinpointing the circuitry that composes ideas, or isolating the electrochemical reactions that make decisions, or tracing the creative currents that spawn new discoveries.

Intelligence is not a static condition of being or a particular juxtaposition of brain cells. Intelligence is a dynamic process. We must treat it accordingly if we have any hope of simulating it. And so we will not attempt to define intelligence, but instead to describe it: Intelligence is the continuous process of acquiring, sifting, sorting, and interpreting information.

Still more words, certainly, but perhaps there is something more tangible in this description, something we can get a handle on. We know what information is: It is the sum of all the facts, figures, data, and terms we have invented and collected to create our mental representations, or models, of the world. Acquiring information, then, is the process of gathering the world into ourselves through the senses. But not all input is relevant or important, so we sift the barrage of sensory input, keeping some of it and discarding the rest. The retained portion is then *sorted*—a term we use loosely to describe the process of imposing order upon random fragments of information. It is here that raw information is processed into knowledge as objects are classified, relationships are formed, and governing rules are established. Finally, stored knowledge is retrieved and interpreted to solve problems, make decisions, and assimilate new information.

Notice that three of the four stages in the simplified model in Figure 2.1 are involved with the building of a large base of knowledge. This is significant. Most psychologists and experts in AI agree that intelligent behavior, in humans and computers alike, is dependent more upon on the size and quality of the knowledge base than on the power of the reasoning scheme employed.

We already knew this, of course. When we set out to "become intelligent" in some new field or discipline, most of our conscious effort is spent learning everything we can

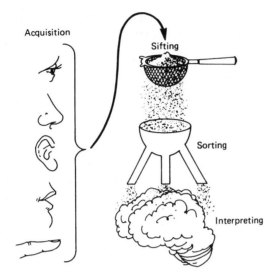

Acquisition

Sifting

Sorting

Interpreting

Figure 2.1 A simplified model of the mind.

about it. Once the existing body of knowledge is acquired, we seem to unconsciously know how to apply it.

The unconscious ease with which we interpret knowledge is what makes intelligence so difficult to simulate. While it's true that we have developed inference and decision-making tools, such as propositional logic and predicate calculus, these methods are weak and inflexible compared to the mysterious reasoning mechanisms of the human mind.

When we make a decision, we can usually explain why our proposed course of action is the best one. But it is not so easy to give a detailed accounting of *how* we reached our conclusion. Most decisions are reached with more than purely logical inference. They include excursions into the nebulous realms of the mind where emotion, creativity, and intuition are at work.

Inference chains facts together to get from point A, a statement of existing conditions, to point B, the hypothesis of goal conditions. But consider the decision-making process of a juror in a murder trial. He must weigh the evidence both pro and con, resolve contradictions in the testimony, make subjective assessments of the character and integrity of the witnesses, and evaluate and apply the relevant rules of law. Pure logical inference is clearly insufficient.

Yet the goals of AI must be to simulate all the intelligent machinery of the mind, for if we are to entrust even moderately complex judgments to computers, we must endow them with as many of our decision-making techniques as possible.

BUILDING A KNOWLEDGE BASE

Artificial intelligence leaves behind the comfortable algorithmic certainty of conventional computer programming. Instead of simply computing our answers, problems are now so complex that we must search for solutions as humans do. There are no guarantees that the search will yield an answer, or if it does, that the answer will be correct. But AI experts agree that the chances for success are greatly enhanced if the system contains considerable knowledge of the subject of inquiry. The first step in making an informed decision is to become informed.

Human beings possess knowledge in a great many areas, but are usually considered knowledgeable in only a few. During the last century, civilization has undergone a knowledge explosion, and it has become impractical, if not impossible, for an individual to gain expertise in every area of human endeavor. With very few exceptions, we are a species of specialists.

Intelligent computer systems must specialize also. Given the infrequent appearance of the Renaissance man throughout human history, it is unrealistic to try to design a ''Renaissance computer'' capable of expertise in several fields. Instead we must focus the system's intelligence on a single, carefully chosen, clearly delineated subject. This subject is usually known as the *domain of discourse* in the AI community.

Setting the Focus

The selection of a domain of discourse is dependent upon several factors. Foremost, of course, are the goals that have been established for the AI system.

First realize that no computer system to date has reached the level of omniscience that you see in the movies. Unless you have all the answers to the great mysteries of the universe and understand how you got them, no computer system you build will have them either.

With this in mind, what specific role should your computer play to benefit you most? Should it monitor and control a manufacturing process? Diagnose disease and prescribe treatment? Deduce molecular structures from mass spectogram data? Schedule the maneuvers of a spacecraft en route to the planets? All of these things are possible today.

Once goals for the system are established, they should be examined to see if they are realistic. Remembering that all knowledge in the system must come from human beings, we must make certain we have access to cooperative human beings who possess the knowledge we need. If adequate knowledge is not available, the goals of the system cannot be achieved.

Assuming that complete knowledge of the subject is available, we must decide on the depth of knowledge required. For example, if we were designing a system to troubleshoot automotive breakdowns, we could include knowledge down to the *system* level (e.g., electrical system, fuel system, brake system), or down to the *component* level (e.g., spark plugs, carburetor, master cylinder), or down to the *physical* level (e.g., the laws of electricity, thermodynamics, friction).

The depth of knowledge given to a system depends largely on the depth of the questions you will ask of it. There is no need to clutter the system with ''deep'' information if it is not required to solve the types of problems you will pose to the system. But if the nature of your inquiries is not well known, it's best to include as much knowledge as possible, as you never know to what level you must plunge to come up with a solution.

Another matter to consider is the time investment required to feed knowledge into the system. If the domain of discourse is broad or complex, hundreds of thousands of information fragments may be needed before the system can function at intelligent levels. Many times it is advisable to narrow the domain, at least initially, to get the system running and tested in a more reasonable time frame. Additional knowledge can always be added later.

Finally, there is the practical consideration of hardware limitations. If the proposed AI system requires an extensive knowledge foundation to operate, it may exceed the available memory and mass storage of the computer system. Most AI systems in operation today require several million bytes of memory.

In sum: Start small; expand later. As we will see in Chapter 4, AI development systems are designed around this premise and make modular, layered designs easy and natural to implement.

Gathering Knowledge

Once the domain of discourse has been sufficiently focused, the next step is to build up a core of knowledge about the chosen subject. In AI terminology, this is known as building a knowledge base.

When human beings set out to acquire knowledge in an unknown subject, they have several avenues open to them. They can gain knowledge directly through observation and draw inferences and conclusions from what they see. Alternatively, they can gain knowledge indirectly through some kind of tutor—either another person or a book, film, recording, or some other audio and/or visual medium. Finally, they can gain knowledge through discovery, combining old knowledge in new ways to develop new ideas and hypotheses.

The AI community would like to make these means of knowledge acquisition available to computers. While significant strides are being made, no model of human learning has been implemented with a level of performance that even approaches that of a human. Instead, most computers acquire knowledge through the passive means of programming, which loads knowledge directly into the computer's memory. Several obstacles prevent computers from using more active and independent methods of knowledge acquisition. Let's first look at the problems of learning by observation.

Obtaining knowledge through observation is being studied by a branch of AI known as *computer vision* or, more recently, *image understanding*. The goal of such systems is to computationally transform the image received from a video camera into a high-level description of the scene.

Researchers in image understanding have found that decoding a visual scene requires an enormous store of general knowledge of the world—information that human beings often call ''common knowledge.''

Before an object can be identified, the observer must have a mental image of the object stored away in his memory. The mental image was created by a previous encounter with the object. When an observed object matches one of these mental images, an identification is made.

Even when a large repository of world knowledge is present, other, more fundamental, problems arise. Before an object can be identified, it must first be recognized as an object. In other words, the first order of business in image understanding is to extract all objects that are present in the scene. While human beings take this talent for granted, the ability to separate a scene into its component objects does not come naturally to a computer. Object recognition, then, begins by finding all the ''edges'' in a scene and then deciding which edges define the boundaries of objects. Once the boundaries of an object are found, it can be pulled out of the scene, examined, and (perhaps) identified.

Object identification has its complications, too. Even if the observed object is known, several factors can alter its appearance, making identification difficult. Distance, for example, can change the apparent size of the object. The object's orientation with respect to the observer may present an unknown perspective of the object. And the direction and intensity of the light source can change the shading of the object, altering or eclipsing some of its features.

Because of these other factors, an observed object rarely matches exactly the corresponding mental image of the object. We cannot simply superimpose the observed image of the object over the mental image of the object and hope for a precise fit. Instead, matching is achieved by manipulating the observed object using our understanding of the effects of distance, shading, orientation, and so on, until the object is transformed into the mental image of the object.

Given these and other complications too numerous to mention here, it is not surprising that the most successful computer vision systems are found in industrial environments, where lighting and object orientation can be controlled and where the number of possible objects is small. Development of a successful general-purpose computer vision system is unlikely to happen for several years.

Given the state of computer vision, observational learning by computers is currently not a viable option. Learning by tutor and learning by discovery are still possibilities, however. We can dismiss learning by discovery rather quickly, for discovery requires creative thinking to generate new hypotheses, followed by an evalution of each hypothesis to see if it is consistent with known facts. While the ''generate-and-test'' principle can be implemented on a computer, it has been successful only in extremely well defined domains of discourse, such as mathematics and molecular chemistry. When the domain contains uncertainty and ambiguity (as most do), this method breaks down. We do not understand the creative processes of the brain well enough to emulate them. Nor can we provide a computer with enough ''common knowledge'' and ''common sense'' to judge whether a new hypothesis is valid or totally ridiculous.

The tutorial approach to learning, where computers gather knowledge by reading or listening, is making strides, but it runs against another of the great obstacles facing artificial intelligence today: natural language understanding.

Because most AI research is taking place in the United States, Great Britain, and other English-speaking countries, *natural* language usually refers to the *English* language, although technically it refers to any human language.

The goal of this branch of AI is to develop computers that can understand English, and thus can both receive and report information in a way that is ''natural'' for human beings (or at least for English-speaking human beings).

One of the most efficient ways for human beings to gather new information is to hear it or read it in their native language. Psychologists believe language is indigenous to our thought processes, which suggests that our mental representations of information may well contain words and phrases. At the very least, we use words as a convenient symbolic currency for the objects and ideas that we keep within our minds.

Since intelligent computers must communicate with people—both to receive information and to convey their results—having them speak our language would greatly enhance this relationship. People have been condescending to computers for decades, learning their digital dialects; now the movement is underway to make computers conform to our standards of communication.

But natural language, and English in particular, does not easily lend itself to computational dissection. Early efforts sought to process language by simple translation: Merely look up the words in a dictionary and analyze the sentence structure using the rules of grammar. These early attempts found there is much more to language than syntax and definitions—semantics and world knowledge are heavily involved.

For example, one early thrust in natural language processing was to use a computer to translate from one language into another. One experiment attempted to translate an English phrase into Russian and then back into English again. When given the phrase, "The spirit is willing but the flesh is weak," the computer performed the double translation and replied: "The wine is good but the meat is spoiled."

Missing in these early efforts was an understanding of context clues—the invisible inferences people draw from their "common knowledge" to make sense of sentences. Consider the following pair of sentences:

He struck the boy with the club.

He struck the boy with the red hair.

Structurally, these sentences are identical, yet their semantics are totally different. In the first, "with the club" describes the agent of the action, "struck." In the second, "with the red hair" describes a characteristic of the receiver of the action, the "boy."

There is nothing inherent in these sentences that tells us how to interpret them. Only our knowledge of the world—of what makes sense and what doesn't—guides our understanding. Thus far in their development, computers lack common sense and so are greatly disadvantaged when confronted with human conversation.

Natural language understanding has made considerable progress in the last decade, but much remains to be done. As with computer vision systems, a general-purpose natural language processor is far out on the horizon. However, systems have been designed that can converse quite well in English, provided the domain of discourse is restricted. Since AI systems are confined to a well-defined domain of discourse anyway, this does not present a significant handicap.

Even so, the effort and expertise required to build and test even a limited natural language processor is great. Thus the natural language interface is likely to be an add-on-later feature, rather than an initial system requirement.

Knowledge Engineering

Since we are not yet to the stage in AI development where we can command a computer to gather its own knowledge, we must gather the information for it, then load it into its memory. Given this, how is the transfer of knowledge from human being to computer to take place?

First we must find a person or group of people who individually or collectively have expert-level knowledge of our chosen domain of discourse. Then we must find a way to extract this knowledge from them. However, most people are taken aback when asked: "Tell me everything you know about . . . " It's difficult to state in an orderly fashion everything you know about a topic. It's difficult to know where to begin. And, in many cases, it's difficult to put into words exactly how judgments relating to the subject are made.

This need for someone skilled at extracting knowledge from people has given rise to the new profession called *knowledge engineering*. The knowledge engineer is an unusual cross between a talk-show host, a psychologist, an actor, and a computer scientist. Like a talk-show host, the knowledge engineer is adept at putting his subject at ease and is an expert interviewer. As a psychologist, he is sensitive to what his subject is saying between the lines, drawing him out, and encouraging him to be introspective. As an actor, he must feign utter ignorance about the topic under discussion, asking for clarification of every uncertain point. Finally, as a computer scientist, he must decide how this knowledge can best be represented in a computer, and how to emulate the thought processes of the subject using artificial intelligence programming techniques.

For the remainder of this chapter, we will follow the knowledge engineer's process of knowledge acquisition. In so doing, we will gain a better understanding of what constitutes knowledge, how it is gathered, and how the components of knowledge can be assembled to construct an increasingly powerful knowledge base.

In the following example, we will excerpt a fictional interview between an expert automobile mechanic and a knowledge engineer. The goal of this interview is to find out how the expert diagnoses and repairs engine problems. The domain of discourse is the world of engine parts and tools, and all the rules that describe how an engine works, how to troubleshoot it when it fails, and how to fix it, when the problem is found. Don't be concerned if you know nothing about car repair; our purpose is to discover how knowledge is built, not how to replace a fuel pump. (As a matter of fact, we strongly discourage you from using the following example to try to fix your car. The authors will not be held accountable for any damage that ensues or hours that are wasted.)

Objects, Attributes, and Classes

The interview between the knowledge engineer and the expert subject is a question-and-answer session. The knowledge engineer asks a question, and the expert answers it. The answer is likely to spawn a swarm of new questions, the answers to which will spawn still more questions, and so it goes until the domain of discourse is well defined.

The knowledge engineer's feigned naiveté may frustrate the expert, particularly in the initial stages of the interview where so many minuscule, but fundamental, details are clarified. The dialogue might begin like this:

KNOWLEDGE ENGINEER: What do you do first when troubleshooting an engine problem?

EXPERT: First I test the engine to determine which subsystem seems to be malfunctioning.

KNOWLEDGE ENGINEER: What is the ''engine'' exactly? What does it look like? And what are ''subsystems''? How many subsystems are there? What relationship do they have to the engine and to each other? Do the subsystems have any component parts? What do they look like? Where are they in relationship to one another? How do they work? Why . . .

A knowledge engineer would not overwhelm his subject like this, of course, but our point is clear. The initial, general question is cascading into a series of questions of increasing specificity. Also, *every* term the subject mentions is considered undefined. Even the term *engine,* which the knowledge engineer himself used, is tossed back to the expert for clarification.

There is good reason for this approach. The computer, which is to be the recipient of the expert's knowledge, has no prior experience or frame of reference with which to make sense of new terms. The words *engine* and *subsystem,* if typed at the keyboard, would return the error message: ''Undefined variable.'' The knowledge engineer plays the role of computer advocate, eliciting precise definitions from the expert in the computer's behalf, even though these same terms may be taken for granted by humans.

Thus an important step in knowledge acquisition is to precisely define all terms in order to establish a working vocabulary for the domain of discourse. The process entails attaching names to the physical objects (e.g., the actual engine) that populate the domain.

When human beings are introduced to a new object, they build a description of it in their minds and attach the name of the object to this description. For example, when we mentally decode the word *engine,* we call up a host of images, smells, sounds, ideas, and concepts that we associate with the object. The process works in reverse as well, taking a description of an unknown object, matching it against our mental data base of description patterns, and extracting the associated name (e.g., the word *engine*).

In AI terminology, the collection of characteristics associated with an object (name) are called the attributes of the object. The knowledge engineer and the expert could continue for days naming objects and defining them by giving their attributes. Eventually, however, two or more objects will be found that are so similar they deserve to have the same name. Suppose, for example, that the mechanic has a collection of 100 adjustable wrenches of various sizes that he uses to make repairs. It would be ludicrous to give each a completely different name, calling the first one ''adjustable wrench,'' the second one ''zorp,'' the third one ''zollup,'' . . . the hundredth one ''watu.'' Each of these objects differs by only one characteristic: size. Therefore, we create a class called ''adjustable wrench'' and include each of 100 wrenches as members of the class. To specify an individual wrench, say the ⅜-inch wrench, we simply specify it by its distinctive attribute: "Give me the adjustable wrench whose value for the attribute 'size' is ⅜-inch," or more simply, "Give me the ⅜-inch adjustable wrench."

Classification imposes a hierarchical order upon the world and prevents an unwieldly proliferation of terms. We could imagine the hierarchy shown in Figure 2.2, which illustrates various classes of objects; the circled entires show the path taken through the hierarchy to specify a particular object. Each level down in the hierarchy is more specific than the previous one. The dialogue between the knowledge engineer and the expert who built this hierarchy might proceed something like this:

EXPERT:	You take the tool and . . .
KNOWLEDGE ENGINEER:	Which tool?
EXPERT:	The wrench tool. You take it and . . .
KNOWLEDGE ENGINEER:	Which wrench tool?
EXPERT:	The *adjustable* wrench tool. Like I was saying . . .
KNOWLEDGE ENGINEER:	Which adjustable wrench tool?
EXPERT	The *English-calibrated* adjustable wrench tool!
KNOWLEDGE ENGINEER:	Which English-calibrated adjustable wrench tool?
EXPERT:	The *⅜-inch* English-calibrated adjustable wrench tool!!
KNOWLEDGE ENGINEER:	Thank you.

At last, the expert worked his way down through the subclasses until he specified a single object, not a group of objects.

As this example shows, subclasses are defined by the values of the attributes of the preceding class. Here's what we mean: The class "Tool" has an attribute called "Type." The possible values this attribute can assume are "Wrench," "Hammer," "Screwdriver," and so on. Each of these possible values defines a subclass of "Tool." The subclass "Wrench" is further subdivided into subclasses "Open-end," "Adjustable-end," and "Box-end," as defined by the attribute "End-type."

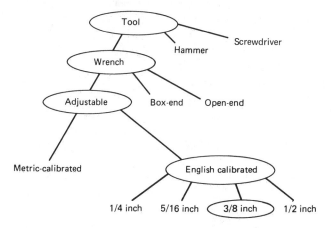

Figure 2.2 The tools hierarchy.

And so it goes, down through the hierarchy, until the sum of all attribute values specifies a subclass with only one member—that is, a single object.

One last observation about classes before we move on. Classes may have constant-value attributes: attributes that have only one possible value. For example, the class "Tool" may have a constant-value attribute called "Made of" that always has the value "Steel," meaning that tools are made of steel. Furthermore, this means that *all* subclasses of "Tool" are made of steel, right down to the ⅜-inch English-calibrated adjustable-end wrench tool.

Put another way, all subclasses beneath "Tool" inherit the value of the attribute "Made of," even though they do not explicitly contain this attribute. This avoids the repetition of constants down through the hierarchy.

Let's look at another example to make this clear. We could have a class called "Dogs," which includes the subclasses "Spaniels," Terriers," "Shepherds," "Collies," and so on. Since all dogs have four legs, we can give the class "Dogs" a constant-value attribute called "Number of legs," and assign it the value "Four." There is no need to give the subclass "Terriers" the attribute "Number of legs"—since all terriers are dogs, they automatically inherit four legs.

Thus, the complete set of attributes that describe a subclass consists of all local attributes plus those of its parent class. If both the subclass and its parent class contain the same attribute, the local value overrides the parent's value. If there existed a subclass of "Dogs" called "Hopalongs" that had only three legs, this subclass would also contain the attribute "Number of legs" with value "Three." The local value of "Three" overrides the parent's value of "Four," which is another way of saying that Hopalongs are an exception to the general rule that dogs have four legs.

Before we continue, let's pause to survey the extent of our knowledge thus far. To help visualize the current condition of the knowledge base, imagine the knowledge engineer as an artist. As the expert talks, the knowledge engineer creates a painting. The more information the expert provides, the more detailed and lifelike the painting becomes. At this point, he has progressed through the following stages:

As the expert mechanic mentions unfamiliar words, the knowledge engineer puts a blotch of paint on the canvas and labels it. A blotch is the best we can do at this stage, for the word has no meaning until the expert defines it. Part of the painting might look like Figure 2.3.

Next, the knowledge engineer asks the expert to define his terms. He does so by describing the objects in terms of their attributes. Now the painting begins to take shape, as objects are given form, color, texture, size, and so on. The painting now looks like Figure 2.4.

As the process continues and more objects are defined, classes begin to emerge. Often what was once thought to be a single object is revealed instead to be a group of objects. Subclasses are then created with additional attributes. The additional attributes make the subclass more specific than its parent. The introduction of classes rearranges the objects on the canvas, grouping them according to similarities. Connections between groups are also formed, establishing a hierarchical structure. The painting now looks like Figure 2.5.

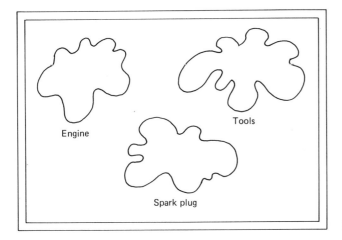

Figure 2.3 The "blotch world."

Notice that precise descriptions are possible only at the lowest (single object) level of the hierarchy, where the greatest amount of definition exists. In the preceding illustration, the knowledge engineer can say of objects in the class "Tool" only that they consist of a handle attached to some kind of appendage, so we show a generalized picture of a handle with a cloud surrounding the unknown appendage. Move down one level to the subclass "Wrench," and the knowledge engineer adds that the appendage is curved, making the objects in this class more precise and reducing the amount of cloudiness in the drawing. Note that the handle shown in this subclass was inherited from the parent class. And so it goes until all the relevant features are completely described, the class is narrowed to a single object, and the cloud is completely removed.

At this stage of knowledge development, the knowledge engineer has created what is usually called a *data base* or *information base* in computer science. Such a system can respond to requests like:

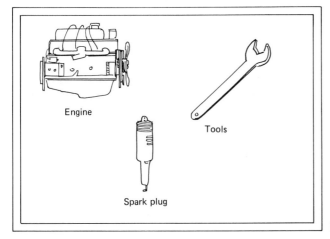

Figure 2.4 Objects and their attributes.

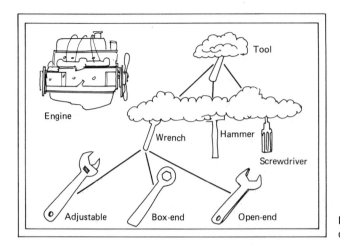

Figure 2.5 The hierarchy of object classes.

- Provide a list of all red tools that are less than two inches long.
- Tell me if there are more metric-calibrated tools than English-calibrated tools.

Certainly this is useful, but it hardly requires intelligence. Data base operations rarely involve more than a search for objects based on criteria described in the problem statement. This is a good foundation for an intelligent, knowledge-based system, but the knowledge engineer has a long way to go yet.

Relationships

A glance at the painting tells the knowledge engineer what is missing. All objects in the domain of discourse have been defined and sorted into neat little piles (classes). The result is a completely dismantled engine and a neatly organized toolbox. But the goal is to acquire knowledge of engine troubleshooting and repair. This requires an assembled engine.

Never having seen an engine, how do you build one given only a sorted pile of component parts? Ask the expert mechanic:

KNOWLEDGE ENGINEER: How do all these parts fit together?

EXPERT: Well, the exhaust manifold is connected to the cylinder head. The cylinder head goes on top of the cylinder block. The oil pan goes under the cylinder block. The distributor is mounted on the left side of the cylinder block. The high-voltage cables run between the distributor and the spark plugs. These cables carry electricity from the distributor to the spark plugs . . .

Gradually, all of the components are assembled and the engine takes form. Assembly takes place as relationships are defined between objects.

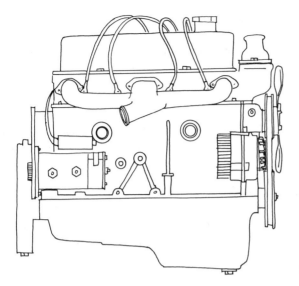

Figure 2.6 The role of relationships.

Generally speaking, relationships link two or more objects together (see Figure 2.6). Relationships come in several varieties, depending on the nature of the link. Some show the position of one object relative to another (above, below, between, etc.). Others link objects functionally, as in ''cables *carry* electricity. . . . '' Whatever their form, relationships take two or more objects and associate them in some way.

Relationships may have attributes, just as objects can. For example, the connection between the cable and battery may be described as ''dirty,'' or ''bad,'' or ''good.''

It is sometimes difficult to distinguish between a statement of a relationship and a statement of membership in a class. The statement, ''A collie is a dog'' clearly links two objects together, suggesting a relationship. But a clear examination shows that the statement establishes two names for the same object, showing membership in a class.

States

The knowledge engineer has now created a three-dimensional painting of an engine. Although the theory of operation of the engine is defined by the sum of all functional relationships, the engine is not yet operating. To get it started, we need to change its state.

The state of an object at any given moment is defined by the values of its attributes. For example, an engine whose state is ''running'' has attribute values that are different from an engine whose state is ''not running.'' A battery whose state is ''fully charged'' is different from a battery whose state is ''discharged.''

Adding states to the painting creates a need for attributes that were not present before. These new attributes exist only to indicate the state of an object and thus are often called ''state attributes'' or ''state variables.'' For example, all wires now need a state attribute called ''has current'' which has the value ''true'' if there is current along the wire, or ''false'' if there is no current present. We should also add a state attribute ''temperature'' that holds the value of the temperature of the engine at any given moment, and the state attribute ''gas'' that tells how much fuel is in the gas tank.

States add the dimension of time to the model. The painting has now come to life; it is now a working model and not a mere image.

Twenty Questions

The knowledge engineer has now achieved a level of knowledge equivalent to that of a graduate of Auto Mechanics 101: Engine Anatomy and Function. He can name all engine parts, list their properties, group them according to their similarities, assemble them into an engine, describe their functions and their various states. Yet even with all of this information at his command, he still cannot troubleshoot an engine that fails to run:

KNOWLEDGE ENGINEER: What happens if the car won't run?

EXPERT: You figure out what's wrong.

KNOWLEDGE ENGINEER: How?

EXPERT: You play ''Twenty Questions.''

KNOWLEDGE ENGINEER: Huh?

EXPERT: You play the kids' game ''Twenty Questions'' where you try to solve a problem by successively narrowing the range of possible solutions. You do this by asking questions. You start with a general question. The answer you get eliminates a lot of possibilities and narrows your search. The next question narrows it even further. You keep asking questions until there's only one possibility left, and that's your answer. That's how it works in principle, anyway. It doesn't always work in practice.

KNOWLEDGE ENGINEER: How do you know which questions to ask?

EXPERT: Experience.

KNOWLEDGE ENGINEER: How do you know what the answers mean?

EXPERT: Experience. That's the next thing I need to give you: the benefit of my experience.

KNOWLEDGE ENGINEER: Tell me.

EXPERT: OK. If the engine doesn't turn over, the problem may be the ignition system, or you may be out of gas, or you may have a flooded engine. Check the fuel gauge first—always try the simple things first. And here's a little trick: Tap the gauge a few times if it shows fuel in the tank—those gauges get stuck sometimes. If there seems to be gas in the tank, check the battery for charge. An easy way to do this is to turn on the wipers. If there's no response, make sure the cables are connected and the connection is clean. . . .

The expert is giving rules of thumb, strategies, tricks, and estimates on how to best troubleshoot an engine problem. Collectively, these devices are known as *heuristic rules,* or just *heuristics*. The purpose of heuristics is to guide the search for a solution by eliminating unlikely possibilities based on experience and knowledge of the domain. Heuristics don't always work, but they usually do.

Heuristic rules have an "if-then" structure. The "if" part gives a set of conditions. The "then" part gives a set of actions. If all the conditions in the "if" part are met, then all the actions in the "then" part are carried out.

In artificial intelligence, we are usually faced with problems that have an enormous number of possible solutions. Heuristics help to focus the search for a solution by extracting clues from the statement of the problem.

To illustrate this, imagine we have a car that has sensors connected to all its parts. By collecting readings from each of the sensors, we can determine the state of the entire car. Now consider the following problem:

"My car is broken. What's wrong with it?"

This doesn't give the expert much to go on. He doesn't know if the car has a flat tire or an engine on fire. It is difficult to know where to begin searching for a solution.

Without a heuristic that tells where to start in such cases, the expert's search would come screeching to a halt. Fortunately, he has a rule of thumb that states:

Rule #1: If you don't know where to start, begin reading sensors, starting with sensor A, until an abnormal reading is detected.

That gets him started. Then when an abnormal reading is found, his next rule kicks in:

Rule #2: If an abnormal sensor reading is detected, investigate possible malfunctions in the associated part.

This last rule sets him off on another line of reasoning and another rule, which will eventually lead to the solution. In both cases, the rules keep the expert going in the face of uncertainty and eliminate a great number of blind alleys.

As we mentioned before, heuristics don't always work, and it may be that the search proceeds down a blind alley. When this happens, the expert must have another heuristic that says, "OK, guys, we made a mistake, so let's back up to where we started this wild goose chase and try another path."

If the problem statement is better defined, the expert should take advantage of it. If, instead of the vague problem description given above, he were told:

"I had just filled the tank with gas and was pulling out of the service station when the car just died. Why did my car stop?"

Here our expert would extract clues from the statement, such as the full gas tank and the fact that the car started properly and then died suddenly. He would have rules that state:

Rule #3: If the car has gas, don't bother checking the gas gauge.

Rule #4:   If the car starts and quickly dies, don't bother checking the cooling system or the ignition system.

Rule #5:   If the car dies suddenly, it is probably an engine problem.

Rule #6:   If the car starts and quickly dies, check the fuel system.

Rule #7:   If checking the fuel system, start with the fuel pump.

In just five rules, he has narrowed his search down to a single component, the fuel pump. Notice that rules 3, 4, and 5 appear to be superfluous, since Rule 6 matches the conditions of the problem statement exactly and guides the search directly to the fuel system. These rules will be needed later, however, as we follow this example a bit further.

By narrowing the search to the fuel pump, the expert has, in effect, created a new statement of the problem. He is no longer concerned with the details of the original statement; he is now considering only the following problem:

"Is the fuel pump malfunctioning?"

Let's suppose the fuel pump is fine; he has run into a dead end. So he backs up to the point where he went astray, which is the last rule listed above. Then he backs up one more step to see where to go next. Rule 6 sends him back to the fuel system; Rule 7 sends him back to the fuel pump, which he knows is fine.

Our expert is caught in an infinite loop because we overlooked a very important point. When the expert determined that the fuel pump was not at fault, he *updated* his *knowledge base* with that information. In his mind, he has a state attribute for each component called "status" that he sets to "OK" when the component is functioning properly, or sets to "bad" when something is wrong. He also has a heuristic that says: "If you've already checked a component and found it to be OK, don't check it again."

With this straightened out, the expert is no longer caught in an infinite loop, but he doesn't know where to go, either. Rule 7 is no longer in effect, but Rule 6 is still applicable since the entire fuel system has not been checked. If each remaining component of the fuel system is just as likely to fail as any other, then we can add the heuristic:

Rule #8:   If the fuel pump is "OK," check the remaining fuel system components in the order they appear in the knowledge base.

This gets the expert going again and keeps him going for quite some time. He proceeds through the fuel system, and at each step, he creates a new problem statement (e.g., Is the fuel injector clogged?), updating his knowledge base with the results.

After an hour, all fuel system components have been checked and found to be working normally. The expert now backtracks to Rule 5, which tells him to check the engine. Rules 3 and 4 are important also, for they eliminate the need to search the cooling and ignition systems of the engine. The expert then uses another rule that directs him to investigate the lubrication system.

Now, to make things interesting, let's introduce a bug into the system of rules. Suppose the expert has just checked to make sure the oil filter has not fallen off. The rule is:

Rule 75: If the oil filter is present, then get a beer.

The oil filter is found to be intact. The expert then creates a new problem statement, which says:

"Where's the beer?"

Hold it! Unless some kind of internal monitoring system is present, the expert mechanic may abandon his search for the solution in the quest for a beer, and if there is no rule that states, "After drinking a beer, go back and fix the car," he may never return!

As each new problem statement is created, it must be compared with the original problem statement to make sure it is moving in the direction implied by the original problem statement. If it is not, then backtracking is in order. If it is, then we are still closing in on the solution.

The mechanic gets back on track, checks every component in the engine, and finds nothing wrong. Now what? Remember that the cooling system and the ignition system were removed from consideration by Rule 4. But heuristics are "soft" rules, not hard and fast axioms. Sometimes they are incorrect, and if all other avenues have failed to produce fruit, it's time to reconsider the givens. We need another rule:

Rule #90: If all components are functioning normally, and you have run out of components to search, and there are some components that were excluded from the search by a rule, examine all unexamined components.

This rule reopens the cooling and ignition system components as suspects in the search. Upon close examination, it is found that the distributor cap fell off.

But is that the solution? Is the distributor cap an essential component to a running car? Could its absence cause a car to stop? We could have a rule to provide this answer, but there comes a time when the expert stops depending on rules and starts making a few inferences of his own, based on his knowledge of the domain. With this, we leave the realm of existing knowledge (the knowledge base) and enter the realm of reason.

THE LOGICAL MIND

Actually, we've been in the realm of reason throughout this example. While the rules guide the expert's search for a solution, something must guide the search for the proper rule. That something is reason, logic.

Consider rules 1 and 2, with which we began the example:

Rule #1: If you don't know where to start, begin reading sensors, starting with sensor A, until an abnormal reading is detected.

Rule #2:   If an abnormal sensor reading is detected, investigate possible malfunctions in the associated part.

Notice that there is nothing in Rule 1 that tells the expert to go to Rule 2 when an abnormal reading is detected. Yet he does it anyway, because it is logical: One follows naturally from the other.

The logic here is simple: When the conditions of the problem statement match the conditions of a rule, use the rule. At the time Rule 1 is invoked, the problem is no longer "What's wrong with the car?" but "Where do I start?" The initial problem statement has been set aside and a new subproblem, which must be solved first, has been created. The condition of the subproblem matches the condition of Rule 1, therefore Rule 1 is selected.

When Rule 2 is invoked, the problem of where to start has been solved (by Rule 1) and the new subproblem is: "I have an abnormal reading—what do I do now?" Thus, Rule 2 is selected.

Even though this is a simple strategy, it is nonetheless important. Without it we would have an algorithm—a rigid step-by-step procedure incapable of adjusting to changing conditions. By using this simple matching strategy, our system can adapt to changing conditions and "discover" the path (chain of rules) that leads to the solution.

The essence of this scheme is:

1. Match the conditions of the current problem statement to the conditions of a rule.
2. Select that rule and execute it.
3. Update the knowledge base with the results obtained by executing the rule, and formulate a new problem statement.
4. Begin again at step 1.

Of course, this process has to stop sometime, or the solution to the original problem statement will never be found. There must be a *terminating* or *goal* condition that signals the end of the search, that a solution has been found.

The goal condition is usually formulated from the original statement of the problem. In an earlier example, the expert examined the problem statement:

"My car is broken. What's wrong with it?"

Here the goal condition is simply to find a part of the car that is malfunctioning. We might define a malfunctioning part as one whose sensor reading is out of the normal range. Thus, as soon as this condition is met, the corresponding part is reported as a solution.

The second problem statement that the expert is now pursuing is more specific:

"I had just filled the tank with gas and was pulling out of the service station when the car just died. Why did my car stop?"

The goal condition here is not merely to find a malfunctioning part, but to find a malfunctioning part whose malfunction is capable of stopping the engine. The first part of meeting this goal is to find a defective part—a *search* problem. The second part is to prove that the defective part caused the engine to fail—a *theorem-proving* problem.

The expert has already found a defective part using heuristic rules to guide his search toward the goal condition. The next step is to use logical inference to prove or disprove his conjecture that the distributor cap is indeed the source of the problem.

Logical Inference

Logical inference is the technique of showing that a hypothesis logically follows from a given set of facts. The expert's hypothesis is that a missing distributor cap is a sufficient condition to prevent an engine from running. His facts are contained in his knowledge base and include the parts of the engine and the physical and functional relationships that exist between parts.

Let's follow the expert's logic as he extracts facts from the knowledge base and chains them together:

Condition: The engine is not running.

Hypothesis: The malfunction in the distributor cap is responsible for this condition.

Problem #1: Why won't the engine run?

1. **Fact:** An engine that is not running means that no combustion is taking place in the cylinder block.
2. **Fact:** Combustion requires air, gasoline, and a spark.
3. **Aha!:** If there is no combustion, then at least one of the necessary conditions for combustion is not being met.

Problem #2: Which condition for combustion is not being satisfied?

4. **Fact:** Air and fuel are provided by the carburetor.
5. **Fact:** The spark is provided by the spark plugs.
6. **Fact:** The carburetor is part of the fuel system.
7. **Fact:** The spark plugs are part of the ignition system.
8. **Fact:** The distributor cap is part of the ignition system.
9. **Conclusion:** The distributor and the spark plugs are part of the same subsystem.
10. **Fact:** Parts of the same subsystem are functionally related.
11. **Aha!:** Since the spark plug and the distributor cap are functionally related, and the spark plug provides a necessary condition for combustion (the spark), maybe the distributor cap provides a necessary condition for the spark plug to produce a spark.

Problem #3: Does the distributor cap provide a necessary condition for the spark plug to operate?

12. **Fact:** The spark plug requires electricity to produce a spark.

13. **Fact:** The distributor cap provides electricity to the spark plug.

14. **Fact:** A malfunction in a component means that the component is not performing its primary function.

15. **Aha!:** If the distributor cap is malfunctioning, it provides no electricity to the spark plug, and the spark plug cannot produce a spark!

Conclusion Cascade: The answer to Problem 3 is yes, the distributor cap provides a necessary condition for the spark plug to operate.

The answer to Problem 2 is the condition for combustion that is not being satisfied is the spark, because the distributor is not meeting a necessary condition for the spark plug to produce a spark.

The answer to Problem 1 is the engine is not running because the distributor is not producing a necessary condition for the spark plug to produce a spark, which is a necessary condition for combustion, which is a necessary condition for the engine to run. Therefore, the missing distributor cap is preventing the engine from running. This proves the hypothesis.

Mathematicians and logicians will throw up their hands at the unruliness of this reasoning process, and that's just fine. People rarely use pure formal logic, either consciously or subconsciously, when making a decision or proving a conjecture correct. While mathematics and formal logic certainly have their place in reasoning techniques— indeed, many of their methods were used in this example—they are not sufficient to solve complex problems, nor are they entirely compatible with the human mind. And in the final analysis, who can contest the success of the human mind when it comes to solving complex problems. We must be doing something right.

All of this aside, let's call attention to some of the methods used in this exercise. First, the expert uses the same process of creating smaller, more manageable subproblems that he used in his heuristic-driven search for a defective component. Second, he collects facts pertinent to the current problem statement until he can reach an ''Aha!'' and generate a new problem statement or reach a conclusion that answers the subproblem. Third, once one subproblem was solved, the others followed. This shows that the subproblems were well chosen. Finally, unlike heuristic-directed search, the goal of this process was not to match the conditions of the initial problem statement, but to independently generate the hypothesis by drawing conclusions from the knowledge base.

BEYOND LOGIC

Up to this point, everything has been reasonably well defined. Our domain of discourse is exact, our knowledge base complete. Most everything about the domain is understood. We have no inconsistencies or contradictions to settle, no superfluous information to lead us off the track, no fuzziness to resolve in the relationships between objects or in their suitability for membership in a class. Everything either is or isn't. All in all, a fairly typical example of the types of problems human beings must deal with.

Dream on.

Logic and mathematics were designed to explain and model the purely rational behavior of nature and philosophers. But we, unfortunately, must deal with reality. When we make decisions and solve problems, our information is usually incomplete, full of inconsistencies, and replete with conflicting subjective assessments. Somehow, we must bound over these obstacles. Rationality helps, but it is not enough.

Consider oil exploration for an example. We have compiled an extensive array of indicators that help us determine whether oil is likely to be found at a given location. We can extract core samples and study the geologic history of the area and perform all kinds of studies that predict with a certain degree of confidence that an oil deposit will be found at a particular depth and in sufficient quantities to make the drilling investment worthwhile.

But what of the economic climate? What if a depression returns and people stop driving their cars? What if OPEC crumbles? What if war prevents the oil from being transported to refineries? What if the current government is overthrown and the new regime decides to nationalize all industries and throw out all capitalists? What if, indeed.

And finally, all other things aside, there is that gut feeling that says, "I don't care what the figures say, *I know* there's oil there. Let's do it!"

The human race has proven itself to be a pretty successful species, and much of the credit goes to scientific developments. But even science, mathematics, and logic owe their progress to those unruly, illogical qualities of the human mind: creativity, imagination, intuition, and emotion. No one has explained how these . . . *things* . . . work. We must call them *things* for lack of a better description. Everything else we have dealt with in this chapter could be called a method—a method for representing objects, a method for grouping objects, a method for relating objects, a method for narrowing a search, a method for proving a hypothesis. We cannot always define how the method works, but we know it is a method.

Creativity, imagination, intuition, and emotion seem to defy methodology. They are like spontaneous by-products of the mind over which we have no control. To turn on imagination, for example, we more or less relinquish control of our minds and leave them to their own mysterious devices. We sit idly by, watching as a stream of images and ideas float by, waiting and hoping that we will find one we can use.

The ramification of AI, of course, is that there may be a limit on the level of intelligence that can be programmed into a computer. Certain mental processes seem to defy codification. But perhaps we have been going about it all wrong; perhaps we are examining these processes far too logically. Maybe we should turn our imaginations loose on these questions. Maybe then these problems would literally solve themselves.

DIGITAL DIALECTICS

Now that we have defined some of the components and processes of human intelligence, we are ready to address the next challenge: How can these components and processes be represented inside a computer?

The mind's mechanism for storing and retrieving knowledge is fairly transparent to us. When we "memorize" an orange, we simply examine it, think about it for a while, and perhaps eat it. Somehow, during this process, all the essential qualities of the orange are stored. Later, when someone mentions the word "orange," our senses are activated from within, and we see, smell, touch, and taste the orange all over again.

Computers, unfortunately, are not as adept at forming internal representations of the world. As we saw in the last chapter, computer senses (e.g., vision via a video camera), are not yet well developed. Instead of gathering knowledge for themselves, computers must rely on human beings to place knowledge directly into their memories.

This suggests programming, but even before programming begins, we must decide on ways to represent information, knowledge, and inference techniques inside a computer. That's what this chapter is all about.

Let's look at an example.

THE GAME OF DARTS: A WARM-UP EXERCISE

Suppose we wanted to simulate the game of darts in a computer. We have a dart board that looks like that shown in Figure 3.1.

The game is played by throwing darts at the dart board. Whenever a dart sticks in a

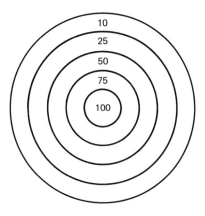

Figure 3.1 Dart board.

region of the dart board, the corresponding score is awarded. The object of the game is to get the highest score.

Our problem is to transform this tangible object into an abstract computer representation. We begin by extracting the "essence" of the game.

A dart board is composed of five concentric circular regions. Each region is associated with a score (number). The larger the region, the smaller the score. If we assume that the player of the game is unskilled, the probability of hitting a large region is greater than the probability of hitting a small region. Put another way, the likelihood of getting a low score is greater than the likelihood of getting a high score.

To represent these ideas in a computer, we must first "store" the dart board in the computer's memory. For this example, think of a computer's memory as a large grid, as shown in Figure 3.2.

Each box or location in the grid represents one memory location. Each location is specified by a unique index, which is a pair of numbers. The first number in the index gives the row number of the location; the second number gives the column number of the location. Row numbers are marked along the top of the grid; column numbers are marked along the left-hand side of the grid. For example, the cell in the upper left-hand corner of the grid has an index of (1,1) because it is in the first row and first column of the grid. Each cell in the grid can contain one number.

Now let's place the dart board in the computer's memory by superimposing this memory grid over the dart board (see Figure 3.3).

We can now get rid of the physical dart board by storing scores in memory locations. If a memory location is contained within a region, it receives that region's score. (Notice that some memory locations span region boundaries in this illustration. Don't be concerned with this; we can minimize the problem by using a finer grid. For now, concentrate on the concepts.)

The memory representation of the dart board is shown in Figure 3.4.

The memory representation maintains the basic structure of the original dart board. But is the physical structure of the dart board important? If it is not, perhaps we can reduce the representation by another level of abstraction.

To answer this, we need to define how we will represent the action of throwing a

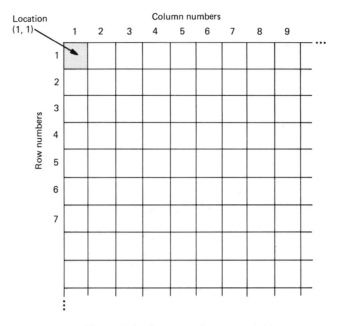

Figure 3.2 A computer's memory grid.

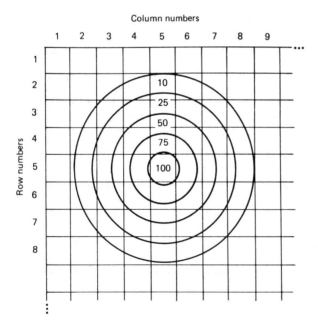

Figure 3.3 Dart board in memory.

Column numbers

Row \ Col	1	2	3	4	5	6	7	8	9	10	11	
1				10	10	10	10	10				
2			10	10	25	25	25	10	10			
3		10	10	25	25	50	25	25	10	10		
4		10	25	25	50	75	50	25	25	10		
5		10	25	50	75	100	75	50	25	10		
6		10	25	25	50	75	50	25	25	10		
7		10	10	25	25	50	25	25	10	10		
8			10	10	25	25	25	10	10			
9				10	10	10	10	10				
10												

Row numbers

Figure 3.4 Memory representation of dart board.

dart. Given our simplifying assumption that the players of the game are totally unskilled, every dart thrown will strike the board randomly. Therefore, every location in our grid is equally likely to be selected (hit).

To select a location, we must specify its index, which consists of two numbers: the row number and the column number. The procedure looks like this:

1. Randomly generate a number between 1 and the largest row number of the grid. This is the row number of the location.
2. Randomly generate a number between 1 and the largest column number of the grid. This is the column number of the location.
3. Combine the numbers generated in steps 1 and 2 to create the index for the selected location.

Once the index is computed, we need only read the number in the selected location to determine our score.

How does this technique affect our representation? Since the action of throwing a dart is merely a matter of computing a random location, we can simplify the process by converting our two-dimensional grid into a one-dimensional sequence of locations. With

1	2	3	4	5	6	7	• • •	13	14	15	• • • • •	39	40	41	• • • ~ •	74
100	75	75	75	75	50	50	• • •	50	25	25	• • • • •	25	10	10	• • • • •	10	

Figure 3.5 One-dimensional representation of the dart board.

only one dimension, we need compute only a single number for the index instead of two. The dart-throwing procedure would then look like this:

1. Compute a random number between 1 and the total number of locations in the board. This is the index to the selected location.

Let's do some counting. In our current grid there are:

- 32 locations containing the score 10
- 24 locations containing the score 25
- 8 locations containing the score 50
- 4 locations containing the score 4
- 1 location containing the score 100

Our one-dimensional representation would then look like Figure 3.5.

Of course, we could throw away the dart board altogether and programmatically represent the throw of a dart with the following:

1. Randomly generate a number between 1 and 74.

2. *If* the index is between 40 and 74,   *then* score is 10, *else.* . .
If the index is between 14 and 39,   *then* score is 25, *else.* . .
If the index is between 6 and 13,   *then* score is 50, *else.* . .
If the index is between 2 and 5,   *then* score is 75, *else.* . .
If the index is 1,   *then* score is 100.

REPRESENTING KNOWLEDGE

The purpose of the preceding example was to show how we can extract the essence of the real world in order to represent it abstractly in a computer. We will now apply this same principle to build up representations for the knowledge base that we developed in Chapter 2.

Objects and Attributes

In the last chapter, we began building the automotive knowledge base by defining all objects in the domain of discourse. We all have an intuitive idea of what an object is, but we must now make these ideas explicit in order to represent them in a computer.

To define an object, we have to do two things:

1. Create a name for the object, and

2. Define the attributes of the object and the values for these attributes.

For example, we could define a headlight as follows:

OBJECT NAME:	Headlight
ATTRIBUTES:	Made of: Glass
	Function: Produce light
	Location: Front of car
	Shape: Round

Headlight definition.

This scheme seems explicit enough, and it conforms well with our intuitive definition of a headlight. But in computer science, an object definition includes more than just a name and a description—it also includes a set of operations that are defined on the object. There is a good reason for this.

In the old days of structured programming (say, five to 10 years ago), the programmer would define objects and the operations on those objects separately. He would define an object, say a headlight, and then define a set of modules (procedures) that manipulate the headlight. Because each module manipulated the object directly, each had to know the details of its structure.

In object-oriented programming, the details of an object's structure are hidden from the rest of the program. This is achieved by bundling the object, and all operations on the object, together. Let's look at an example.

Suppose we have a headlight switch object. The operations defined on this switch are:

• Throw the switch one way to turn the headlights on.

• Throw the switch another way to turn the headlights off.

Using the structured programming approach for our diagnostic program, we might have several modules that turn the headlight on or off as part of their diagnostic procedure. For example, the procedure that tests whether the battery is dead might turn the lights on, as would the procedure that tests the generator, as would the procedure that tests the wires running to the headlights, as would the procedure that tests the headlights themselves, and so on.

Each of these diagnostic procedures must know how to turn the headlights on, which means they must have knowledge of the structure of the switch used. Let's say the headlight switch is a rocker type located on the dashboard to the left of the steering wheel. Then every module that manipulates the switch contains the following knowledge:

- To turn the headlights on, push on the top half of the switch.
- To turn the headlights off, push on the bottom half of the switch.

This works fine, until the automobile manufacturers decide to change the structure of the switch. Now, instead of a rocker switch, they change the design to a push-in/pull-out knob. The knowledge needed to operate the switch has now changed to:

- To turn the headlights on, pull the knob out.
- To turn the headlights off, push the knob in.

Every module that manipulates this switch must now be reprogrammed with this new technique. If there are one hundred modules that turn the headlights on or off, all of them must be changed.

   In the object-oriented approach, all operations defined on an object are bundled with the object. Thus, the headlight switch object might look like this:

OBJECT NAME:	Headlight switch
ATTRIBUTES:	Made of: Plastic
	Type: Rocker
	Function: Turn off/on headlights
	Location: Left of steering wheel
OPERATIONS:	Turn on headlights: push upper half
	Turn off headlights: push lower half

Conventional headlight switch definition.

Using this approach, all modules that manipulate the headlights simply say:

- Turn headlights on, or
- Turn headlights off

The details of *how* this is done are now hidden from the modules—the modules no longer need to know what kind of switch they are dealing with. They need only issue a command to the object. The object then finds the command in its OPERATIONS section and executes the appropriate action.

   Now suppose the switch design is changed:

OBJECT NAME:	Headlight switch
ATTRIBUTES:	Made of: Plastic
	Type: Push-in/Pull-out knob
	Function: Turn off/on headlights
	Location: Left of steering wheel
OPERATIONS:	Turnon headlights: pull out knob
	Turn off headlights: push in knob

Object-oriented headlight switch definition.

When the design of the headlight switch is changed, only the object is altered. All modules that use the object are unaffected; they still issue the same commands, either to "Turn on headlights" or "Turn off headlights."

Object Instances vs. Object Definitions

We can now define any of the objects in our automotive knowledge base by giving the object a name, listing its attributes and assigning values to them, and giving all operations that are defined on the object. Using this technique, we can define a spark plug as follows:

OBJECT NAME:	Spark plug
ATTRIBUTES:	Made of: Ceramic, metal
	Function: Produce spark for ignition
	Location: Side of cylinder head
	Gap: .02 inches
OPERATIONS:	Produce spark: supply current, current jumps gap, produces spark

Spark plug definition.

While this might be an adequate general description, it does not account for the fact that there are more than one spark plug in an engine, and that each spark plug has individual characteristics. There is a subtle distinction to be made here: The object description given above is a *definition* of an object, but it is not the object itself.

Computer scientists distinguish between the act of defining an object and the act of creating an object. When an object is defined, all its characteristics and operations are specified, but the object itself does not yet exist. You can think of an object definition as a mold or template that can be used to create an object. When the object is created, the object definition is "cloned" to create an *instance* of the object. An instance of an object is an actual, individual object, such as the third spark plug or the left wiper blade.

Some of the attribute values of an object definition will be different from those of an instance of the object. The object definition contains "default" or "generic" attribute values—values that are typical of the object. The instance of the object replaces these default values with actual values. Consider the spark plug definition and instance shown below:

OBJECT NAME:	Spark plug
ATTRIBUTES:	Made of: Ceramic, metal
	Function: Produce spark for ignition
	Location: Side of cylinder head
	Gap: .02 inches
OPERATIONS:	Produce spark: supply current, current jumps gap, produces spark

Spark plug definition.

OBJECT NAME:	Spark plug
ATTRIBUTES:	Made of: Ceramic, metal
	Function: Produce spark for ignition
	Location: Side of cylinder head, third cylinder
	Gap: .041 inches
OPERATIONS:	Produce spark: supply current, current jumps gap, produces spark

Spark plug instance (third spark plug).

Notice that the instance replaces the definition's generic values for **Location** and **Gap** with the actual values for the third spark plug.

Classes: The ako Slot

The object concept gives us a powerful yet simple scheme for representing the components in the domain of discourse. The next step is to establish classes, to link the objects together by similarities in their attributes.

Returning to the tools example we used in Chapter 2, we present the following object definitions:

OBJECT NAME:	Tool
ATTRIBUTES:	Made of: Plastic
	Function: Dismantle, assemble engine
	Location: Toolbox
	Appearance: Has a handle
OPERATIONS:	Pick up:
	Put down:
	Rotate right:
	Rotate left:
	etc.

Tool definition.

OBJECT NAME:	Wrench
ATTRIBUTES:	Made of: Metal
	Function: Tighten, loosen nuts and bolts
	Location: Toolbox
	Color: Silver Appearance. Has a handle with curved appendage
OPERATIONS:	Pick up:
	Put down:
	Put around nut:
	Rotate right:
	Rotate left:
	etc.

Wrench definition.

OBJECT NAME:	Adjustable Wrench
ATTRIBUTES:	Made of: Metal
	Function: Tighten, loosen nuts and bolts
	Location: Toolbox
	Color: Silver Appearance. Has a handle with an adjustable C-shaped appendage
	Calibration: (English or metric?)
	Size: (?)
OPERATIONS:	Pick up:
	Put down:
	Put around nut:
	Adjust
	Rotate right:
	Rotate left:
	etc.

Adjustable wrench definition.

Each of these object definitions has some characteristics in common and some that are unique. In general, as we move from tool to wrench to adjustable wrench, the definitions become more precise as more attributes are added and values become more resolved.

We finish this progression by adding an instance of an adjustable wrench, defined as follows:

OBJECT NAME:	Adjustable Wrench
ATTRIBUTES:	Made of: Metal
	Function: Tighten, loosen nuts and bolts
	Location: Toolbox
	Color: Silver Appearance. Has a handle with an adjustable C-shaped appendage
	Calibration: English
	Size: 3/8-inch
OPERATIONS:	Pick up:
	Put down:
	Put around nut:
	Adjust
	Rotate right:
	Rotate left:
	etc.

⅜ English adjustable wrench instance.

Here, the instance-dependent attributes **Calibration** and **Size** have been resolved, and we have created the ⅜-inch English-calibrated adjustable wrench tool that was discussed in Chapter 2.

At the moment, however, there is nothing linking the object definitions together. We need some way of showing that an adjustable wrench is a kind of wrench, and that a wrench is a kind of tool. We can do this by adding an *ako slot* (ako stands for "a kind of"). With this simple addition, we can build a complete hierarchy of objects to any level of complexity we desire.

Our object definitions now look like this:

OBJECT NAME:	Tool
AKO:	None
ATTRIBUTES:	Made of: Metal
	Function: Dismantle, assemble engine
	Location: Toolbox
	Appearance: Has a handle
OPERATIONS:	Pick up:
	Put down:
	Rotate right:
	Rotate left:
	etc.

Tool definition.

OBJECT NAME:	Wrench
AKO:	Tool
ATTRIBUTES:	Made of: Metal
	Function: Tighten, loosen nuts and bolts
	Location: Toolbox
	Color: Silver Appearance. Has a handle with a curved appendage
OPERATIONS:	Pick up:
	Put down:
	Put around nut:
	Rotate right:
	Rotate left:
	etc.

Wrench definition.

OBJECT NAME:	Adjustable Wrench
AKO:	Wrench
ATTRIBUTES:	Made of: Metal
	Function: Tighten, loosen nuts and bolts
	Location: Toolbox
	Color: Silver Appearance. Has a handle with an adjustable C-shaped appendage
	Calibration: (English or metric?)
	Size: (?)
OPERATIONS:	Pick up:
	Put down:
	Put around nut:
	Adjust
	Rotate right:
	Rotate left:
	etc.

Adjustable wrench definition.

This excerpt from the hierarchy of tools is fine, but it doesn't take advantage of the inheritance property of classes. Notice, for example, that each of the object definitions has the same value for the attribute **Made of.** If indeed all tools are made of metal, we can eliminate the **Made of** attribute from all object definitions except Tools. The same argument applies to the attribute **Location** and to many of the operations (e.g., pick up, put down, etc.).

By making use of the inheritance property of classes, we can devise the following representation:

OBJECT NAME:	Tool
AKO:	None
ATTRIBUTES:	Made of: Metal
	Function: Dismantle, assemble engine
	Location: Toolbox
	Appearance: Has a handle
OPERATIONS:	Pick up:
	Put down:
	Rotate right:
	Rotate left:
	etc.

Tool definition.

OBJECT NAME:	Wrench
AKO:	Tool
ATTRIBUTES:	Made of: Metal
	Function: Tighten, loosen nuts and bolts
	Color: Silver Appearance. Has a handle with a curved appendage
OPERATIONS:	Pick up:
	Put down:
	Put around nut:
	etc.

Wrench definition.

OBJECT NAME:	Adjustable Wrench
AKO:	Wrench
ATTRIBUTES:	Function: Tighten, loosen nuts and bolts
	Appearance: Has a handle with an adjustable C-shaped appendage
	Calibration: (English or metric?)
	Size: (?)
OPERATIONS:	Adjust:
	etc.

Adjustable wrench definition.

Now suppose we are asked:

"What is an adjustable wrench made of?"

First we would look in the object definition for Adjustable Wrench. Not finding a **Made of** attribute there, we follow the ako link to the object definition of Wrench. Again, failing to find the **Made of** attribute, we proceed up the ako link to Tool. There we find the **Made of** attribute and return the answer: metal.

Similarly, if we were told to "pick up" the ⅜-inch English-calibrated adjustable wrench tool, we would begin with this particular instance of an adjustable wrench object and follow the ako links up the hierarchy until the "pick up" procedure is found. Note that object instances also have ako links because they are cloned from object definitions.

Relationships

The next phase of building the knowledge base is to find a representation for relationships. Relationships, you'll recall, provide the links that assemble objects into functionally and physically accurate models of the domain of discourse.

Relationships are best thought of as statements of fact that tie objects together. For example:

The spark plug produces a spark.

This statement relates two objects, *spark plug* and *spark*. The relation that connects the two objects is *produces*. This statement conveys an action—if given complete object definitions of spark plug and spark, we can almost see the spark appearing at the tip of the spark plug.

Another example:

A high-voltage cable connects the spark plug with the distributor.

Here we have a three-way relation, *connects*, that links the objects *high-voltage cable, spark plug,* and *distributor* together. This relationship literally shows how these objects are linked together—we can see how the high-voltage cable runs between the spark plug and the distributor.

And another example:

Current flows through the high-voltage cable from the distributor to the spark plug.

Here the relation is *flows,* and it has four components:

- The transporter of the flow, *high-voltage cable*
- The object that flows, *current*

- The source of the flow, *distributor*
- The destination of the flow, *spark plug*

This relation conveys both an action and a spatial relationship. Not only can we see the physical linkage of the components, but we also "see" current moving through the system, in the direction from the distributor to the spark plug. By combining all these statements, we get a pretty good picture of how this segment of the engine is put together and how the parts work.

But how can we represent these relationships in a computer? Recall from Chapter 2 that natural language understanding by computers has not yet been perfected. We must, therefore, look for some other, simpler representation.

One commonly used method for representing relations in a knowledge base is to use *first order predicate logic*. With this scheme, relations are viewed as functional predicates and objects are the arguments to the predicate.

For example, the statement:

The spark plug produces a spark.

translates into:

Produces (spark plug, spark)

More generally, the relation *produces* takes the form:

Produces (object that produces, object that is produced)

The statement:

A high-voltage cable connects the spark plug with the distributor.

becomes:

Connects (high-voltage cable, spark plug, distributor)

The general form of connects is:

Connects (object that connects, object being connected, object being connected)

And finally, the following statement:

Current flows through the high-voltage cable from the distributor to the spark plug.

becomes:

Flows (current, high-voltage cable, distributor, spark plug)

And the general form is:

Flows (object that flows, transporter of flow, source of flow, destination of flow)

This representation is nice because it is easy to translate English statements into a predicate logic form and because various inference rules exist for manipulating such statements. We cannot stop here, however. We may have found a simplified representation for English statements, but we haven't yet specified how this representation contributes any additional knowledge to our knowledge base.

At the moment, we can express any relationship in simple form. But we cannot simply allocate a huge region of memory and randomly store these relational statements in it. We need a scheme for integrating the knowledge contained in these statements into the knowledge base.

One way might be to create a relational data base within our knowledge base. Each relation would have its own table in which all statements of that type are stored. For example, there might be a *Produces* table:

Produces:

Object that produces	Object that is produced
Spark plug	Spark
:	:
:	:

And a *Connects* table:

Connects:

Object that connects	Object being connected	Object being connected
High-voltage cable	Distributor	Spark plug
:	:	:
:	:	:

And a *Flows* table:

Flows:

Object that flows	Transporter of flow	Source	Destination
Current	High-vltage cable	Distributor	Spark plug
:	:	:	:
:	:	:	:

With this scheme, when a certain relationship is needed, the appropriate table is searched and the desired relationship is located and restored to its predicate logic form (if necessary).

Another scheme is to use the relational statements to add knowledge to object definitions and/or instances of objects. For example, we could add a RELATIONSHIPS section to our object definitions that contains all relationships involving that object. Thus, when we make the statements:

- Produces (spark plug, spark)
- Connects (high-voltage cable, spark plug, distributor)
- Flows (current, high-voltage cable, distributor, spark plug)

the definition of the spark plug object becomes:

OBJECT NAME:	Spark plug
ATTRIBUTES:	Made of: Ceramic, metal
	Function: Produce spark for ignition
	Location: Side of cylinder head
	Gap: .02 inches
OPERATIONS:	Produce spark: supply current, current jumps gap, produces spark
RELATIONSHIPS:	Produces: Spark
	Connects to: High voltage cable
	Receives: Current

Spark plug definition with partial relationships.

The problem with this scheme is that only the part of the relationship that involves the object is represented. For example, the original *Connects* relationship shows the connection between three objects: the high-voltage cable, the spark plug, and the distributor. The *Connects to* relationship stored in the spark plug definition, however, shows only the portion of the *Connects* relationship that directly relates to the spark plug. We cannot say that the spark plug connects to the distributor because it doesn't: The spark plug connects to the high-voltage cable, which connects to the distributor.

We can, however, reconstruct the entire *Connects* relationship by following the link to the high-voltage cable definition. Because the high-voltage cable is, in effect, the "center" of the *Connects* relationship, the object definition for the high-voltage cable contains the entire relationship. Thus, the *Connects to* relationship in the high-voltage cable definition looks like:

RELATIONSHIPS: Connects to: Distributor and spark plug

A similar situation exists for the current object definition. Current is the "center" of the *Flows* relationship. Therefore, it contains the following RELATIONSHIPS section:

RELATIONSHIPS: Flows through: High-voltage cable
Flows from: Distributor
Flows to: Spark plug

Do you see another problem here? Current flows through the entire electrical system. The relationship we defined above covers only one small portion of the circuit. How can we include this fact in this representation?

There are at least two ways. One is to create several instances of the current object, one for each leg of the entire circuit. Thus you would have one instance that covers from the battery to the ignition switch, another instance that covers from the ignition switch to the coil, and so on. Each instance would have a different set of relationships, depending on which part of the circuit it defines.

Another method uses a single instance of the current object, but creates several *Flows* relationships, one for each segment of the circuit. Thus, *Flows1* might cover from the battery to the ignition switch, *Flows2* might cover from the ignition switch to the coil, and so on.

A Short Breather

This last section on relationships became rather complicated, so we'd like to pause a moment and put things in perspective. The point of having relationships is to show how objects relate to each other. Any scheme that efficiently accomplishes this goal is fine. One way is to include relationships as part of an object definition, just as you would do with attributes and operations. If, for example, you will be tracing a network of objects in search of a defective part, this scheme will work well.

In the engine troubleshooting example, you might test an object, move on to the next, test it, move on, and so forth until a defective part is found. If relationships are embedded in your object definitions, you can test the ATTRIBUTES section of an object definition for abnormalities, then if there are none, use the RELATIONSHIPS section to find the next part in the network.

Another way is to collect all relationships of a certain type together in a table. This has the advantage of keeping complex relationships intact for manipulation by inference techniques.

There are unquestionably more ways to represent relationships. Do whatever comes naturally to the situation.

States

States bring the concept of time to the knowledge base. Certain attributes of an object change over time—these we represent with *state* attributes.

For example, the spark plug definition might include the state attribute *Has current* to indicate the pressure of current in the spark plug:

ATTRIBUTES: Has current: (True or False)

When an instance of the spark plug object is created, the *Has current* attribute takes the value True if there is current present, or False otherwise.

Demons

Adding states to the knowledge base creates a need for a mechanism to keep the knowledge base up to date. Since a full complement of state attributes allows us to represent the condition of the domain of discourse at any given time, we must make sure that all state variables contain accurate values if this information is to be useful. One way to accomplish this is through the use of *demons*.

A demon is a watch dog that springs into action when certain changes in the knowledge base occur. If, for instance, the battery were to lose its charge, its state variable *Has current* would be set to False. But since the battery is the source of all current in the electrical and ignition systems, all components in these systems should have their *Has current* attributes set to False.

A demon is a rule that accomplishes this. The rule in the above example might be:

If Has current is False, *then* find all other Has currents and set them to False.

This rule is invoked every time the value of the state attribute *Has current* in the Battery definition is changed. If the condition becomes true, then it sets into action a process that will search through all objects in the electrical and ignition systems and set all *Has current* attributes to False.

Rules

Demons, being a form of rule, bring us to the issue of representing rules in the knowledge base. Fortunately, this task is fairly straightforward.

Let's look at the demon rule just mentioned. Stated in English, it looks like:

If Has current is False, *then* find all other Has currents and set them to False.

This example is typical of all rules in that it has an *if* part, which specifies a condition, and a *then* part, which specifies an action to be carried out if the condition is met. As with relationships, the problem with representing rules is to find a way to translate an English statement into a concise, computer-readable representation.

If we take the same approach used to represent relationships, we can use predicate logic to extract the essence from the English statement. First let's rephrase the *if* part to be more specific:

If the attribute Has current in the object Battery has a value of False . . .

We can now represent this statement by defining a predicate:

IS-FALSE?(Battery, Has current)

The predicate *IS-FALSE?* takes as its arguments the name of an object and the name of one of the object's attributes and returns a value of True if the value of the attribute is False, otherwise it returns a value of False. For example, if the battery is discharged, the value of Has-Current is False, and the value of *IS-FALSE?* in the statement above is True.

We can now represent the conditional part of our rule as:

IF IS-FALSE(Battery, Has current)

The first action in the *then* part of the rule is a search procedure for the attribute Has current. Thus, we can define a procedure called INTELLIGENT-SEARCH and invoke it as follows:

SEARCH-AND-REPLACE(Battery, Has current, False)

The procedure INTELLIGENT-SEARCH takes as its arguments the name of an object, the name of an attribute, and a replacement value. The object is the origin of the search, the attribute is the thing being searched for, and the replacement value is the value that will be given to the attribute once it is found. The strategy of the procedure is to search for the attribute in all objects that are directly or indirectly connected to the origin of the search. Once the attribute is found, it is set to the specified value. The implementation details of this search are omitted, but we can state that the procedure will use connection relationships to trace outward from the origin of the search.

The rule now has its final form:

IF IS-FALSE(Battery, Has current) THEN SEARCH-AND-REPLACE(Battery, Has current, False)

As with relationships, we cannot simply throw all our rules randomly into a pot and hope to find them quickly. Rules must be grouped in a way that reflects how we will search for them.

There are two ways to search for a rule. The first is a forward chaining or data-directed search, which begins with a statement of initial conditions and searches forward for a solution that explains these conditions. The second is a backward chaining or goal-directed search, which starts with a statement of the goal (hypothesis), and searches backward to find the conditions that establish the goal.

The example in Chapter 2 used both of these techniques. When searching for the source of an engine malfunction, we used forward chaining to move from the conditions given in the problem statement to an object (i.e., the distributor cap) that appeared to explain these conditions. However, we still had to prove that the distributor cap was indeed capable of causing an engine failure, so we used backward chaining to show that our hypothesis could create the conditions described in the initial problem statement.

When forward chaining is used, rules are selected by matching the *if* part (the conditions) to the conditions given in the current problem statement. When backward chaining is used, rules are selected by matching the *then* part (the actions) to the next desired state of the goal.

The implications for grouping (classifying) rules is to group them according to the way you will search for them. For instance, if you will use a forward-chaining search, then group the rules according to the objects they contain in their *if* parts. Thus all rules involving the ignition system in their conditionals would be grouped together, all rules involving the suspension system would be grouped together, all rules involving the tires would be grouped together, and so on.

REPRESENTING REASON

Reason is the technique of using knowledge to solve problems. The strategy of reason is to break big problems into smaller subproblems, which are in turn broken into even smaller subproblems, and so on. When a level of subproblem is finally reached where the answer is readily available from the knowledge at hand, the solution tends to bubble up through the hierarchy of subproblems until the original (topmost) problem is solved.

Decision Trees

A decision tree is a graphical representation of the problem-solving process just described. It begins with a statement of the problem. This is called the root node (Figure 3.6).

Emanating from the root node are decision paths that lead either to a new problem statement (subproblem) or to a solution (Figure 3.7).

If the decision path leads to a new subproblem, more decision paths are encountered. The process continues until a solution is found (Figure 3.8).

Most problems have so many possible decision paths that a purely blind search strategy would take years to perform, even at the near-light execution speeds of a computer. The purpose of heuristic rules, then, is to guide the search by eliminating decision paths that are unlikely to produce a solution. Heuristics are said to prune the decision tree of unproductive branches.

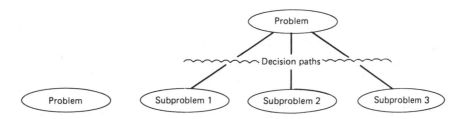

Figure 3.6 Root node of decision tree.

Figure 3.7 Decision paths from root node.

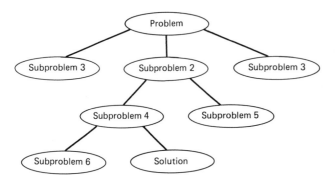

Figure 3.8 Decision path to solution.

Reasoning techniques, then, are responsible for generating the decision tree and selecting the appropriate heuristic rule to guide the search down the most promising path. There are several steps in this process:

1. Phrase the problem statement.
2. Select from the knowledge base those rules that are relevant to the problem.
3. Select from the knowledge base those objects that are relevant to the problem.
4. Match the conditions of the selected rules against the attributes of the selected objects.
5. If step 4 yields more than one candidate rule, evaluate candidates and select the one most likely to proceed toward a solution.
6. Perform the actions specified in the chosen rule.
7. If a solution is found, then quit. If a dead end is reached, back up to the point where your logic went astray and begin again at step 5. Otherwise, go back to step 1.

Let's run through one cycle in detail, using a real example.

Step 1   Phrase the problem statement.   The initial problem statement is:

The trunk of my car won't close. Why?

Since this is given to us, we have finished this step.

Step 2   Select from the knowledge base those rules that are relevant to the problem.   Our knowledge base contains hundreds, if not thousands, of rules, and there is no need to look at all of them. It would be ludicrous, for instance, to consider any rule involving the engine as having any bearing on this problem. We would hope that rules are grouped (classified) according to the objects they operate on, and that we can simply find the group that deals with trunk problems and eliminate the rest.

Step 3   Select from the knowledge base those objects that are relevant t o the problem.   This is the same principle as in step 2, but it pertains to objects instead of rules. Since our problem deals with the trunk, we want to focus on the trunk object, as well as any other object that is linked to the trunk via relationships. We can discard all others.

Step 4 Match the conditions of the selected rules against the attributes of the selected objects. The trunk object has a state attribute (call it Will close) that tells whether or not the trunk will close. In this case, the value of this attribute is False: The trunk will not close.

The group of rules we have selected include some with conditionals that begin:

IF IS-FALSE?(Trunk, Will close) . . .

Thus, this subset of rules contain conditions that match the relevant state attribute of the object.

Step 5 If step 4 yields more than one candidate rule, evaluate candidates and select the one most likely to proceed toward a solution. This selection process may be arbitrary or quite formal. Each rule that qualified in step 4 represents a decision path. One way to proceed is to generate the next level of the decision tree by "looking ahead" at the subproblems each candidate rule will generate if selected. Each subproblem is then evaluated in some way to determine its distance from the solution. The rule generating the subproblem judged to be nearest the solution is then selected. If several rules appear equally good, one is selected by some systematic but arbitrary scheme. However, no rule is selected twice.

In this example, we might have the following candidate rules:

IF IS-FALSE?(Trunk, Will close) THEN CHECK(Lock, Jammed)
IF IS-FALSE?(Trunk, Will close) THEN CHECK(Trunk, Too full)

The predicate CHECK has two arguments: an object to be checked and the state attribute of the object whose value is to be read. If the value of the attribute is True, then the predicate returns true and the problem is solved, else the predicate returns false and the problem is unsolved.

Since both rules are equally good, we choose the first one.

Step 6 Perform the actions specified in the chosen rule. Execute the selected rule and do its bidding. This will ultimately result in a solution to the problem, in changes to the knowledge base (e.g., new values for state attributes), in a new subproblem statement, or in a dead end.

In this example, the action part of the rule says:

THEN CHECK(Lock, Jammed)

The Jammed attribute of the object Lock is then read. The value returned is False: The Lock is not jammed.

Step 7 If a solution is found, then quit. If a dead end is reached, back up to the point where your logic went astray and begin again at step 5. Otherwise, go back to step 1. Naturally, if the rule generated a solution to the problem, we are finished—at least with the current subproblem. There may be higher-level subproblems that are still unsolved, however, which were waiting for these lower-level, intermediate results before the search for their solution could continue.

On occasion, a heuristic fails and leads to a dead end. In this case, we must mark this decision path as a failure and backtrack to the point where it diverged. If there are additional, untried, candidate rules at this level, select one of them. If there are none, continue backtracking until you find one.

If we have not yet found a solution but still appear to be on track, go back to step 1 to develop a new problem statement and run through another cycle of the process.

In this example, we have reached a dead end. The problem statement remains the same, but we have exhausted all resources along the current decision path for solving it. Therefore, we back up to step 5 and select the other candidate rule for resolving the current problem statement. This rule yields the solution.

REPRESENTING UNCERTAINTY

There is one last topic we must touch on briefly before leaving this chapter: that of representing uncertainty. In the real world, we are rarely 100 percent certain of our knowledge. Our data is incomplete; our rules are conjectural; our knowledge is approximate.

Uncertain knowledge may lead to uncertain conclusions. If our conclusions cannot be directly tested, it is wise to attach an indication of our degree of confidence in them. There are several ways to do this.

One method attaches *certainty factors* to each rule. The certainty factor is a number between 0 and 1 that represents the expert's level of confidence in the rule. A certainty factor of 1 represents fact; a certainty factor of 0 represents impossibility. As rules are chained together to form a conclusion, certainty factors are combined to calculate the overall level of confidence in the final conclusion.

Another method uses the concept of *fuzzy sets* to soften the value of an attribute. People often use inexact and relative values to describe the world. A tree may be "tall," but it's exact height is not known. You may be "low" on fuel without knowing exactly how many ounces are left in the gas tank.

There are many instances where the exact value of an attribute is not important—only the attribute's relative value need be considered. A fuzzy set allows for this. Instead of strict limits for inclusion in a set, fuzzy sets express the *degree* of inclusion in a set.

Consider, for example, the set of all tall trees. In conventional set theory, a tree six inches tall would not be included in this set. But with fuzzy set theory, this tree is included in the set, but its degree of inclusion is "very low." A two-hundred-foot tree, on the other hand, has a degree of inclusion that is "very high."

Whatever scheme is used, the important consideration is to qualify the accuracy of a decision according to the accuracy of your information.

LISP: A VEHICLE FOR ARTIFICIAL INTELLIGENCE

In the last chapter, we explored some ways to represent knowledge in an intelligent computer system. The next step, of course, is to program these representations into the computer using the appropriate programming language. In the United States, this programming language is Lisp.

While you may not be as familiar with Lisp as you are with FORTRAN, BASIC, or Pascal, Lisp is not a new language. It is actually one of the oldest in the lineage of programming languages, second only to FORTRAN.

Lisp was created by John McCarthy at M.I.T. in 1958. Since its inception, Lisp has become the language of choice of universities and research institutes involved with artificial intelligence. Its evolution has been marred by the failure of the computing community to set standards for the language, and as a result several dialects of Lisp exist today, varying widely in their features and emphasis. The dialect INTERLISP, for example, strives to provide the best of all programming environments; it compromises execution speed and memory efficiency to achieve this end. MACLISP, on the other hand, stresses efficiency, flexibility, and easy development of AI tools.

The features of Lisp we introduce in this chapter apply to most any dialect.

SPECIAL FEATURES OF LISP

What makes Lisp so convenient for developing AI applications? Contrary to what you might expect, Lisp is not a complicated language, but derives its power from its simplicity. The syntactic and semantic rules of Lisp can be learned in a matter of minutes. In addition, there are a number of other features that contribute to Lisp's suitability to AI.

Symbolic vs. Numeric Orientation

Unlike many conventional languages that were designed as efficient number-crunchers, Lisp was designed to deal with symbols and symbolic expressions (called *S-expressions* in Lisp). Symbols are words that represent objects and concepts. Thus, Lisp is ideal for creating the kinds of representations discussed in Chapter 3.

Lists: One Data Structure for All

The name Lisp is derived from *List programming language,* so it should come as no surprise that the fundamental data structure in Lisp is the list.

A list is just what you think it is. A grocery list, for example, might look like:

- Milk
- Bread
- Butter
- Cheese
- Eggs

In Lisp, lists are enclosed by parentheses, and the objects in the list are separated by spaces. The list above would look like this:

(Milk Bread Butter Cheese Eggs)

Each item in the list is called an *element* of the list. List elements can be symbols (words) as shown above, or they can be numbers, or they can be other lists. This list contains a nice assortment of elements:

(COUNT OFF (1 ONE) (2 TWO) (3 THREE))

There are five elements in this list: two symbols and three lists. Because lists can contain other lists as elements, they can get quite complex:

(((HOW)) (MANY ((ELEMENTS (ARE)) IN (THIS))) LIST)

The deep nesting of parentheses makes it difficult to determine how many elements this list contains. Lists are delineated by their outermost level of parentheses, so the list above contains the following three elements:

- The list ((HOW))
- The list (MANY ((ELEMENTS (ARE)) IN (THIS)))
- The symbol LIST

A list can have zero elements, as in:

( )

This empty list is called *nil*. Nil is a very special object in Lisp because it is both a list (when represented as ( )) and a symbol (when represented as **NIL**). But that's not all: In expressions involving truth, NIL is the symbol for False.

Equivalence of Data and Programs

One very remarkable feature of Lisp that has important consequences for AI programming is the fact that both programs and data share the same representation—both are represented as lists.

Consider, for example, the following list:

(DEFUN INCREMENT X (PLUS 1 X))

This is a list of four elements: three symbols and a list. It also happens to be a Lisp program. This uniformity among programs and data has the following ramifications:

1. Programs manipulate lists.
2. All programs are lists.
3. Therefore, programs can manipulate programs.

In Lisp, it is easy to create programs that create or modify other programs. This is very important to some artificial intelligence applications. For example, one of the goals of AI is to design programs that learn from their experience. Learning involves modifying the knowledge base and reasoning algorithms to suit new information. Thus, learning systems can make good use of this feature.

Modular Organization and Extensibility

Lisp programs consist of functions. Functions take a certain number of values (arguments), manipulate these values in some way, and then return a value. For example, PLUS is a function in Lisp. When given the values 2 and 4, PLUS returns the value 6.

The function-based design of Lisp enforces modular programming practices. Lisp programs are built by successively defining new functions in terms of existing ones. When a function is invoked (called), it may in turn invoke other functions, which may invoke other functions, and so on. Top-level functions in powerful programs may cascade into hundreds of function invocations, and yet when all is through, they return a single value.

The function-based design also makes Lisp very extensible. While Lisp provides certain "core" functions as part of its definition, users may (and do) define new functions to suit their programming needs. There is no difference between a core function and a user-defined function; indeed, the user may redefine a core function if he or she chooses. In essence, Lisp allows you to create your own custom language definition.

Evaluation Rules

Since programs and data share the same list structure, every expression in Lisp must be evaluated. The rules for evaluating symbolic expressions are as follows:

1. If the expression is a list, the first symbol inside the left parenthesis is considered to be the name of a function, and all other elements of the list are considered arguments of the function. If a function has not been defined with that name, an error occurs.
2. All numbers evaluate to themselves, as do the special symbols T (true) and NIL.
3. All other symbols, whether they appear by themselves or as elements of a list, are considered variables and are evaluated to determine their values.

In general, arguments of a function are evaluated according to these rules and the resultant values are passed to the function. If the argument is a list, it is considered a function call and is evaluated according to rule 1. If the argument is a number, or T or NIL, it is evaluated according to rule 2. If the argument is a symbol, it is considered a variable and is evaluated according to rule 3.

There are exceptions to these rules, some of which will be discussed later in the chapter. In general, however, they are good guiding principles for understanding how Lisp works.

Recursion

Lisp functions may, and often are, defined recursively. A recursive function is one that is defined in terms of itself, that is, it calls itself. You might think this design is circular, that the function would call itself forever and never return a solution. This often happens during a program development, but a well-designed recursive function is efficient and compact.

The idea of recursion is very similar to the problem-solving strategies we discussed in the last chapter. The approach is to successively divide a complicated problem into simpler subproblems until the subproblem is simple enough to solve.

Let's look at a simple example. Suppose we know how to add 1 to a number. Our problem, however, is to add 4 to 10. Thinking recursively, we can solve the problem this way:

1. The problem is $10+4=?$ But $4=3+1$. Therefore, we can break the original problem into two additions: $(10+3)+1=?$ We can add 1, but cannot add 3, so send the subproblem $10+3$ through the loop.

2. The problem is $10+3=?$ But $3=2+1$. Therefore, we can break this problem into two additions: $(10+2)+1=?$ We can add 1, but cannot add 2, so send the subproblem $10+2$ through the loop.

3. The problem is $10+2=?$ But $2=1+1$. Therefore, we can break this problem into two additions: $(10+1)+1=?$ We can add 1, so we can solve this problem. The result of the first addition, $(10+1)$, is 11. The result of the second addition, $11+1$, is 12. Therefore, $10+2=12$.

4. We know from step 3 that $10+2=12$. We can use this answer to solve the problem in step 2: $10+3=(10+2)+1=12+1=13$.

5. We know from step 4 that $10+3=13$. We can use this answer to solve the problem in step $1:10+4=(10+3)+1=13+1=14$. This is our final answer.

The key to successful recursion is to test for the terminating condition each time the function is invoked. In this example, the terminating condition is the knowledge of how to add 1. As soon as the terminating condition is detected, we can produce a solution instead of another subproblem. The solution is then used to solve the preceding subproblem, whose solution is used to solve the preceding subproblem, and so on, until the original problem is solved.

SOME COMMON LISP FUNCTIONS

Lisp functions have the following general form:

(function-name argument1 argument2 argument3 . . .)

The number of expected arguments varies from function to function, as does the argument type.

Let's briefly survey some of the more fundamental Lisp functions.

Quote

The function Quote takes one argument. The argument may be any symbolic expression: a symbol, a number, or a list. Quote returns its argument, unaltered, as its value.

Some examples:

(QUOTE HARRY) returns HARRY

(QUOTE (A B C)) returns (A B C)

A function that simply returns its argument seems rather pointless. Yet the real value of Quote is that it "turns off" the evaluation rules mentioned earlier in this chapter. We will see the value of this feature as we look at some of the other functions.

Many systems allow Quote to be abbreviated by using a single quote mark ('). Thus, the two expressions below are equivalent:

(QUOTE (1 2 3))
'(1 2 3)

We will use this abbreviation throughout the rest of this chapter.

Car

The function Car takes one argument, a nonempty list, and returns as its value the first element in the list.
Some examples:

(CAR '(A B C)) returns A
(CAR '((A) (B) (C)) returns (A)

Notice the use of Quote here. In both of these examples, Quote keeps the argument of Car from being evaluated. If we were to remove the quote mark in the first example, for instance, the Lisp system would try to evaluate (A B C). Since this is a list, it would expect A to be the name of a function by evaluation rule 1. Since A is not a function, an error would be reported.

Cdr

The function Cdr takes one argument, a nonempty list, and returns as its value its argument with the first element removed.
Some examples:

(CDR '(A B C)) returns (B C)
(CDR '((A) (B) (C)) returns ((B) (C))

Put another way, Cdr applied to a list returns the list with its Car removed.

Cons

The function Cons takes two arguments. The first argument may be any symbolic expression: a symbol, a number, or a list. The second argument must be a list. Cons inserts its first argument as the first element of its second argument and returns the resultant list.
Some examples:

(CONS 'A '(B C)) returns (A B C)
(CONS '(A) '((B) (C)) returns ((A) (B) (C))

Cons allows you to construct new lists from existing ones.

Predicates

Lisp has a full complement of predicate functions. Predicates are functions that return a value of true or false. As mentioned earlier, NIL is Lisp's symbol for false. True, however, may be represented by the symbol T, or it may be any symbolic expression except NIL. Thus, the following are all representations of truth in Lisp:

    42
    (1 2 3)
    A
    T

Some of the predicates in Lisp are:

Atom.   The function Atom takes one argument of any type and returns T if the argument is a symbol or number, or returns NIL if the argument is a list.
Some examples:

    (ATOM 'NIL) returns T
    (ATOM '(A B C)) returns NIL

Zerop.   The function Zerop takes one numeric argument and returns T if the number is 0, NIL otherwise.
Some examples:

    (ZEROP 14) returns NIL
    (ZEROP 0) returns T

Greaterp.   The function Greaterp takes a list of numbers and returns T if the numbers are in descending order, NIL otherwise.
Some examples:

    (GREATERP '(10 9 8 7 6)) returns T
    (GREATERP '(6 7 8 9 10)) returns NIL

Cond

The function Cond is the Lisp version of a conditional statement. It has the form:

    (COND (condition1 expression1)
         (condition2 expression2)
         (condition3 expression3)
                 :
                 :
         (conditionN expressionN)

The conditions and expressions in the Cond function can be any symbolic expression. Cond works by evaluating the conditions in order until a non-NIL value is found. If a condition evaluates to a non-NIL value, the corresponding expression is evaluated and the resultant value is returned as the value of the Cond function.

Although it is not required, most Cond functions contain an "If all else fails" clause at the end. This clause contains a condition that always evaluates to a non-NIL value. Thus if all other conditions fail, the last one, at least, will succeed.

Consider this example of a Cond function:

```
(COND ((EQUAL X 1) 'ONE)
((EQUAL X 2) 'TWO)
((EQUAL X 3) 'THREE)
(T 'UNKNOWN-NUMBER))
```

The symbol X is a variable, and has some value. If the value of X is equal to 1, then the first Cond condition is satisfied and the expression 'ONE is evaluated and returned as the value of the function. Similar actions occur if the value of X is equal to 2 or 3. If the value of X is not 1, 2, or 3, the final condition is evaluated. It is always non-NIL (T ensures that), so if all else fails, the Cond function will return UNKNOWN-NUMBER.

Setq

The Setq function takes two arguments. The first must be a symbol; the second can be any symbolic expression. Setq returns as its value the value of its second argument.

Some examples:

```
(SETQ LETTERS '(A B C)) returns (A B C)
(SETQ ONE 1) returns 1
```

Setq seems rather useless. It merely returns the value of its second argument, similar to Quote, and appears to ignore its first argument completely. What makes Setq valuable is not the value it returns, but rather its side effect.

A side effect is an invisible by-product of a function. Setq's side effect assigns the value of the second argument as the value of the first argument. Thus, Setq is Lisp's version of the assignment statement found in conventional programming languages.

In the examples above, the value of LETTERS is now (A B C) and the value of ONE is now 1.

Setq is also an exception to the evaluation rules discussed earlier. Notice that Setq's first argument is not quoted. This is because the first argument in a Setq function is not evaluated, hence it does not need the quote mark to suppress evaluation. This is an exception to rule 3.

Defun

The function Defun allows us to define new functions. It returns as its value the name of the function being defined, but like Setq, the important thing about DEFUN is its side effect.

DEFUN has the form:

(DEFUN *function-name (argument-list) (function body)*)

For example, we might define Second, a function that returns the second element of a list, in the following way:

(DEFUN SECOND (X) (CAR (CDR X)))

The argument list contains dummy arguments—just place holders for the real arguments. The function body contains a Lisp expression that performs the ''work'' of the function. We can now invoke the function SECOND as we would any other function:

(SECOND '(A B C)) returns B
(SECOND '((A) (B) (C)) returns (B)

When the function is called, the actual argument is *bound* to the dummy argument X in the function definition. This means that X is temporarily assigned the value of the actual argument in the function call, just as if a Setq had been performed. The function body can then be evaluated using this assignment.

BUILDING FUNCTIONS IN LISP

The last example shows how new Lisp functions are built using existing ones. The function Second is defined in terms of the functions Car and Cdr. When the function body of Second is evaluated, Car is called. When the argument of Car is evaluated, Cdr is called. The value returned by Cdr is used as the argument to Car, and the value returned by Car is used as the value returned by Second. This is what we meant earlier by cascading function calls.

USING LISP TO REPRESENT KNOWLEDGE BASE COMPONENTS

Representing Objects and Attributes

Now that we have a basic repertoire of Lisp functions, let's translate some of the representations developed in Chapter 3 into Lisp expressions. Lisp's symbolic nature and simple list data structure makes this much easier than it would be with conventional programming languages.

There are several ways to represent objects in Lisp. Perhaps the most natural way is to translate an object definition directly into a list.

For example, in Chapter 3 we created a definition of the object Tool. The object definition looked like this:

OBJECT NAME:	Tool
ATTRIBUTES:	Made of: Metal
	Function: Dismantle, assemble engine
	Location: Toolbox
	Appearance: Has a handle
OPERATIONS:	Pick up:
	Put down:
	Rotate right:
	Rotate left:
	etc.

Tool definition.

Translating this into a list, we get:

```
((OBJECT-NAME Tool)
(ATTRIBUTES   (MADE-OF METAL)
              (FUNCTION DISMANTLE-ENGINE ASSEMBLE-ENGINE)
              (LOCATION TOOLBOX)
              (APPEARANCE HAS-HANDLE))
(OPERATIONS   (PICK-UP)
              (PUT-DOWN)
              (ROTATE-RIGHT)
              (ROTATE-LEFT)))
```

We can now give the definition a name, call it Tool-definition, using Setq:

```
(SETQ TOOL-DEFINITION '((OBJECT-NAME Tool)
                        (ATTRIBUTES (MADE-OF METAL)
                                    (FUNCTION   DISMANTLE-ENGINE
                                     ASSEMBLE-ENGINE)
                                    (LOCATION TOOLBOX)
                                    (APPEARANCE HAS-HANDLE))
                        (OPERATIONS (PICK-UP)
                                    (PUT-DOWN)
                                    (ROTATE-RIGHT)
                                    (ROTATE-LEFT))
```

The value of Tool-definition is now the list structure.

Knowing the structure of the object, we can use Lisp functions to extract pieces of information. For example, to find out what the tool is made of, we can use Car and Cdr in the following way:

```
(CAR (CDR (CAR (CDR (CAR (CDR TOOL-DEFINITION))))))
```

Let's step through the evaluation of this expression to see how it works:

1. Evaluate the innermost list first. This is (CDR TOOL-DEFINITION). TOOL-DEFINITION evaluates to the list structure, the Cdr of which is:

```
((ATTRIBUTES (MADE-OF METAL)
             (FUNCTION DISMANTLE-ENGINE ASSEMBLE-ENGINE)
             (LOCATION TOOLBOX)
             (APPEARANCE HAS-HANDLE))
 (OPERATIONS (PICK-UP)
             (PUT-DOWN)
             (ROTATE-RIGHT)
             (ROTATE-LEFT)))
```

2. The result of step 1 is passed on as the argument to Car. The Car of the list in step 1 is:

```
(ATTRIBUTES (MADE-OF METAL)
            (FUNCTION DISMANTLE-ENGINE ASSEMBLE-ENGINE)
            (LOCATION TOOLBOX)
            (APPEARANCE HAS-HANDLE))
```

3. The result of step 2 is passed on as the argument to Cdr. The Cdr of the list in step 2 is:

```
((MADE-OF METAL)
 (FUNCTION DISMANTLE-ENGINE ASSEMBLE-ENGINE)
 (LOCATION TOOLBOX)
 (APPEARANCE HAS-HANDLE))
```

4. The result of step 3 is passed on as the argument to Car. The Car of the list in step 3 is: (MADE-OF METAL)

5. The result of step 4 is passed on as the argument to Cdr. The Cdr of the list in step 4 is: (METAL)

6. The result of step 5 is passed on as the argument to Car. The Car of the list in step 5 is: METAL
   This is the answer to our question, what is the tool made of?

If this is a question that might be asked often, we can make a function out of it:

```
(DEFUN WHAT-IS-THE-TOOL-MADE-OF (X)
       (CAR (CDR (CAR (CDR (CAR (CDR TOOL-DEFINITION)))))))
```

And we can now ask the question by calling this function:

```
(WHAT-IS-THE-TOOL-MADE-OF TOOL- DEFINITION)
```

Representing Classes

As we discussed in Chapter 3, classes can be created by adding the ako (a kind of) slot to our object definitions. This is easy enough to perform. But how can we follow ako links from one object to another?

One way is to define a function similar to the one above that extracts the ako link from an object definition. A call of the function to extract the ako link for an adjustable wrench might look like this:

(GET-AKO ADJUSTABLE-WRENCH)

This function call finds the parent class of the adjustable wrench. With this information, the object definition of the parent class could then be examined to determine the value of an inherited attribute, for example.

Representing Relationships

Lisp is equally good for representing relationships written in a predicate logic form. In the last chapter, we used relationships like:

Connects(high-voltage cable, spark plug, distributor)
Flows(current, high-voltage cable, distributor, spark plug)

This translates almost directly to the form of a function call:

(CONNECTS HIGH-VOLTAGE-CABLE, SPARK-PLUG, DISTRIBUTOR)
(FLOWS CURRENT HIGH-VOLTAGE-CABLE DISTRIBUTOR SPARK PLUG)

Representing relationships as function calls makes sense. The functions invoked by these function calls could handle all the bookkeeping details involved with integrating this information into the knowledge base.

Representing Rules

Heuristic rules also find a natural representation in Lisp. Since rules consist of conditions and actions, we can use the Cond function.

In Chapter 3, we created the following rule:

IF IS-FALSE(Battery, Has-current) THEN SEARCH-AND-REPLACE(Battery, Has-current, False)

In Lisp, the rule looks like:

```
(COND ((EQUAL (GET-STATE BATTERY, HAS-CURRENT) TRUE)
(SEARCH-AND-REPLACE BATTERY, HAS-CURRENT, FALSE)))
```

The rule has only one conditional and one action, and so does the Cond function. The function GET-STATE is assumed to be defined. It extracts the state variable given in its second argument from the object definition given in its first argument. The predicate function EQUAL then tests to see if the state, HAS-CURRENT, is true. If it is, then the action part of the rule is evaluated. If the condition is false, evaluation of the Cond function simply terminates.

EXPERT SYSTEMS

ORIENTATION

Previous chapters introduced artificial intelligence and Lisp, the base language for AI. This chapter talks about expert systems, an evolving application of Lisp. You get answers to these questions:

- How did expert systems get started, and what are they like today?
- What is an expert system anyway?
- What can I do with an expert system?

We hope our discussion of Lisp and artificial intelligence, up to this point, has shown the connections between computer systems, Lisp, and artificial intelligence. This chapter extends those connections to expert systems. It begins with the invention of Lisp and ends with the steps you take to develop an expert system. We use this background to discuss AI systems in general in subsequent chapters.

BACKGROUND INFORMATION

If you examine expert systems, be prepared to look at most dimensions of AI. An examination of expert systems leads to an examination of dialects of Lisp, which leads to an examinaton of types of artificial intelligence, which leads to a study of specific computer systems and funded projects, which leads to a discussion of Lisp experts, which leads to . . . . You can get into an endless cycle and not know when to exit.

To help you get a complete picture, we synthesized information from a broad base and consolidated the information to form a sequence that begins with the invention of Lisp and ends with today's expert systems. We felt this was necessary because the development of expert systems occurred partly by accretion and partly by design. If you do not look at expert systems in relation to the whole of artificial intelligence, it is difficult to know what an expert system does and how you could use one.

Relatively few people belong to the artificial intelligence community. Relatively few people are Lisp experts—knowledge engineers, as they are called today. The Lisp and artificial intelligence communities are mostly one and the same, and the community is very exclusive.

You can become a member if you are willing to spend years working with established experts and learn the inner workings of AI. This condition is a verity. Since 1960, Lisp experts have plied their trade in think-tank environments in universities, large corporations, and special agencies. The experts know each other personally, and they know what other experts do. Today there is a critical shortage of knowledge engineers. Many knowledge engineers believe the world is not yet ready for AI. Others believe AI is not ready to be released to the world. Marketing people believe AI is ready. Whatever, you are most likely to encounter AI in the form of an expert system.

We hope you do not bypass this section and go directly to a definition of an expert system and a discussion of how you can use one. We believe it is necessary for you to understand how the world got expert systems before you look at them. You need a perspective before you think about using an expert system. Let's take some time to look at this. Let's set the stage for defining and discussing expert systems.

THE SETTING FOR EXPERT SYSTEMS

While the Lisp experts often disagreed with each other as AI was developed, they always worked to extend the frontiers of AI and bring Lisp up on state-of-the-art computer systems. The experts conducted research in the truest overall sense of the concept, but like many people, they had strong egos.

The Lisp experts worked in relatively exclusive and free environments where they were not subjected to continuous public scrutiny. They invented ideas that no other people in the world understood, but to place the development of expert systems into an adequate personal perspective, you must realize that the Lisp experts were driven to succeed by distinct, but related, outside factors.

On the one hand, the experts knew they were inventing computer systems that had immense power, but they were afraid that people would not accept their systems or would misuse them. On the other hand, groups of experts within the Lisp community thought they were developing the best systems and that other groups within the community were not doing the most significant work.

As you read on and as you examine particular expert systems, you will see the effects of the overall setting in which AI developed in these ways:

- Many dialects of Lisp were developed. Each group of experts thinks their dialect is best suited to the development of an expert system.
- Lisp was brought up on varied types of hardware systems. Each group thought their system was suited to the development of expert systems.
- Collectively, the Lisp community created many types of software, but particular groups thought their software was best suited to creating or using expert systems.

Throughout your examination of expert systems, be aware that each system you look at has "roots." The roots will contain three elements: the dialect of Lisp used to create the system; the particular variation, or type, of system being developed; and the components of the system. Below, each element is described in a subsection.

The invention of Lisp created much interest, within the select environment we just described, in the pursuit of artificial intelligence. Consequently, new features and capabilities were added to the original Lisp language.

The development of new features created a stream of Lisp experts, but the experts did not agree about what should be developed (tools, compilers, applications, internals, and so on). It doesn't matter whether you know what these things are. The important thing is that the development of Lisp diverged, it did not converge. Consequently, Lisp experts formed camps.

Some of the camps were like laminar streams which do not interact, but which flow in about the same direction. The individual camps went their own ways, but the collective camps used Lisp to create software in which artificial intelligence and knowledge were used to solve problems normally solved by human experts. The software that eventually became an expert system, or became a tool kit that could be used to develop an expert system, was developed in a dual atmosphere in which experts had divergent opinions about how to create expert systems, but their work converged to create the systems. The experts were driven to disagree, but they were also driven to create systems that people could use. Unlike most Americans, the experts were free to diverge and examine any interesting element of AI; but like most Americans, the experts were pragmatic at times.

The streams of thought about AI flowed along separately, but they were funneled into a single reservoir, a reservoir which today contains myriad expert systems and tool kits for developing expert systems. Consequently, the reservoir that contains expert systems is like a reservoir in which you can catch trout, bass, pike, and salmon. You need to determine which type of expert system you need, get properly equipped, and go fishing.

Before you learn about expert systems per se, the next few subsections discuss parts of the overall setting in which you should examine expert systems. Each subsection discusses an element that shaped the development of expert systems. After you read the subsections, think about the type of expert system you might purchase. Will you need a user-friendly application system, or are you able to hack around in a system and do your own work? Will you need a large or small system? Will you need a dialect of Lisp containing many functions that provide I/O, or will you need a dialect containing functions that do graphics? You can raise many questions. Our point is this: Take time to raise questions before you go to a trade show and look at existing expert systems.

The Invention of Lisp

John McCarthy, an M.I.T. associate professor of communications, got the idea for Lisp in 1956 when he attended a conference. His idea evolved and incubated for two years. Armed with a grant from IBM and a small building on the M.I.T. campus, McCarthy and a few graduate students began development of a Lisp language in 1958 (programmers refer to this as implementation of a language). McCarthy Lisp (actually called Lisp 1.5) was implemented by 1962. McCarthy described this development in the article:

> McCARTHY, JOHN. "History of Lisp," *ACM SIGPLAN Notices* (Association for Computing Machinery, Inc.) 13, no. 8, August 1978.

while he was at the Artificial Intelligence Laboratory at Stanford University in Palo Alto, California. During this initial work, McCarthy received much help from Marvin Minsky, a professor of mathematics at M.I.T.

After McCarthy invented Lisp, the language was altered in many ways as associates, disciples, and rivals developed new dialects.

Dialects of Lisp

Despite everything you hear or read, Lisp 1.5 became essentially two dialects: MacLisp (at M.I.T.), and BBN-Lisp (at the Xerox Palo Alto Research Center), but there were many spin-off dialects. The developers of MacLisp focused on low-level system features such as arbitrary precision arithmetic (things that go on deep within the software system). The developers of BBN-Lisp, which was renamed InterLisp, focused on programmer tools and applications software. At present, some Lisp experts are consolidating MacLisp and InterLisp into an "industrial-strength Lisp" called Common Lisp. We'll get back to this "industrial-strength" Lisp later.

Let's look at the development of Lisp, which led to the development of expert systems, in more detail. Notice the splits, spin-offs, and consolidations.

Early on, the MacLisp people, who were at M.I.T. or who came from M.I.T., used two criteria to develop Lisp. One, they implemented whatever features they wanted. Two, they brought up Lisp on new hardware as soon as it was invented. As an example of new hardware technology, Digital Equipment Corporation (DEC) invented the PDP-6 minicomputer. MacLisp was brought up on this computer. Then MacLisp was implemented on the DEC PDP-10, DEC PDP-11, DEC TOPS 10, and DEC TOPS 20 computer systems as soon as these systems were developed. As an example of implementation of assorted features, programmers worked for some time to enable MacLisp to process numbers of arbitrary precision, even though some people discounted the value of doing this.

When the DEC VAX minicomputer was invented, a new dialect of MacLisp was implemented on the VAX. The DEC VAX implementation of Lisp was called VAX NIL (for New Implementation of Lisp). By the way, you may remember that NIL is an important Lisp function. Many Lisp experts thought this was funny, an inside joke, if you please.

To illustrate how Lisp dialects were propagated and specialized, the VAX NIL version of Lisp was taken to the University of California at Berkeley and implemented on a new DEC VAX. The name was changed to FranzLisp, and FranzLisp became the *de facto* standard Lisp for DEC VAX computers.

Meanwhile, back at M.I.T., several changes were made in MacLisp to create another dialect, which was called the M.I.T. Lisp Machine Lisp. This new dialect was then taken to Carnegie-Mellon University as part of the SPICE project (Scientific Personal Integrated Computing Environmnent). Several new features were added, and the new dialect was called SPICE Lisp.

As you can see, one group of Lisp experts took McCarthy's Lisp 1.5 and changed it into MacLisp. Then they changed MacLisp into other dialects in accordance with technological advancement and their needs and interests.

Switch gears now, and we'll talk about the other group; they developed InterLisp. McCarthy's Lisp 1.5 was taken to the West Coast and changed into Lisp 1.6 (often called Standard Lisp). This Lisp was changed into InterLisp and brought up on the Dolphin and Dorado computers made by Xerox Corporation.

The InterLisp experts on the West Coast were interested in the portability of Lisp (being able to run one dialect of Lisp on different computers). For example, InterLisp was brought up on the DEC PDP-10, in addition to being up on the Xerox Dolphin and the Xerox Dorado computers. The term *portability* refers to having a core of program code that can be used by different computers. That is, a language is portable when the same version of the language can run on different computers.

Notice that the InterLisp experts did two things differently from the MacLisp experts. One, they focused their attention and tried to develop software along certain guidelines. The MacLisp experts developed whatever they wanted to develop. Two, the InterLisp people worked on software that sits on top of an operating system. The MacLisp experts worked on core programs and internal features as much as they worked on anything else. Let's look at some examples:

- **Focused Attention**: If you accept some operating system such as UNIX, and then try to implement software that runs on any UNIX system, you are focusing your attention on software portability. That is, you are looking beyond the computer you are using and focusing on other computers. The InterLisp people did this more than the MacLisp people.

- **Unfocused Attention**: If you bring up Lisp on new hardware systems as they are created, and implement a separate dialect of Lisp on the specific operating system used by each hardware system, you are not focusing attention on a general concept. The MacLisp people did this more than the InterLisp people.

- **Tools and Applications Software**: Tools are programs such as editors, formatters, and translators that let you use a computer efficiently for many, varied purposes. Applications are programs that perform specific tasks such as accounting, job costing, and statistical analysis. People use these types of programs directly. The InterLisp experts created types of programs.

- **Core Software**: Core programs make the computer system work in the fundamental sense. The programs that drive a printer or plotter, the programs that perform computations, the programs that display characters on a screen, and the programs that execute a command are core programs. Programmers spend a lot of time creating and then optimizing these programs. That is, they try to make a computer work efficiently. The MacLisp experts created core programs.

You will see examples of this when you look into expert systems. Some marketing people will tell you how fast a computer works and how you can set it up so it will do anything. These people will talk about myriad specific features that enhance the capacity of the computer system to perform. These people relate to the MacLisp school of thought. Other marketing people will tell you how easy it is to use their systems. Everything is done by pushing a button. The system is very user-friendly. These people relate to the InterLisp school of thought. Of course, there is a lot of overlap. We discussed basic tendencies to let you know what to look for.

We do not want to alarm you, but you will discover as you read more and more information about AI that it becomes difficult at times to know exactly what someone means by terms such as drivers, kernels, core programs, tools, applications, heuristics, objects, and knowledge bases. The terms are not the problem. The problem is that the people who created AI came from many different disciplines, and then, once they became experts in AI, they divided into several camps. Here are some things to consider that help you avoid confusion:

- Many terms in AI had to be invented. Since the field is new, precise definitions are often not available. Be patient. Look at the context. Read several different articles or books and compare notes.

- Many people describe the wonderful world of AI. AI experts know all the nuances related to a term because they visit with the experts who coined the term. When the experts write articles, they assume the reader knows what they are talking about. Other reporters, like us, are not AI giants. These reporters interpret AI and report their findings according to myriad criteria.

- Much work in AI is conceptualized as it is done. For example, during the development of an expert system, knowledge engineers encounter problems and invent concepts they hope will solve the problems. They name the concepts and apply them, but things never work out exactly as planned. Thus, the concepts are altered as solutions are formulated. This causes shifts in meanings and the addition of more terms, some of which are project-dependent. Recall our earlier discussion of predicating and subjecting. It is still done much of the time and it may affect an expert system you purchase.

- Companies compete with each other. A company who calls a rule interpreter an "inference engine" creates a first that other companies do not want to acknowledge. Consequently, other companies invent a similar type of program, but give it a different name.

- Some terms have precise definitions, but most people never seem to really understand them. *Heuristics* is such a word. The problem is that heuristics are an integral part of AI. Some other terms in this category are *facilitate, efficacy,* and *taxonomy.* Examine the context in which these terms are used and do the best you can to interpret what they mean.

- Work in AI is done by people who have very diverse backgrounds. Some terms which have one meaning in mathematics have similar, but different, meanings in philosophy, English, or computer science. Many experts know about the subtle differences, but ordinary people are not so informed. It is difficult to deal with this problem because you often have no way of knowing about an expert's background. Again, be aware of the context and the overall situation.

These factors combine to increase the potential for confusion in direct proportion to the number of people who talk about AI. This potential is magnified as marketing people promote the use of AI in industry, education, and business. The ancient maxim, Let the buyer beware, applies more to AI than to automobiles, because you will be less familiar with AI products.

We tried to maintain some consistency, but at the same time we fudged here and there in the usage of some terms. In places where you feel there are severe discrepancies, consult the Glossary. It contains comprehensive definitions of the major terms in AI.

Getting back to our discussion of the development of Lisp, you can see there was no cohesive effort to develop it. The InterLisp experts claim they were more organized and advanced. The MacLisp people claim they were more creative and did more to improve Lisp. Other experts did their thing in assorted environments throughout the world.

When you shop for an expert system, be aware that a dialect of Lisp or any of several tools may have been used to develop the system. The nature of the expert system is shaped by how it was developed, but this is not bad. Actually, this is good, because present-day developers of expert systems have a variety of means for creating a system. This means that you can examine many different types and sizes of expert systems.

In writing this book, we reviewed more than 50 Lisp dialects. After a while they begin to look pretty similar. All dialects have CAR, CDR, and CONS functions, but some dialects let you find the CADDDR of a list; others only let you find the CADR of a list. At a surface level, this may look like a trivial difference. Beneath the surface, the difference can be important, depending on what you intend to do with your dialect of Lisp.

Variation in Expert Systems

Much more could be said about dialects of Lisp, but let's stop and focus on expert systems. We talked about the development of Lisp and the orientations of its developers to let you see that any expert system you examine will have ''roots.'' The ''roots'' (InterLisp, MacLisp, Standard Lisp, and such) affect how your expert system works. To see this, let's discuss variations in expert systems. As you look at the variations, remember that we alluded earlier to an ''industrial-strength'' Lisp. We are working up to that Lisp and to a definition and description of an expert system, but we are not quite ready to discuss them. There are expert systems and there are expert systems for these reasons:

- No two Lisps are alike. What you get, and consequently what you can do, is partly dependent on the dialect you obtain and the computer system on which the dialect runs. Thus, your expert systems will have characteristics. The characteristics accrue from processor capabilities (e.g., its speed and register sizes), availability of tools (e.g., the type of editor you get for writing Lisp programs), and the number and type of functions in the Lisp dialect (e.g., macro functions, I/O functions, define functions). Select a system that has the characteristics you need.
- There are no standards for what a dialect of Lisp should do. Consequently, there are no standards for what an expert system should do. If you ''get into'' expert systems, you'll venture into a new area that people have not explored. You'll be a pioneer in the truest sense. If you are a corporate executive, it's possible that you'll perform tasks for which there are no legal or policy precedents.
- Lisp is a very plastic language. It is easy for an expert programmer to extend or alter a dialect of Lisp. Consequently, the expert system you purchase initially will have certain features, but a programmer can add new features or customize existing features. Look at what is built into your Lisp environment, determine what your programmers must do to get a system started, and then relate these things to your resources and constraints. It takes months, or years, for Lisp programmers to effect significant changes in the capability of an expert system.

Wait a minute! This looks like a mess. Did we just contradict ourselves? On one hand, we said that you can alter a dialect of Lisp and then create just about any expert system. On the other hand, we said that what you can do is limited to what your dialect of Lisp provides. Actually, there is no contradiction, but there are several relationships you should examine:

- A dialect of Lisp resides on some operating system (e.g., UNIX, TOPS 10). The dialect you buy provides certain core commands and functions. You also get an editor (for writing Lisp programs), a library of utilities (a program debugger, compiler, documentation browsers, program formatters), and access to other programming languages (Fortran, C, Pascal). These things vary among Lisp environments (dialects); they limit how a dialect of Lisp can be extended. Therefore, you should consider the total environment in which your expert system will function to determine what can be developed. For example, having a program that lets you create an expert system is more powerful than having a ready-made expert system, but it takes more expertise in AI to use the first program.
- Within a total expert system environment, a dialect of Lisp fits in between several distinct types of software in the environment. That is, a dialect of Lisp interfaces with software above and below its place in a hierarchy of software. A core program that operates the hardware always sits on the bottom of the hierarchy. Tools and

applications programs reside above Lisp in the hierarchy. There will be some limitations in how the dialect of Lisp interacts with software above and below Lisp in the environment. Also, all the software in the environment must run on some particular hardware. People often say that software is portable, but this is not entirely true. Software can be portable within limits. Beware of media hype in this regard.

As you consider an expert system, examine the total environment in which a dialect of Lisp can be used. The total environment determines how you can create or use an expert system, and it determines how the expert system will work. The total environment also determines how easy it is to customize or alter the software you purchase.

Components of Expert Systems

You do not just purchase an expert system. The simplest expert systems contain several components. The total system works as efficiently as the least efficient and capable component. Let's see what is required.

In general, you need the following things to develop an expert system:

- The hardware system must have a high compatibility factor. It should be easy to connect computers, monitors, disk drives, printers, plotters, modems, measurement instruments, robots, networks, graphics tablets, and so on. You do not want to be concerned about drivers (programs that enable devices to talk to each other) and connectors (devices that contain pins to let you hook one device to another). Before you purchase anything, be sure all hardware in the system can be connected.
- The operating system is a set of programs that runs the computer system. The operating system should provide easy access to all the software in the expert system environment. The operating system should also perform tasks efficiently and rapidly. For example, some Lisps run on top of the UNIX operating system. Others run on their own Lisp operating system. Your Lisp should not run slower or lose any capability when it operates on top of UNIX.
- The dialect of Lisp needs "industrial strength." This means its built-in functions should do these things: handle all types of data, provide interpretation and compilation of programs, provide access to features of its operating systems, access other programming languages and routines, provide for networking (sharing computer resources), provide access to tools software (editors, formatters, debuggers), and provide extensibility. Extensibility means that functions are available that enable a programmer to create new functions or program segments for development of expert systems. Common Lisp is emerging as the "industrial-strength" Lisp. More on this later.

Our setting is complete. We can define an expert system. Take a moment before you read the definition to think about what we said. We don't want you to become alarmed. On the other hand, we don't want you to spend a million dollars for the wrong system.

Let's see. Start with a dialect of Lisp. Run the dialect on top of an operating system which itself runs on a computer hardware system. Obtain additional software that runs on top of Lisp that either is a fully functioning expert system or contains assorted programs that can be used to create an expert system. Oh, my! The slogans and media hype made this sound easy. It looks like this is getting complicated. What definition of an expert system can incorporate all these things: dialects of Lisp, variations among expert systems, components, and who knows what else? Move on, gentle reader. It's not as bad as we made it sound.

DEFINITION OF EXPERT SYSTEMS

Webster's dictionary has no definition of an expert system, but it does define each term separately:

- An *expert* is a person with a high degree of knowledge about or skill in a certain subject.
- A *system* is a group of interacting, interrelated, or interdependent elements forming or regarded as forming a collective entity.

Although nothing about an expert system is human, the two terms do imply the nature of an expert system. In general, an expert system is defined by these features:

- A human expert feeds knowledge about an area such as heart diseases, teaching, or oil exploration into a computer. This information forms what most people call a knowledge base. Since most knowledge is recorded in sentences, as opposed to mathematical equations, the computer system must process symbolic data as opposed to numerical data. For example, in the area of heart diseases, an expert might feed this statement into the computer: The human heart has four chambers. Here's the point: An entire sentence, rule, or set of statements or rules can be a piece of information in an expert system.
- The knowledge given to the computer is divided into categories: facts, assumptions, and heuristic rules. Stating that the human heart has four chambers is a fact. Stating that problems with the aorta are caused by such and such is an assumption. The term *heuristic* means "helping to discover or learn." Thus, heuristic rules relate the facts and assumptions about an area to a problem situation and then attempt to find a solution to a problem.
- Once the knowledge has been stored according to an appropriate scheme for a given area, information about a problem that needs to be solved is fed into the computer. Then the heuristic rules are used to relate the knowledge to the problem situation or vice versa. Finally, the computer suggests a solution or provides a report that humans can use to determine a solution.

Several things are important when you think about an expert system. The subject area or domain must be carefully defined. It must be possible to classify knowledge as belonging to the area or not belonging to it. The facts must be established with a high degree of certainty and reliability. Something cannot be a fact in one context and an idea in another. It is not sufficient to just specify the rules. The structure that fits the rules together must be part of the expert system. The assumptions on which facts and rules are based must closely model the realities associated with the area. There must be some external method of verifying the reliability of proposed solutions to problems.

These ideas are combined to form this fundamental definition: An expert system is a computer system with sufficient hardware capability to run programs that do these things:

- A knowledge base is stored in memory or mass storage. The knowledge base can contain any type of knowledge, but it usually contains an elaborate set of rules which have an *if this . . . then that* format. A human supplies the knowledge that is placed in memory. The knowledge is placed in memory according to an exact format. For example, an expert system that operates an electric power plant could monitor the use of electricity and have a rule such as: If the available electricity falls below 40 megawatts, then turn on the auxiliary power switch. This is simplified, but it illustrates the idea.

- A human interface lets a person describe a problem situation and enter it into the computer system. Several schemes are used to let the human describe and enter a problem situation. The human might fill in fields in a frame, type entries for a series of prompts, or create a window and type a description of the problem.

- An inference engine or rule interpreter relates the knowledge base and the problem situation entered by a human. The knowledge in the knowledge base and the problem situation are related in a manner that emulates human intelligence. This is a critical factor. This program must perform the same tasks as are performed by a human expert who listens while a human describes a problem and then uses unique expertise to arrive at a solution to the problem. The expertise can include using expert common sense, specialized knowledge, complex skills, or old-fashioned intuition (the kind Captain Kirk had on *Star Trek*). You might suspect that expert systems do some of these things better than others. Whatever, an expert system does not just calculate statistics or reconcile account balances. It solves problems. It must incorporate elements of human intelligence.

- An interface displays, prints, plots, or transmits a solution to a problem in a manner that can be understood by humans or can be used by another machine. The humans do not have to be knowledge or domain experts, but they must be capable of understanding the proposed solution. When solutions are transmitted to other machines, the machines incorporate the solution and adjust what they were doing.

Since this is a general definition, expect to find many variations as you examine actual expert systems. Also, expect the definitions to vary. Here is a typical definition offered by Annie Brooking, director of the Knowledge-Based Systems Center at South Bank Polytechnic in London, England: A marketable expert system is a computing system that embodies organized knowledge about some area of human expertise which enables it to perform as a skillful and cost effective consultant.

We included this definition because it defines an expert system in relation to knowledge and human expertise, as most people do, but it also includes a reference to marketing and cost-effective considerations. This is admirable because you should probably not buy a million-dollar expert system to solve problems that can be solved by employing a consultant for a low retainer.

At the 1984 AAAI National Conference in Austin, Texas, John Seely Brown, now at PARC in Menlo Park, California, described the virtue in using an expert system to solve the "right size" of problems. You don't want to give the computer more than it can handle; on the other hand, you don't want to use an expert system to solve simple problems.

An expert system will cost from $15,000 to several million dollars. This is part of its definition, because the cost gives you a good indication of the range and complexity of problems that can be solved by the system. For example, if you are an executive who monitors the commitment of resources for oil exploration on a worldwide basis, a $15,000 expert system will not provide the range of capabilities you require. Expect to spend at least $500,000. On the other hand, if you use an expert system to process employment applications for a small company of one thousand people, then the $15,000 expert system should work very well.

More than any other factor, the performance of your personal expert system will relate to how well you match the nature and complexity of the problems to be solved by the expert system to the cost and components of your expert system. Try to effect a slight overkill so your expert system can grow as the complexity of your problems increase and as you think of more things to do with the system. Do not under any circumstances buy an expert system that is too small to do its job.

Notice the implication in this. We have provided a general definition. You will read definitions provided by other people. But the critical definition is the one you identify in which your expert system and the problems it solves are matched. There is an immense range in the capabilities of expert systems. Part of the definition of your personal system must include getting a system that is the "right size" for the problems it solves.

Let's see how this definition works with some typical, general models.

A GENERAL MODEL FOR EXPERT SYSTEMS

Before we look at models for expert systems, here is a general model for software developed with conventional languages. Notice the term *conventional languages*. AI experts often use this term when they talk about a language other than Lisp.

Most computer software developed with conventional languages works like this:

- A programmer writes a program (code) that performs a specific overall task (process numbers, process words, keep records, or do accounting).
- The program usually provides many functions that are called via menus, key interrupts, softkeys, or commands.
- A user provides inputs, and the program provides predictable outputs. You do not

expect a conventional program to change the way it handles inputs over a period of time. Nor do you expect a conventional program to add information to itself, although expert programmers can make programs do this to an extent (a spelling program can let a user add words to its dictionary).

Although capability to deal with branching can be built into conventional programs, such programs do not provide rule-based, variable, and situational output based on user inputs.

We know that many programmers will scream about this description, especially since many claim to have written expert systems in languages such as BASIC, Pascal, and FORTRAN. These programmers are justified to a degree, and we do not wish to belabor the point or get into a long discussion of the merits of this or that language. Perhaps the benefit of using Lisp for writing expert systems lies in how it processes inputs, not in whether it allows a programmer to do something that cannot be done with a conventional language. In any case, here is a general model for an expert system:

- A user provides inputs in the form of antecedents. For example, the computer display might prompt the user to enter a series of IF-antecedent statements concerning a problem situation. In particular, on IF prompts, a user might type:

  IF: The strain of the organism is gramneg, and

  IF: The morphology of the organism is rod, and

  IF: The patient is seriously burned.

Notice that all antecedents, except the last, end in, and. The use of *and* directs the expert system program to consider all the antecedents as a block and look for a consequence (diagnosis) that is related to the collective antecedents.

- A *rule interpreter* or *inference engine* compares the antecedents with rules found in a knowledge base until it finds a match or until it determines there is no connection between what the user typed and what the knowledge base contains. The rule interpreter is the general reasoning mechanism of the expert system. The rule interpreter matches the antecedents against entries in the knowledge base (the source of the rules).
- If all the antecedents match something in the knowledge base, the rule interpreter links the matching knowledge set with an appropriate consequence, which is displayed on a screen or output to a printer. In particular, in reference to the above antecedents, a consequence might be:

  Weak suggestive evidence (.4) of pseudomonas

- Many things can happen when no match is found. They are discussed later in the chapter on how computers learn.

- Exactly how the enabled rules are found and exactly how the rules are applied is the control strategy, which is operated by the rule interpreter program. There are several strategies. Choice of the correct one is up to your knowledge and Lisp experts.

One strategy is to scan through rules until one is found whose corresponding antecedent matches an assertion in the knowledge base. The rule is applied and the knowledge base is updated. This process continues until a consequence can be stated, or not stated.

Notice that in this strategy, the expert system responds directly to user-supplied antecedents about a problem. Thus, it is a *data-driven* control strategy. This is called a forward-chaining or antecedent reasoning strategy, depending on who you talk to. This strategy is equivalent to saying, ''I have a problem characterized by these things. What can I do to solve it?''

A different strategy is to state a goal to be achieved (perform a double valve bypass on a heart patient) and scan the rules to find those antecedents whose corresponding consequent actions can achieve the goal. Each appropriate rule is tried out in turn. If the antecedents for a rule—which, by the way, are stored in the knowledge base—match existing facts supplied by the user, the rule is applied and the goal is achieved (i.e., the problem is solved). If the system encounters an unmatched antecedent, the user proceeds through a series of steps designed to provide necessary facts, and then the new rule is recorded in the knowledge base and the rule is also applied recursively (i.e., it is applied to itself to solve the problem).

Notice that in this strategy, the expert system responds to the goals the system is trying to achieve. Thus, it is a *goal-driven* strategy, and is called a forward-chaining or consequence-reasoning strategy, depending on who you talk to.

These are the two major types of strategies, but there are many variations. Expect your knowledge and Lisp experts to know about these strategies and know how to select an appropriate strategy or variation thereof.

Many authors who write about AI discuss the validity of assorted strategies. They are justified in discussing this because the efficacy of your expert system depends on how well your knowledge and Lisp experts utilize a strategy that fits both the types of problems you must solve and the nature of your knowledge base. This is a difficult aspect of using AI.

Separating the knowledge base from the rule interpreter is important because, over a period of time, you can do these things:

- The rule interpreter can be altered so that it changes or updates the knowledge base as your knowledge and Lisp experts discover more efficient relationships between the antecedents, the consequences, and the types of problems being solved by the expert system.
- The knowledge base can be updated in the same manner as in the above item.
- The overall structure of the functions that are called by the rule interpreter can be expanded so that as problems are solved, any new information that accrues from solving the problem is automatically added to the knowledge base; thus, the expert

system learns from its own actions. By the way, much of this capability is provided by the define, cond, car, and cdr functions in Lisp that were discussed in Chapter 4. How your dialect provides these functions is part of having or not having an industrial-strength Lisp.

This is the overall, general model of an expert system. Notice that the model is very flexible. You, or whoever you employ, have many alternatives for creating your personal expert system. In the same vein, people who create specific expert systems which are then marketed must make many choices. Their choices determine the nature of the expert system they create.

As you examine available, specific systems, be aware of the subtle nuances that distinguish one system from another. To see this, examine the details in the makeup of specific expert systems that we discuss at the end of this chapter. In general, be aware of differences in these things:

- The size of the knowledge base determines the horizontal and vertical scope of an expert system to a large degree. For example, when the expert system named R1 had a few hundred rules, it could be used to configure DEC VAX computer systems. In terms of horizontal scope, as more rules were added, R1 could configure other DEC computers. In terms of vertical scope, as other rules were added, R1 could configure assorted brands of computer systems.
- The details related to how the rule interpreter works determine how the interpreter works. Some of these details are extremely technical and lie far beyond the scope of this book. We are talking about fundamental implementation details with regard to system interrupts, flags, commands, and system variables. This should not be a concern other than to ensure that the rule interpreter has appropriate capabilities.
- The control strategy determines how the expert system works. This determines how you give a problem to the system and the type of solution you get. Determine the types of problems you need to solve first. That is, determine if you need solutions when you have certain conditions or you need to know the conditions for reaching a certain goal.
- Determine the matrix of tools and related programs you need to either set up an expert system or use an existing system. This matrix will contain an operating system, a dialect of Lisp, and assorted other programs. The ''assorted other programs'' can vary to an extreme degree. Editors, tools, utilities, applications, interfaces, and such are included in the assorted other programs.

To get a visual picture, Figure 5.1 shows an illustration of an expert system. Take a moment to think about the model and how you solve problems. This overall method of reasoning has worked quite well so far, probably because it mimics the way humans make decisions. For example, if your car won't start, the headlights are dim, and the battery water is low (the antecedents or conditions), then your knowledge base (all the things you know) and your rule interpreter (the way you think about the world) supplies a consequent: The battery is almost certainly bad.

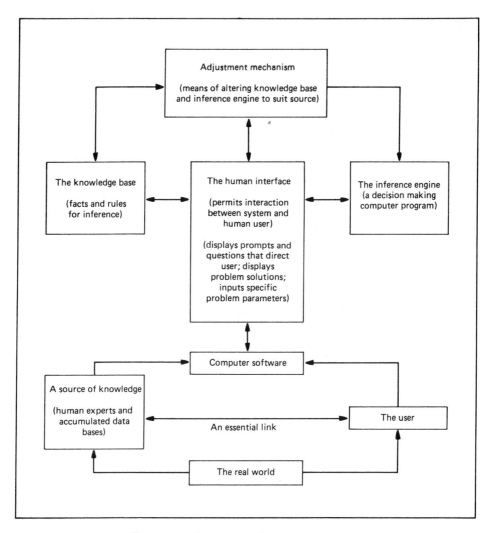

Figure 5.1 General model of an expert system.

The personal rule interpreter of some people tells them to solve the problem by replacing the battery. But this is not a universal solution. Other people have a rule interpreter that says, "Oh my gosh. The battery is bad. What do I do now?" A few people, who are usually thought to be weird, have a rule interpreter that says, "So the battery is bad. Aha! Maybe I can tinker around with it and get the thing working again."

AI systems are no different. You must be aware that how the rule interpreter of your AI system works will be determined partly by how your knowledge and Lisp experts set it up and partly by the capabilities of your Lisp programming environment. The need to have assorted types of knowledge bases, rules, and rule interpreters obtains from how you personally need to move up and down within the scope of human endeavor. Let's look at this.

A MODEL OF HUMAN ENDEAVOR

It is one thing to create assorted types of expert systems and quite another to examine how humans function. Humans function in the real world. The real world is apparently a combination of real matter (water, earth, trees, animals) and phenomena (light, gravity, sound, and electricity). All this gets mixed up some, and many categories are not mutually exclusive for many reasons. An expert system will not perform adequately unless it fits in with some well-defined human endeavor.

You must remember that people do not see the world. As Robert Davis described so accurately when he was at Syracuse University, people map the world into their cognitive schemas. This means that people use their sensing mechanisms to detect stimuli. People have no guarantee that they detect all the stimuli sent out within the universe. They only detect what their nervous systems let them detect. The stimuli that are detected are filtered a great deal by the nervous system before they get to the brain, where mental mechanisms such as cognition and biases change the stimuli into perceptions of the world. A lot can happen. It is this phenomenon that shows why a referee can make a decision in a football game that is accepted by some and rejected by others.

What people think they know about the world is not necessarily correct. It is certainly not fixed. Instead, what people think they know is determined and shaped by many factors. Here are some of them:

- The knowledge accumulated by people is shaped by the actual matter and phenomena they study, by the types of data they collect, and by the methods used to analyze the data. Recall that Aristotle once said there were four elements: earth, fire, water, and air. Today, people say that Aristotle used inadequate methods to arrive at his conclusions, but this contention does not change the fact that people used Aristotle's knowledge as a basis for their thinking for many centuries. Now, due to the work of Dalton, Lavoisier, and others, people believe there are about 100 elements. Thus, people talk about oxygen, hydrogen, and iron. But people have probably not observed and noted all the types of matter or phenomena that make up the universe. Our knowledge about elements is probably incomplete.

- Knowing is not equivalent to thought. How people think is shaped by how they perceive knowledge. It is no accident that people study philosophy and epistemology (the study of the validity of knowledge). People don't just want knowledge. They also want to know what knowledge is worth and how it can be used. They want to know how certain categories of people view knowledge. People strive to go beyond knowledge; they have an innate drive to do this. This is one of the same phenomena that drove certain people to travel the road that led to AI.

- Besides knowledge, perception, and orientation, individuals develop unique ways of sensing the real world and responding to what is sensed. Individuals develop mental schemas that they use to map the real world into the mind. The schemas are a combination of values, morals, ethics, biases, common sense, and apparent facts. Thus, for example, one person sees a shooting and says, "Oh. That poor man. How awful!" Another person sees the same shooting and says, "Now that's justice. The man deserved to die.'' Each person creates a unique orientation to viewing the world that is independent of the world per se.

- Knowledge is never the things or the phenomena. Knowledge is always how things and phenomena are envisioned and represented. Knowledge, whatever its basis, is always metaphysical. Consequently, it is always somewhat categorical, somewhat taxonomical, and never a total representation of the real world.

Collectively, these things illustrate a need for you to select an appropriate model for an expert system. It is necessary to obtain a close match between the type of expert system you create and the manner in which you translate the real world into knowledge, rules, and rule interpreters in your subject area.

The whole issue of how you interpret the world, identify a subject area, and create a knowledge base is so important that AI experts created a concept within AI specifically called *common sense*. Under the umbrella of common sense, AI experts look at the validity of knowledge, the validity of models, and the means by which human experts ply their trades. Experts in AI do not just look at whether or not they can create an expert system. Instead, they look at many models, many types of knowledge, many interpretations, and many heuristics used by domain experts and try to use the best knowledge, the best models, and the best heuristics. Expect your personal domain and knowledge engineers to do the same things.

We don't want to get on a soapbox, but we hope you see the need to identify appropriate models for expert systems and relate them to appropriate models for how people function. Your examination of expert systems should encompass an examination of human ways of learning and thinking about the world.

Once you have interpreted the real world, collected data about that world, changed the data into information, and used the information to create knowledge, then you can use the knowledge to make decisions. Making decisions is equivalent to solving problems or answering questions. Thus, one rather functional model of human endeavor looks like that shown in Figure 5.2. The model assumes that humans function at successively higher levels as they move up the scale.

Take a moment to examine the categories in the model and note how lower categories relate to higher categories. The model for human endeavor can help you in these ways:

- In observing the real world, be sure your domain experts use the latest and best available means to determine the nature of that world. Even in such stable areas as physics, chemistry, and mathematics, the fundamental concepts have been revised—and changed altogether in some cases—as new means of detecting the universe have been developed. There is no room for bias and tradition in observing phenomena and physical objects.
- In gathering data, use adequate and appropriate instruments. Remember that the term *instrument* covers a lot of ground. It's obvious that a voltmeter is a measurement instrument, but so are a questionnaire and a multiple-choice examination. It is not helpful to detect a new phenomenon and then use antiquated or inadequate

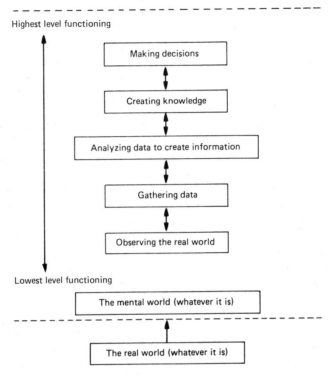

Figure 5.2 A model of human endeavor.

methods to gather information about it. The major principle is this: The capability of an instrument to measure must exceed the range within which a phenomenon can vary. Many people are adept at selecting an appropriate measurement unit and scale, but many people do not allow for the range over which a phenomenon can vary. For example, while studying human respiration in distance running, researchers knew about the effects of lactic acid for years, but until recently they did not allow for its range in extreme cases. Then, allowing for an adequate range, researchers discovered that numerous agents could counteract the accumulation of lactic acid.

• Once data about a subject area has been gathered, the domain and knowledge engineers analyze the data and create knowledge. In creating an expert system, two things are done. One, appropriate models must be used to analyze the data. Your experts must shift gears here and think more about sorting and searching through symbolic data than numerically or statistically analyzing numerical data. Two, the information is translated into the rules that go into a knowledge base. This translation can become very technical, but it must be done. You cannot just have knowledge. You must have knowledge in a form that can be understood by your inference engine or rule interpreter.

• Once you get to the level of creating knowledge, several things happen at once. The process of developing the rules for a knowledge base amounts to using data to create usable knowledge. On the other hand, given a knowledge base that can be used in an expert system, the process of using the expert system creates conditions that cause you to go back and update the knowledge or create entirely new knowledge. An expert system can become its own self-perpetuating system in which knowledge is used to provide solutions, and feedback from using the solutions can lead to updating knowledge, eliminating inadequate knowledge, and creating new knowledge. Be sure your expert system permits these things.

- The solutions generated by an expert system become your basis for making decisions. For some people, this is a radical departure from the way they usually make decisions. Some people rely on experience. Others use luck. Some claim to have special powers of intuition. Ancient people used incantations. You must change the way you make decisions when you use an expert system. Therefore, you will probably want proof that an expert system works. The benefit derived from an expert system is directly related to how well it helps you make decisions, compared to the methods you previously used. In this regard, the original expert did very well. In most cases, they performed better than teams of recognized experts and performed much better than managers or executives when the criterion was percentage of correct decisions.

We chose this model of human endeavor because it provides guidelines and still lets you use any of several other models for observing phenomena, gathering and analyzing data, and creating and using knowledge. It's easy to carry this model around in your head where it can help you keep things in perspective.

A MODEL EXPERT SYSTEM

Now that we have defined an expert system, discussed types of systems, and provided a model for organizing human endeavor, here is a hypothetical, but complete, model for an expert system (Figure 5.3). Your expert system will probably not have every component shown below, but it should have the major parts.

Notice the dividing line labeled *Portability Layer*. Every actual system has this layer. Below this layer, the software is machine-dependent. That is, the software will only run on a certain hardware system. Above the portability layer, software can be purchased from assorted sources and modified so it runs on a particular system. The modification usually amounts to configuring the software so it works with certain operating systems, monitors, keyboards, terminals, disk drives, printers, plotters, and assorted instruments.

Notice the position of the operating system and the dialect of Lisp in the total model. Again, you need industrial-strength software in this position. Also, notice the central role of the human interface as a means of accessing higher- and lower-level software. You need a state-of-the-art human interface. A poorly designed and inefficient human interface can really slow you down.

Use this model as a basis for evaluating actual AI systems you investigate. Check

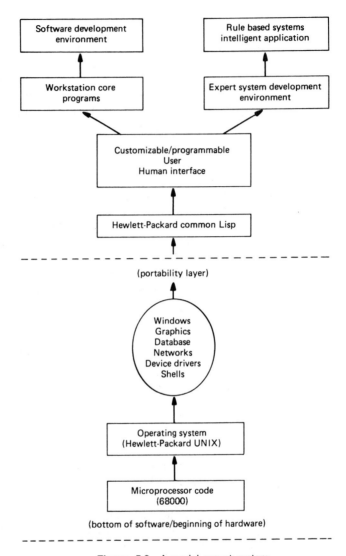

Figure 5.3 A model expert system.

actual systems for completeness, functionality, efficiency, ease of use, and compatibility. Shop around. Get an expert system that meets your needs.

EXISTING AI SYSTEMS

Here are some actual, representative expert systems. Each of them contains some of the components mentioned in the previous section. We'll provide a brief description first; then we'll select one system and discuss it in depth. That way, you should get a comprehensive picture of what assorted expert systems look like:

- MYCIN was developed at Stanford University to diagnose infecting organisms in blood in regard to meningitis. It prescribes an antibiotic treatment. MYCIN uses about 400 diagnostic rules and about 50 therapy rules.

- DRILLING ADVISOR uses knowledge to solve problems with drilling for oil. The system contains information about well formation, sticking problems, bottom hole assembly, and related things. Information about a well is fed into the computer. Then rules are applied to provide advice for drilling. For example, one rule determines whether there is a conical hole in the well. The rule provides that if the action is drilling, the bottom formation is hard, and a certain bit was used, then there is a conical hole in the well.

- R1 configures complex computer systems. The term *complex* means that about 10,000 parts are available, and a sales rep needs to know which parts to order for a customer. R1 uses a forward-chaining strategy to accept antecedents concerning configuration and to produce consequences concerning how to configure a system. Here is a typical rule in R1.

> If: Currently assigning devices to the unibus modules, and there is an unassigned dual-port disk drive, and the type of controller it requires is known, and there are two such controllers still unassigned,

> Then: Assign the disk drive to each of the controllers, and note that each controller supports one device.

Using about 14,000 rules, R1 determines if an order for a computer is complete, defines the spatial relationships among the components in an order, and adds necessary, but unspecified, components to the order. R1 has been able to configure a computer successfully much better than human experts; in particular, R1 does not forget the details related to cables, ports, and connectors.

- DART performs diagnoses that determine whether the components in a hierarchically related set of components are connected correctly. DART is an important expert system because it shows how knowledge engineers take an important concept, the d-Algorithm, which is used to determine whether transistors in a circuit are correctly connected, and elevate the level of abstraction of a concept so it works for general models or hierarchies. DART uses propositions from predicate calculus that let you work with general, hierarchical design models which could simulate related specific models. Imagine this problem. You are designing a circuit board that contains millions of AND gates and OR gates. To get an output of 1 at a certain node, you must have certain inputs, a 1 or 0, at preceding gates, depending on how the AND gates and OR gates are connected and the values of the inputs. This could get out of hand. DART helps engineers test general, hypothetical situations. From these tests, a specific circuit board can be designed. DART is a good example of the use of a heuristic, high-level strategy, and a model in this case.

- STEAMER was developed to train steam plant operators. At first blush, this does not sound like much. But if you visit a steam plant, examine the maze of ways in which pipes are connected, and realize that the pipes carry steam at high pressure and temperature, you get the idea. STEAMER employs sophisticated graphics, schematics, and illustrations to show trainees how a steam plant operates. STEAMER has the capability to show the operation of the plant at many levels, and it can simulate critical situations. Thus, it provides dynamic, not static, instruction. Using STEAMER, you believe you are operating a steam plant, not just talking about running a steam plant.

- WEST illustrates a different level of use of an expert system. WEST teaches mathematics to elementary school children. That is, it teaches elementary-school-level mathematics. WEST accounts for the needs of individual students and customizes the instruction they receive. Besides individualizing the instruction, WEST teaches heuristics (strategies) for solving elementary problems in a dynamic and interactive manner that is quite different from the worksheets most teachers use.

Notice that in each of these systems, humans collect information about something and feed it into a computer. Then the computer applies knowledge, rules, heuristics, and common sense (or combinations of these things) to solve a problem, guide a dynamic process, or direct a complex process to a desired end. To see this in more detail, let's examine one expert system. We chose an expert system called R1 because it had a solid evolution and was the first expert system to go into daily use.

As you read the description of R1, imagine that you are creating your own expert systems. Imagine that you have the same types of problems and that you employ assorted resources to effect solutions.

- **The Beginning**: As Digital Equipment Corporation (DEC) developed their lines of minicomputers, and as they created more peripheral devices, the configuration of a system got to the point where a human expert, trained by DEC, made numerous mistakes. Therefore, DEC contacted John McDermott and others at Carnegie-Mellon University to discuss the possibility of creating an expert system that would configure the DEC computers. This process was not one-sided. John McDermott was looking for a problem that could be solved by using an expert system. Both groups were happy.

- **The Situation**: Initial discussions focused on selecting an appropriate computer system. Should the expert system configure the DEC PDP-11 or the DEC VAX 11/780? The 11/780 was chosen because the problem was serious, there was too much variety in the peripherals supported by the PDP-11, and the volume of orders for the VAX 11/780 was low. John McDermott and others thought the VAX 11/780 offered them the best chance to create a significant expert system and not have to cope with too many factors. You will have to do the same thing when you identify an area within your corporation or agency in which you can use an expert system. The trick is to identify a significant problem that is not too overwhelming.

- **The Specifications**: A domain expert from DEC and people from Carnegie-Mellon University (CMU) spent part of a day examining the configuration task. They determined these things:

  a. It took about 1000 steps to configure a VAX 11/780.

  b. Each VAX system had about 50 –150 configurable components per system, chosen from about 5000 available components.

  c. There were about 25 –125 bits of information per component.

  d. The average fan-in and fan-out was three.

- **The Agreement**: Both DEC and CMU agreed that the expert system could be created. DEC agreed to give CMU access to a domain expert, a person who was an expert in configuring the VAX 11/780. CMU agreed to develop a prototype expert system.

- **The Prototype**: The overall problem was to make the expert system recognize situations in the process of configuring a computer system. Therefore, the CMU group selected these things: the OPS language system; a large set of situation-action rules that would be placed in memory; a conditional prefix for each rule that specified conditions under which the rule would "fire"; a space in memory that contained a description of the configuration situation; and an interpreter (an inference engine) that determined which rules were applicable to the current situation. You too will examine a problem situation and go through the same type of selection process.

- **The Interpreter**: In the computer that ran the OPS language system, sections of memory contained rules, configuration situations, and descriptions of VAX 11/780 components. Each rule was linked with a situation and an action. Therefore, if the interpreter fired a rule, which means that a rule was applicable to its corresponding situation, then the corresponding action was taken. For example, if a rule about an unassigned backplane-#4 applied to situation K, then action K was taken. This means that R1 used a forward-chaining strategy. This illustrates another point: You always identify the basic strategy you intend to use.

- **Sample Rule**: With regard to the interpreter above, here is a sample rule. The IF part is the situation and the THEN part is the corresponding action.

  > IF: The current subtask is assigning devices to unibus modules and, there is an unassigned dual port disk drive and, the type of controller it requires is known and, there are two such controllers, neither of which has any devices assigned to it and, the number of devices which these controllers can support is known

  > THEN: Assign the disk drive to each controller and, note that each controller supports one device

- **The Effort**: CMU spent several worker-years to develop the OPS language system. OPS was designed specifically as a tool for creating expert systems. People at CMU wanted to use it. To some extent this means that the language system was selected before the problem situation was selected. In this case, CMU researchers found a problem that could be solved by using OPS. You will probably have a choice: You can select a system and then use it; or you can have a problem and find an appropriate system. CMU researchers talked to the domain expert for two weeks, taking many notes each day. Four months later, R1 could configure a simple VAX 11/780 system. Ten months later R1 could configure most VAX 11/780 systems given to it. Three years later, in 1983, R1 could configure VAX and PDP systems. By 1984, R1 could configure several types of computer systems. R1's name was changed to XCON/XSEL because it left the laboratory and became a product.

- **The Scope and Complexity**: By 1983, R1 had configured 35,000-plus systems and had about 1800 rules. At times R1 had more than 3000 rules. The number of rules varied along three dimensions during the development period. One, new rules were added as the number of components in the computer systems' product lines grew. Two, new rules were added to enable R1 to configure additional computer systems. Three, some rules were eliminated or consolidated when certain new rules were added or old rules were modified.

- **The Evaluation**: A domain expert, who has a strong computer background, takes several months to acquire the knowledge in R1's knowledge base, the descriptions of components. Then domain experts make several errors when they configure a system because the systems are exceedingly complex. R1 consistently produced better results. In particular, R1 did not forget the small details. It's easy to remember that a system needs a 10.5-inch expander box, part number BA11-KV, which provides a space for unibus modules. It's not easy to remember that a system might need a bus terminator, part number M930, which provides unibus integrity. It's the little things that are forgotten, but a system does not run without them. Consequently, a major part of R1's success is that customers spent less time waiting for forgotten parts to arrive.

This is an overall view of one expert system. You will experience the same types of problems when you create or set up an expert system. The steps we outlined should function as a general model. R1 was a resounding success story. In the last analysis, R1 worked faster than people, could configure systems in remote locations easier than people, and last longer than domain experts who specialize in configuring DEC computers. Human experts die, lose interest in their domain of expertise, or go to work for other companies. Expert systems do not do these things, but they do create other problems.

The use of expert systems is based on fundamental concepts or assumptions. Presumably, an expert system can recall and apply more knowledge than a human. An expert system can use rules to diagnose a situation with more comprehension than a human. An expert system can create a more complete solution to a problem than a human, and it can do this work in less time than a human. This is the idea.

Some of the original expert systems have produced spectacular results, but others which have not received much publicity have failed to work as expected. People must still determine whether expert systems will become a significant factor in problem solving or whether they will become computer systems that were like the dinosaurs, unable to perform and adapt to environmental conditions. The development of expert systems was labor intensive when the original systems were created. The development is still labor intensive, and knowledge engineers command high salaries. Time might change this, but for now, expect to spend big money to get an expert system up and running.

If you read between the lines throughout this chapter, you know that the pioneers of AI opened a can of worms when they invented expert systems. Let's discuss them.

PROBLEMS WITH DEFINITIONS

Lisp is a vehicle for development of artificial intelligence. This is not a problem, but it sets up conditions in which people develop numerous misconceptions about AI.

AI is only 25 years old, but it is already a broad area. Under the umbrella of AI, Lisp experts have used assorted dialects to work on natural language systems, intelligent robots, gaming theory, expert systems, vision systems, and voice recognition systems.

It is easy to form misconceptions about artificial intelligence in general and expert systems in particular. Not all applications of AI fall into the realm of expert systems. That is, AI applications and expert systems are not one and the same thing. Expert systems are a small part of the field of AI; they are just the most visible part at the moment. We'll talk about other applications in subsequent chapters.

It was difficult for the pioneers of AI to develop fundamental definitions, even though their community was very small. The pioneers came to AI from assorted disciplines, not just computer science. They had common causes, but they often isolated themselves from other people so they could focus on their work. The pioneers used several concepts that are not easy to define. In some ways, the pioneers were their own worst enemies in this regard, but our research convinced us that many pioneers did not suspect the extent to which outside entities would beat paths to their doors and become confused along the way.

It is more difficult to define fundamental terms in AI as more people enter the field. People such as ourselves, who write about AI without being pioneers of AI, can be guilty of errors of both commission and omission, no matter how well we may be trained in other areas. The problem of defining fundamental terms can get out of hand when marketing people promote AI products via descriptions of features, advantages, acronyms, and such.

Our definition of an expert system focuses on these three things:

- Identification of an area of knowledge that can be specified in such a way as to make the area of knowledge mutually exclusive. For example, R1 configured specific DEC computers. Thus, a unibus was an exact thing; a unibus was not an abstract concept. An identified area must be structured in a manner that lets you store the knowledge in a computer's memory.
- Classification of the knowledge into facts, assumptions, and rules that can be used by a program that functions as a rules interpreter or inference engine.

- Identification of a problem situation that is sufficiently complex to warrant spending the time and money required to get an expert system up and running. The nature of a problem situation must lend itself to the use of software in which you employ a knowledge base, a heuristic (strategy) such as backward-chaining, a user interface, and an inference engine to enter a specific problem situation, and the expert system provides a specific solution.

Beyond this, specific features could be added to alter or extend this basic definition. Therefore, be aware of how a particular expert system may be affected by local definitions and ways of looking at the world.

PROBLEMS WITH THE KNOWLEDGE BASE

In many areas, people do not agree about what is knowledge and what is fiction. Knowledge is better defined in some areas than in others. For example, knowledge about teaching is vague, nebulous, and disputed. Knowledge about human blood has elements of mystery, but many experts agree about fundamental terminology and concepts. Most people probably do not agree on the stuff about Dracula. It is often difficult to differentiate among a fact, a myth, an assumption, and an outright lie.

Facts are not the most troublesome level. It is more difficult to deduce workable generalizations, theorems, or axioms. It becomes even more difficult to agree about effective heuristic rules. Higher yet, people are often totally at odds over judgments of the effectiveness of particular theories. Darwinism is heresy to some people and pure scientific fact to others. Everyone talks about common sense, but what is common sense to one person can be nonsense to another.

The largely symbolic nature of knowledge makes Lisp a natural language for development of expert systems. But the Lisp expert is not often a knowledge or domain expert. Too often, a knowledge expert and a Lisp expert must interact to get knowledge into a computer. In fact, it is easy to get these terms confused. Most people agree that a knowledge expert and a domain expert are one and the same person, someone who is an expert in a particular area or subject. Some people agree that a Lisp expert, an AI expert, and a knowledge engineer are one and the same person, but you can get many dissenting views. We don't make careful distinctions; we have talked about Lisp experts and knowledge engineers as if they were the same thing. We also know that this makes some people furious. Thus, this is an example of the principle we are discussing.

Remember that Lisp uses lists where the first element of a list is a function and the other elements are used by the function—that is, they are arguments of the function. Knowledge must be entered in a computer in a Lisp-like format that only a Lisp programmer knows. By the way, you can find many articles that discuss the validity (often called the epistemology) of how well the Lisp formats for knowledge fit the knowledge. Most people agree that this area is still in a primitive state, but researchers are progressing rapidly in some areas (medicine, law, oil exploration, personnel management). Researchers are progressing slower in other areas (natural languages, voice recognition, vision).

Ideally, a person should be able to enter knowledge via conventional program menus, prompts, and entries. Then a knowledge expert need not be a Lisp expert. This type of software is available, but do not assume it is part of the Lisp environment you purchase to develop an expert system. A salesperson may assume you know how to extend Lisp to suit your needs!

You need a powerful Lisp environment that contains interfaces, libraries, tools, and utilities that ease the burden of creating an expert system. At present, it is still necessary for a knowledge expert to learn some Lisp to be able to create an expert system and use it. This type of software is being developed, but there are many obstacles. Perhaps someday a knowledge expert can create an expert system with little knowledge of Lisp.

These are some of the major problems in identifying a knowledge base. Being able to define your subject area and being able to determine how to convert the subject area into a knowledge base is the most crucial task you must complete before you purchase an AI system. Unless you do this, you must use whatever system you have and hope you can adapt it so the system can function as an expert system. If you know how to deal with your subject area, it is much easier to select an appropriate combination of hardware and software. You'll know how big your computer system should be. You'll also know what software to obtain.

EXPERTS AND EXPERT SYSTEMS

This section describes the fundamental steps in the development of an expert system. We assume you are not a Lisp expert—that is, you are not a knowledge engineer. But you could be anything else. Perhaps you are a subject expert who has just been given the task of creating an expert system. You might be the person who makes management-level decisions about expert systems and hiring knowledge engineers to run them. Perhaps you are a student, taking an introductory class in AI. Whatever, it is important to distinguish between Lisp experts (this includes knowledge engineers) and knowledge experts, managers, or students because Lisp experts know how to modify a Lisp environment and thereby create an expert system. Knowledge experts and managers are often unaware of what is required. This lack of awareness can truly be a case where ignorance is not bliss.

Anyone who has completed some curriculum knows that you learn a lot from the curriculum, but you learn much more from working with the experts who formulated the curriculum. This principle applies directly when you get an expert system up and running and you are not a knowledge engineer. You need some way to compensate for the myriad things you do not know or do not understand. We'll suggest a few strategies shortly.

From 1960 to 1980, expert systems were developed in universities or other special think-tank environments by Lisp experts who corroborated with knowledge experts. These people explored ideas and did not face realities posed by the workaday world. Remember the case of R1. R1 was developed in about one worker-year, but it was refined for about 15 worker-years before it became a viable product. People who work in corporations where projects are completed know about schedules, deadlines, critical paths, limitations, and freeze dates. Such people work under different conditions. They are not free to explore and corroborate. They do these things within definite constraints.

Today, as the need for expert systems extends beyond the laboratory, and as expert systems are used in more subject areas, it is necessary to get the knowledge experts, Lisp experts, and an industrial-strength Lisp environment together. That is, today's managers and executives need heuristics that enable their workers to tap the expertise of the knowledge engineer without taking time to become knowledge engineers. It is not easy to do this.

In our research, we discovered one company that took three years to develop an expert system, and when the system was tested, it did not work. Not willing to give up, the company took two more years to bring some engineers up to speed as knowledge engineers. Another project began. Two years later, the company scrapped the product after Beta site tests. That's seven years of unproductive use of resources.

Here is a strategy you can use to create an expert system. The strategy enables you to proceed systematically in a step-by-step manner. You can get out anytime with minimal difficulty and loss of resources. Here are the basic steps:

- At the executive level, meetings are held to brainstorm situations. Problems are identified. The scope and magnitude of the problems are identified. Then the problems are classified with regard to importance and the degree to which they could be solved by computer systems which emulate human intelligence. In these meetings, those problems that could be solved if you had an expert system are identified. Expert systems are ideal for solving problems in these categories: interpretation, prediction, diagnosis, debugging (computer programs), design, planning, monitoring, repair, instruction, and control, but they are not limited to these categories. You'll just have to be more creative and careful if you identify another category.

- Still at the executive level, but in collaboration with engineers, the problems that look like they could be solved by using an expert system are examined. This is another brainstorming session in which executives, who know about priorities, discuss problems with engineers, who know about solutions. These meetings attempt to identify both problems and subject areas that could be impacted by an expert system. At this stage, characterize the important aspects of potential problems. Examine goals to be achieved, identify resources, note anomalies in problems, and speculate about cost effectiveness.

- Still at the executive level, a problem and subject area are identified and a project is initiated. Notice that considerable work was done to get to this point. If it is desirable to create an expert system, then provide adequate resources.

- The problem situation and subject area are given to a team of engineers. They examine specifications provided by executives and attempt to identify the exact subject area for which the project is suited. The subject can lie in such an area as very large scale integrated circuit design (VLSI), crisis management, mineral exploration, medical diagnosis, chemical data interpretation, sports medicine and training, or experiment planning. But even these categories are too encompassing. For example, if the subject area is equipment failure diagnosis, you would narrow the subject to something like failure of hydraulic oil flow regulators in an arctic environment.

- Once an area is defined, hire a set of experts. Both domain experts and knowledge engineers are needed; the knowledge experts are needed first. These domain experts categorize the knowledge, develop knowledge hierarchies, and reach agreement about what knowledge is important. They identify types of problem situations and determine how knowledge is used to solve problems. Then the knowledge engineers, the Lisp experts, show the knowledge experts how to transform the knowledge into a form an expert system can work with. At this stage of developing an expert system, it is absolutely necessary to do these things: Determine that the knowledge can be translated into a format that can become rules in a knowledge base; identify a strategy that can be used to make the expert system work; determine that software is available to create the expert system, and ensure that the project has a very high probability of completion.

- Here are a few details about the above step, translating knowledge into a format a computer system can use. The selection of specific methods depends on many circumstances, but the expert will probably use methods taken from these areas: predicate calculus, inference techniques, means-ends analysis, state-space searches, blind searches, heuristic searches, solution spaces, generate-and-test, and such. What we are saying is that the methodology for creating an expert system devolves for using these types of areas. These are the areas the experts should examine or know about. If they need training, these are the areas in which they should be trained. This overall process makes up the identification and conceptualization stages.

- If it is not necessary to abort the project, obtain a computer system, a computer operating system, and a total Lisp environment, and then use the system to create a small, prototype expert system that can solve common, easy problems. This is where you need the industrial-strength Lisp. Most companies already have a computer. It is often not feasible to use that computer. It is often better to obtain a computer that is specially suited to expert systems. Networks that allow sharing of hardware and software work very well. We will explain the requirements for the total Lisp environment in the next chapter, but you should be aware here that a skimpy dialect of Lisp will not work effectively. You do not want to pay a Lisp expert to extend your dialect until it can be used to create an expert system.

- As the knowledge and Lisp experts work together to develop a prototype system, test the prototype on a few simple, but representative, problems. Use problems that are test cases where you know what normally happens and what should normally be done. This lets you compare the expert system's prescriptions with your experience. The prototype must do well, otherwise it is not likely to be cost effective. If the prototype does not work, you can abort the project. This is better than testing a complete expert system that does not work. This and the previous overall processes make up the formalization and implementation stages.

- Once the prototype expert system is working, the knowledge base of facts and assumptions is limited by the memory and mass storage capacity of your computer system. The number of rules created and applied by the experts relates the size of the system and the scope of the subject area. About 200 to 400 rules constitutes a rather large expert system. Given time and resources, huge systems that apply more than 1000 rules can be developed. Small expert systems can be created that have about 100 rules. At this point in the project, you should have a feel for the size of system you need. This overall process makes up the testing and finalization stages.

- Use the expert system to solve some apparently routine problems and have a set of experts check the recommended solutions before they are used. Use these comparisons to fine-tune the expert system. This is a research period where the reliability of the system is examined. An expert system should be at least 80 percent reliable in most subject areas. Humans have been about 60 percent reliable. Some expert systems have achieved over 90 percent reliability. When the system is ready, use it.

- Beyond this, engineers can expand the system, maintain the system, or create systems for new areas. One extension which can be very cost effective is to generalize the rule interpreter and human interface so the expert system can use any knowledge base without extensive modification. Try to make your expert systems work at increasingly higher levels of abstraction and generalization. This makes them very powerful.

These things are fundamental. Your exact situation will vary, and you must adjust accordingly. The quality of your expert system depends, accumulatively, on how well each step is executed (e.g., defining an area, hiring experts, defining the knowledge base, and creating and testing the expert system).

This book can discuss the major steps in building an expert system, but it cannot provide the details. There are several sources of details—books, articles, workshops, and courses—but we suggest that your experts will have to solve most of their problems on their own. Situations have a way of being unique. To get a more detailed account of expert systems, we suggest you read this book:

HAYES-ROTH, FREDERICK, DONALD A. WATERMAN, AND DOUGLAS B. LENAT. *Building Expert Systems,* Reading, MA: Addison-Wesley Publishing Co., 1983.

Throughout this chapter, we focused on fundamental information. But we have often taken time throughout this book to discuss pitfalls and problems. We need to do this for expert systems, because you should not get the idea that they are a panacea for problem solving, nor are they likely to replace the human expert in the near future.

Expert systems can help people solve problems in areas where many aspects of a situation are fuzzy. When you have an explicit problem, conventional programs written in conventional language can be used.

Expert systems use massive memory, massive mass storage, and the speed of electricity to perform millions of minute tasks at a surface level. Because a computer works so fast compared to humans, the computer can examine millions of situations in a few seconds and use rather simplistic, shallow methods of "thinking" to solve problems.

But in discussing expert systems, we never really took time to look closely at the solutions. Be aware that the solutions returned to you by expert systems are almost always suggestions for how you could do something. You, the human, must supply the intuition, the experience, and the gut feelings that humans have used for years to effect powerful, significant solutions to problems.

The most powerful computer available today is still a dummy in the areas of intuition, love, compassion, and gut feelings. Computers don't have hunches. Computers cannot look into a person's eyes and see qualities that do not show up on a resumé. Computers cannot see the desperation in some situations that enables some people to perform incredible feats. Only humans can do these things.

We emphatically believe that an expert system can give you powerful options, suggestions, verifications, and diagnoses, but you must run the business, agency, or otherwise handle your situation. There are powerful implications in this with regard to policies and guidelines which we believe you cannot disregard. For example, the federal government is looking into the whole question of using expert systems to prescribe drugs. It will be one thing if they hold people accountable for prescribing drugs recommended by expert systems and quite another thing if they hold the computer responsible. The latter alternative sounds insane on a surface level, but the alternative has been proposed with intense sincerity. You're free to come to your own conclusions.

The next chapter takes a more specific look at hardware and software requirements.

6

TOOLS FOR INTELLIGENCE DESIGN

ORIENTATION

In this chapter, we assume, hypothetically, that you have decided to obtain an AI system and you are the person who makes decisions. That is, you are a company president, an executive, a manager, or other professional who determines whether to purchase an AI system and then determines which AI system should be purchased. We also assume you are not a Lisp expert and want to learn about the nuances of purchasing a system.

The term *AI system* represents any computer system that performs tasks that embody elements of human intelligence. In most cases, this means that an AI system helps people solve problems or otherwise emulates intelligent human behavior in these areas: expert systems, vision systems, voice recognition systems, natural language systems, and robotics systems.

To select, purchase, and use an AI system, you complete a series of steps. You must be realistic in completing the steps and you must know your place in the scope and scheme of things. For example, one of the following steps suggests that you consult with an expert in AI. This is a good suggestion, but you should know that there are currently about 500 to 1000 AI experts; some people say there are only 300 experts. True experts are hard to find. Another step suggests that you set up your system and use it. Again, this is fine, but you must realize that many systems cost $150,000 to $300,000; it can take from 2 to 50 man-years to create an AI system. Eventually, you'll see that several types of AI systems are available, and you can get involved at several levels of scope and complexity. You need to coordinate your needs and your resources, but the steps are essentially the same:

1. Define what your AI system must do. In this step you identify problems that inhibit the productivity of people or machines and then determine how an AI system could solve the problems. For example, you might want an AI system to keep track of maintenance schedules for complex machinery in accordance with the environments in which the machinery was used since the last maintenance.

2. Determine the type of AI system that can perform the required tasks. You'll probably want to research this in several ways.

   a. Invite experts to speak to appropriate personnel about how an AI system might be created to solve problems. The expert system called R1 was an outgrowth of this type of meeting. In this case, you are thinking about developing an original AI system.

   b. Have experts visit with appropriate people to discuss the potential of various systems to meet your needs. In this case, you are looking for an existing AI system that can be adapted to solve your problems.

   c. Attend an AI conference to see what's available and to get a picture of what's happening in the current AI scene.

   d. Read an assortment of materials to get an overall picture of available AI products.

3. Once you determine your needs, select the components for a workable AI system. Depending on the nature and scope of your situation, the selection process can vary from straightforward to extremely complex.

4. Work through the process of installing and configuring your AI system; learn how to use it.

The remainder of this chapter contains fundamental information about how you work through these steps. The intent is to get you started. But you should be aware that in putting together an actual AI system, the level of abstraction in the information you examine increases until you work with heady material that few people have encountered. Reaching the upper levels of abstraction requires time, dedicated study, and resources.

Within the total process of obtaining an AI system you make decisions about several things. Figure 6.1 shows the process. At first, you have near total "opensure." This is the time when you ask questions, look around, wonder about what to do, and get your head around the overall situation. Then, you have successive "closure." This is the time when you make decisions, each of which eliminates certain options. Finally, you have a particular AI system working for you.

Plan to shop around for about one year. Americans were relatively unfamiliar with computers during the 1970s. The rush to use computers began at the end of the 1970s and had a full head of steam by 1982. Very few computer literacy courses were taught in the 1970s. They only became commonplace after 1982, when Americans accepted the viability of personal computers. Americans are even less familiar with computers that use AI to help them solve complex problems. We don't know exactly where you fit into this picture, and you should not be put off by any perceived lack of background if you are aware that the trick, if there is one, is to acquire an AI system that: (1) your people can learn to use

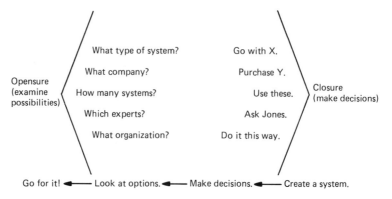

Opensure (examine possibilities)

What type of system?

What company?

How many systems?

Which experts?

What organization?

Go with X.

Purchase Y.

Use these.

Ask Jones.

Do it this way.

Closure (make decisions)

Go for it! ◄─── Look at options. ◄─── Make decisions. ◄─── Create a system.

Figure 6.1 Obtaining an AI system.

effectively, and (2) has enough capability to help you solve particular problems. This will be a compromise, any way you look at it.

About $50 million were spent for AI systems in 1984. It's estimated that over $2 billion will be spent for AI systems in 1990. How many of those systems will sit idle, not fulfilling their intended purpose? If AI systems are like personal computers, the answer is that far too many will sit idle because: (1) the owners do not know how to use them, or (2) the computer system functions inadequately. How bad is this problem? At the personal computer level, about three out of 10 systems are not used after a person gets past the initial experimentation and education phase.

This tragedy could be averted if purchasers steadfastly focus on appropriate factors. Here are two examples of being led astray:

• Stay away from misleading information and outlandish claims. For example, at the 1984 AAAI conference, an onlooker was told that a $15,000 AI system would outperform a $170,000 system, which was displayed across the aisle. Ridiculous! The $15,000 system had certain capabilities, but it also had several limitations.

• Do not lose sight of what your AI system should do. For example, at the 1984 AAAI conference, a potential customer wanted a system that could support several dialects of Lisp and could also use programs written in other computer languages. The salespeople at two consecutive booths, knowing their systems did not provide these features, demonstrated graphics and window capabilities! And the customer endured the demonstrations!

So what are the important factors? They vary, but you find them in the intersection of the particular problems your system must solve, the capability of your people to use a system, and the resources you have to acquire a system. Once you account for these factors, nuances related to processor speeds, operating system macros, and such can be considered. Take your time. Your system needs to create synergy for you.

Once you have identified what your AI system must do, use the following types of questions to help you establish criteria for acquiring an AI system:

- What should the human interface be like? How many interfaces are required? Do we need windows? Is it better for the system to be very user-friendly or is it better to use a cryptic, but powerful, interface?
- What constitutes a muscular, robust AI system? What kind of environment do we need: execution, programming, development, or application? What will our system cost? Can we afford the system we really need? If not, where do we compromise?
- How important is it for the system to be responsive and explain what it does? How important is it for users to intervene and counteract measures taken by the system? Is a turnkey system best?
- Is there an existing turnkey system that can solve our problems, or do we need to build our system? How many people do we need to do the job? Do we need to hire experts or can our people create required solutions?

If you are a manager or an executive, this probably sounds familiar. It should, because you acquire an AI system in much the same way as you acquire any expensive machine. If you keep these types of questions in mind, you should be able to maintain a focused orientation and perspective.

The sections that follow discuss several things about which you make decisions. Read through the sections to see what you'll encounter and get a feel for what will happen as you look for a system. Do not identify and purchase an AI system until you feel you have sufficient background. Be sure to look at both the positive and negative sides of issues.

BASIS FOR INTELLIGENCE

Any AI system you examine will have some means of behaving intelligently. That is, in solving a problem for you, the computer system will emulate human intelligence in some way. The overall manner in which a machine emulates human intelligence relates to the specific type of intelligence it demonstrates. No AI system emulates the entire spectrum of human intelligence. Each machine is specialized. One machine might adjust its behavior according to perceived shapes; another machine might prescribe drugs according to a patient's symptoms. While specifics vary immensely, any AI system has these components:

- **Knowledge Base:** The knowledge base for a particular AI system contains all facts, assumptions, and rules the system needs to behave intelligently. The "all" means all the knowledge that can be reasonably stored and accessed by an appropriate computer system. The format in which this knowledge is stored varies dramatically from one type of system to another. For example, expert systems use rules. Robotics systems use elaborate computations. But all AI systems use some type of knowledge base that provides a basis for intelligent actions.
- **Inference Engine:** The term *inference engine* is most often used in the context of expert systems, but it suggests that an AI system has a way to determine how it should behave intelligently. The inference engine may perform elaborate searches

or sorts, or it might compare particular information against structural models. While implementation details vary, the principle is this: The inference engine performs the tasks that give the system intelligence.

Maintenance Engine: Again, we've borrowed a suggestive term. The maintenance engine is a program that lets you update the knowledge base or the inference engine, or both. "Update" means you can delete knowledge, insert additional knowledge, or modify existing knowledge. It can also mean changing the manner in which your AI system exhibits intelligence. If some glitch causes the system to behave stupidly, you want to be able to eliminate the glitch and insert an intelligent way of behaving. For example, a robot might assemble a part. An engineer might change some locations where holes are drilled. The maintenance engine would let you update the vectors that determine where the holes are drilled. This way, you don't have to drastically modify the overall software.

Your task, in selecting a system, is to examine how these features work and whether they fit your needs. Several variations are available. For example, assume you have a forward-reasoning inference engine that helps you manage huge projects. Knowledge has been entered into the knowledge base as statements related to risk causes. The rules relate to selecting appropriate activities, given certain risk causes. Some risk causes might be:

- Different business practices of customers.
- Project manager misguidance.
- Regulation code changes.

These are the *antecedents* in the forward-reasoning system. Some appropriate selected reasons and actions might be:

- Rule 1012 deduced (contractual defect existed in material standard).
- Rule 3124 deduced (approval delay due to misguiding spare parts amounts).

These are *consequences* in the forward-reasoning system.

Continuing our example, notice that it would be time-consuming to type in the actual antecedent statements in order to obtain the deduced causes. Some systems allow users to enter a short code that corresponds with the antecedent statements. Thus, instead of typing "different business practices of customers," a user could type a code such as "3D03." The codes and corresponding antecedent statements could be kept in a reference manual according to appropriate categories.

This system would have excellent run-time efficiency (the amount of time it takes for the system to deduce a cause, given some antecedents), but dealing with the code is not as easy as dealing with more natural statements.

Other systems do not permit use of codes. Instead, they let the user type whatever Englishlike statement describes a situation. Then the inference engine, or another program, attempts to match what the user types with knowledge in the knowledge base. (Recall that the knowledge base contains facts, assumptions, and rules.) If the inference engine is successful in obtaining matches, it applies rules and returns a cause, just like the system that accepted codes. But you should see the potential problem. With Englishlike statements, it can take a long time for a slow processor to effect a match and then deduce a cause.

The first system, which uses codes, could be inexpensive and have a slow processor, but the user would be locked into a rigid reference procedure. The second system, which allows Englishlike antecedent statements, would be expensive and need an ultrafast processor, but the user would have more latitude in using the system.

This is a brief example, but it illustrates what you will encounter in looking at how a machine emulates human intelligence. In every area of AI, the expert's most difficult task is creating ways for computer systems to emulate human intelligence.

HARDWARE

The hardware requirements of expert systems differ from those of word processing or database systems. Perhaps you can leverage the resources of a company computer, but it is often better to have dedicated hardware. In general, you'll find three hardware trends:

- **Dedicated AI Computer Systems:** These computer systems are optimized to do AI. Their producers do not anticipate that you'd use the system for other purposes.
- **Mini and Mainframe Computer Systems That Provide AI:** Many companies already own such a computer system that can be leveraged for AI.
- **Personal AI Work Stations:** Such work stations can be used for many purposes: AI, CAD/CAM, communications, or documentation. Personal work stations are easily networked.

Very large AI systems might have more than one type of AI hardware.

SOFTWARE

An AI system has unique software requirements. You can leverage some tools, communications, and operating system software from a company computer, but the AI system itself is unique. You'll find an amazing assortment of available software, much more so than hardware. Finding the right combination of software to meet your needs can take time and very particular study.

RESOURCES

Human expertise is your principle resource. Your AI system functions up to the capability of your knowledge and that of Lisp experts, and no higher. Time and money are like necessary evils. You cannot create an AI system overnight. Except in rare and specialized situations, you cannot buy a ready-made AI system. Whatever your need for an AI system may be, its exact nature is probably unique and you will need to create a unique system. This is one reason why you need an industrial-strength Lisp.

PRIORITIES

You either need an AI system or you do not. Do not get one just to be in fashion. If your company or agency processes mostly symbolic (sentences) knowledge rapidly and uses that knowledge to solve problems and make recommendations, then you need an AI system. If you decide to get one, commit the necessary time and resources, and then manage the AI system project much as you would manage any important project.

This is an overall picture. In the remainder of this chapter we discuss the hardware and software requirements. We assume you know how to manage projects and deal with executive matters. We talked about the knowledge and Lisp experts in the previous chapter.

HARDWARE REQUIREMENTS

Two requirements dictate the selection of hardware. First, the hardware must be capable of doing AI tasks. For example, the hardware must process symbolic data rapidly. Second, the hardware must accommodate your specific requirements. For example, your system might need eight megabytes of memory. A system for another person might only need two megabytes of memory.

A complete delineation of hardware requirements could fill a large encyclopedia. Although we are brief, we wanted to make positive recommendations. We solved our problem this way: Most of the recommendations relate to full-blown, but not excessive, AI development systems. A development system is large enough for you to create and develop AI in any area (e.g., expert systems, robotics system). It is more than large enough to run applications programs that perform specific tasks in AI. Types of systems are discussed later in this chapter, in a section called *Types of AI Systems and Applications,* and are defined in the Glossary.

We suggest you develop a checklist of requirements as you examine what your AI system should do. As you read the following sections, which examine the hardware components of an AI system, think about how you should develop and organize your personal checklist.

Processor

An AI system needs a state-of-the-art microprocessor that has excellent speed and is optimized to deal with AI software and hardware. The question is, what does this translate into?

Most processors have 8, 16, 32, or 64-bit registers and operate at clock speeds of 1 to 12 MHz (megahertz). Such processors are found, respectively, in small microcomputers, personal/professional microcomputers, work station computers and minicomputers, and large mainframes. For example, a Hewlett-Packard work station computer has a 32-bit processor. At present, "state of the art" refers to a processor with at least 32-bit registers and a 16-bit data bus. A clock speed of 8 MHz is good; 12 MHz is better.

MHz means megahertz. Mega means one million; hertz means one cycle per second. So 12 MHz means your computer has a clock that permits 12 million electrical pulses to be sent through the hardware system each second. One pulse is a cycle in which one high electrical state is followed by a return to a low electrical state. The high-low electrical states relate to the digital electronics used by computers.

In simpler English, a computer's memory can be altered 12 million times each second when the computer's processor runs at 12 Mhz. At present, this rate is fast. A processor that works at 12 MHz is adequate for sophisticated work in AI. At the other end of the spectrum, some companies advertise AI systems that utilize an 8-bit data bus and a 16-bit processor that run at only 4 MHz. You could take a vacation while waiting for such a processor to complete a large, complex task, but you could use such a system for simple training or demonstrations.

The instruction set for the processor should be optimized for fast processing of strings and numbers. That is, the computer program that operates the processor should be designed to handle large chunks of data, perform rapid calculations, and transport data efficiently. The system must process searches and sorts rapidly. Examining processors can get very technical very fast, but the effort can be rewarding if you need ultrafast processing.

The trend in the design of computer architecture has been to increase the density, complexity, and utility of processors for the purpose of accommodating high-level language constructs. Today's processors have rich instruction sets and are called CISCs (Complex Instruction Set Computers). CISCs have extensive microcode, the machine-language code that makes the processor work, and this microcode lets the processor accommodate software written in assorted high-level languages. That is, it gives a processor flexibility, often at the expense of slower performance.

Realizing this, researchers at the University of California at Berkeley and at Stanford University have been developing RISCs (Reduced Instruction Set Computers). With the drop in the cost of memory, these researchers argue that RISCs execute much faster, as much as 60 percent faster. RISCs incorporate four design concepts:

- One instruction is executed per cycle. This permits fast execution of instructions.
- All instructions are the same size. This simplifies implementation.
- System memory is accessed only by the STORE and LOAD instructions. This simplifies system design.
- The design supports high-level languages by anticipating that some work will be farmed out to peripheral devices.

The RISCs technology is new, and it might emerge as a significant one. Development projects are underway at several major companies: Hewlett-Packard, IBM, DEC, TRW, and Fairchild Semiconductor. If the RISC technology, perhaps coupled or integrated with parallel processing or distributed processing, bears fruit, expect to see immediate utilization of the technology in AI, even though existing AI software would have to be modified.

To get some details, examine:

MARKOFF, JOHN. *"RISC Chips"* BYTE (November 1984) 191–206.

We mention the relationship between CISCs and RISCs here not to give you the details, but to alert you to attempts to create new technologies. The computer industry is not standing still. As another example, some companies are developing technology for parallel processing.

At present, computers use what is called "von Neumann architecture." In this architecture (a term that refers to how a processor is designed), one main processor calls programs and data from memory and controls the processing of instructions. All instructions and data flow through a single bus between the processor and the memory.

In the proposed parallel-processing technology, several processors would be placed on a single chip. A problem could be broken down into identifiable parts so that one processor could work on one part of the problem. This way, several processors could simultaneously compute partial solutions at great speed. The partial solutions would then be combined, returning an overall solution. The potential of parallel processing has dramatic implications for AI. At the current rate of change, we'll probably get to see what happens. The bottom line with regard to the processor is this: The AI microprocessor must hum!

Memory

AI systems require huge amounts of memory. Four or five megabytes is a minimum; more memory is common. A megabyte is 1,048,576 bytes. This translates to being about 1,048,576 characters such as the letter A or the number 7.

By the way, kilobytes, megabytes, and gigabytes can get confusing when you read assorted literature. Computers use a binary system. Consequently, one kilobyte is 2 raised to the tenth power instead of 10 raised to the third power. In short, a kilobyte is 1,024 bytes ($2*2*2*2*2*2*2*2*2*2$); not 1000 bytes ($10*10*10$). One megabyte is not just 1,024 bytes multiplied by a power of 10. For example, one megabyte is not 1,024,000 bytes, as some literature suggests. One megabyte is 2 raised to the twentieth power, or 1,048,576 bytes. One gigabyte is 2 raised to the thirtieth power, or 1,073,741,824 bytes. Relating this to the four-gigabyte memory of some AI systems, you have 4,294,967,376 bytes of memory! That is something, compared to the 128, 256 or 512 kilobyte memories found in most personal computers.

Most knowledge (data) in AI systems is unrelated to numbers. Instead, the knowledge consists of statements written in a language such as English. You process this symbolic knowledge according to rules which themselves may be part of a knowledge base.

Remembering that one byte stores one character, and that one word is usually about six characters, and that statements often contain 10 or more words, you can see why an AI system needs a lot of memory. When intact, addressable memory is not available, your system must employ some means of breaking programs or data files into segments, and then work on the segments. If you have worked with a personal computer, you are probably aware of how often work is interrupted so that a program or data can be loaded into memory.

While a megabyte or two may seem huge, AI programs can be very large. Therefore, it can be necessary for the hardware system to support *virtual memory*. Virtual memory means that your system can extend the address space for memory beyond the physical bounds of your system's memory and incorporate data or programs stored in files on the magnetic media of a tape or hard disk and treat the data or programs as if they were a part of the computer's memory. Such a system has some means of partitioning memory into segments and swapping currently unused segments for required segments. The swapping process slows the system down a bit.

Input Devices

AI systems, like most systems, let you (input) data from numerous devices (keyboard, external instruments, disk drives, mouse). The trick is to select the combination of devices that lets you work effectively. Companies use several schemes for hooking up devices, varying between "You plug it in and it works according to how the company lets it work" to "It works any way you want it to work after you figure out how to connect it." You should not have to rewire connectors, set switches, alter software, and specify addresses to an excessive degree to hook a device to an AI system. Here are several particulars and examples.

Most popular editors, used to develop Lisp programs, employ several special keys. Some companies provide special keyboards that incorporate these keys; other companies use their standard keyboards and accommodate special keys by reassigning the function of nonessential keys. While specialized keyboards are seldom a real requirement, they are very nice because in most cases you press a key and it performs a function according to its label. It is annoying to press the TAB key for the META key, the PAUSE key for the NEWLINE key, and the CONTINUE key for the ESCAPE key.

You need standardized means of accessing external devices. This is a need, not a want. AI systems can become very complex. It must be possible to link every hardware component in the system with minimal difficulty.

Few standards were developed in the early days of the computer industry. Every company thought it had the best system. In time, customers who bought processors from one company, disk drives from another company, and monitors from yet another company, forced the major companies to agree upon some standardized means of hooking up devices.

Most companies complied, but few standards have become absolutes. For example, Hewlett-Packard created and now uses a standardized set of pins (electronic signals) and a standardized connector called HP-IB (Hewlett-Packard Interface Bus) for interfacing devices. As long as you have devices made by HP, you just hook up the connectors and all the devices work fine. In a similar vein, IBM makes huge mainframe computers to which many terminals can be attached. IBM developed their own methods of hooking the terminals to a mainframe. The devices work well as long as you have IBM devices. Still in the same vein, Digital Equipment Corporation (DEC) created their own methods for hooking terminals to their minicomputers. The consequence is that you cannot directly hook up Hewlett-Packard, International Business Machines, and Digital Equipment Corporation devices in many cases. Electrical engineers and programmers circumvent incompatibility problems by creating emulator programs and special interfacing devices. Most of them even enjoy the process, but overall, using interfacing devices and emulators strains your system and slows it down, not to mention the added expense.

Smaller start-up AI companies usually emulate the large companies or go their own way and create their own methods of hooking up devices. A few of the smaller companies borrow an assortment of excellent software and hardware and adapt it. Many of the AI systems created by small companies run very well, especially the turnkey applications systems.

In time, companies, agencies, and organizations set up standardized means of sending electronic signals. Here are the standards you encounter most often:

- **RS 232 C:** The RS-232C standard is a set of pins (wires) that are used for asynchronous serial transmission of electronic signals. RS-232C was developed by the Electronics Industries Association (EAI). You can read all the details elsewhere. The important thing is that the RS 232 standard is used to connect terminals, modems, or printers to computers. That is, RS-232C permits communication among devices.
- **IEEE-488:** Hewlett-Packard developed the IEEE-488 standard in cooperation with the Institute of Electrical Engineers. Other companies adopted the standard to connect computers with disk drives, printers, voltmeters, and assorted measurement devices. Robotics, sensors, and controllers, which employ complex means to determine which device is talking-listening, sending-receiving, controlling-working, and so on, use the IEEE-488 standard. IEEE-488 is often called GPIB (General Purpose Interface Bus).
- **Ethernet:** The Ethernet standards is closely related to the IEEE-802.3 standard. Ethernet, a trademark of the Xerox Corporation, is a *de facto* standard for development of local area networks. "Local Area" refers to a small area within a building where several work stations are connected. To illustrate this, and Ethernet network might have these limits: maximum length of network coaxial cable is 500 meters, maximum number of nodes (work stations) is 100, and maximum node separation from a cable is 2.5 meters. Ethernet is often used with the UNIX (a trademark of Bell Laboratories) operating system or one of its derivatives.

In addition to these standards, you encounter many particular standards. For example, IBM 3270 is an interactive standard companies use for emulators that let you hook up a non-IBM terminal to an IBM mainframe computer. An interactive standard, in this case, consists of hardware and software which enable a terminal or computer to act like a different device so it can interact with another computer. For example, Hewlett-Packard manufactures an emulator that lets their Series 200 computers act like an IBM display station. The emulators are a combination of hardware and software. This way, an HP computer can interact with an IBM mainframe. In a similar vein, Hewlett-Packard created an emulator that lets HP computers act like a DEC VT100 terminal. With an emulator in place, an HP computer can communicate with a DEC minicomputer such as a VAX 11/780.

Most companies that make AI systems use these or similar standards and emulators. It is very likely that you will use several standards and emulators regardless of which computers you purchase because is usually necessary to obtain information or programs from other, external computers. You should deterine which standards are used for interactive communication; also determine the availability of emulators if you intend to obtain resources from assorted external sources.

We mentioned some specific computer companies to make the following points, not to advertise:

- It should not be necessary to rewire connectors or use a variety of connectors to an excessive degree. It is not always easy to determine what is meant by ''to an excessive degree,'' but if your technical experts become very confused, look for another AI system. You should be able to hook up numerous external resources without having to set myriad switches or significantly alter software code.
- At first, computer companies focused on hooking up their equipment. Their standards were, or became, whatever engineers could do at a point in time to make a system work. This created a legacy of not letting different computers interact. Consequently, you must determine the extent to which assorted computers can interact.
- In time, standards were developed that let you hook up assorted devices, but you must be aware that the standards are not rigid. You must examine the technical nuances of how the devices are hooked up. It is one thing for a sales rep to say that brand X interacts with brand Y, and it is another thing to actually hook them up. Don't be paranoid. Just determine what can be done.

Within broad limits, it is best to purchase external devices made specifically for your AI computer. However, do not be dogmatic. There are times when external monitors, printers, and disk drives made by other companies are superior and work very well. It is not always desirable to have all Hewlett-Packard, all IBM, all DEC, or all brand X; it's usually easier just to hook up the devices.

Our discussion of standards for input devices applies equally to output devices discussed in the next section.

By the way, in the area of device compatibility among companies, you should be aware of the difference between supported and nonsupported hardware or software. When you purchase an AI system, the mainframe or computer *is* the system. The overall system can, in many cases, contain devices made by other companies. The company that built the mainframe either supports or does not support other components of the overall system, whether made by themselves or by other companies. Of course, the company supports the mainframe. "Supports" means that the company provides whatever type of service you purchase. This varies from one company to another. You might get installation and configuration, a year of troubleshooting, and the privilege of calling a company service engineer to inquire about problems. You might only purchase installation and configuration. Whatever, "unsupported" does *not* mean device will not work on a company's computer. A device might work very well. But the term "unsupported" does mean that the parent company will not tell you how to make a device or a program work. More important, if you use an unsupported device or program, and your computer blows, you might be staring at some very expensive junk, depending on the fine print of your purchase agreement and the attitude of the parent company.

Output Devices

You should be able to output information to assorted devices. The extent to which you output information depends on the diversity of your AI situation. This diversity determines how you store data, display output, and create printed or plotted material. For example, if you report often to boards of directors, you need a plotter to make overlays, which show information graphically. On the other hand, if you circulate papers in which you report findings drawn from data, a printer is sufficient. If you must communicate information to people in remote offices, you need a modem. Here are the major output devices.

An AI system needs a hard disk drive, with tape backup, for mass storage of programs, data, informations, rules, and so on. About 25 megabytes of mass storage is minimal for most AI systems. Even small AI systems need at least 10 megabytes of mass storage. For many systems, 200 megabytes is optimal; in large systems, mass storage requirements can reach the gigabyte level.

One flexible disk drive is desirable. The flexible disk drive lets you handle small programs and data files. The flexible disk drive is particularly useful for frequent updating of small files.

You'll need a monitor, except with systems that do nothing except monitor assorted devices—and most people want a monitor even then. The 9- to 12-inch monitors used with personal computers are seldom adequate for AI systems. A 17- to 19-inch monitor is more effective because it permits extensive use of windows. Working with the range of available AI systems, we became convinced that a 14-inch monitor is the minimum effective size for any system, and a 17-inch monitor is much better for development work.

Get a monitor that has a soft, as opposed to harsh, display because you spend many hours staring at the screen. Assorted combinations of "black and white" colors are available: white on black, light blue on dark blue, light green on dark green, amber on black, and red on white. All these monitors support the inverse combinations. People have strong opinions about which combination is best. Even we do not agree; one author likes light blue on dark blue, the other likes light green on dark green. The black-on-white combination is very popular. Whatever, get a monitor that has a display your people like.

A window is a rectangular portion of a screen in which information is displayed. By having several visible windows, you can examine information, write programs, display options for commands, and display other things such as helpful information or the status of directories. For example, you should be able to see a Lisp program, a menu of command options, the value returned by the Lisp program, and the status of your active file in separate windows at one time. It is extremely desirable to have a system that provides multiple windows. If you have a window management capability, a mouse makes it easy to move around in the system, but the keyboard is best for heavy-duty work.

A bit-mapped monitor that can show characters and graphics at the same time is desirable, but not required. A color monitor is nice, but not required. If you get a color monitor, a 17- to 19-inch screen works well. It is nice, but not necessary, to have a 21- or 24-inch screen.

Your printer should have very rapid throughput. A line printer is best. AI systems create much hard-copy output. Character printers are adequate for very small systems, but they are too slow to do heavy-duty work.

A plotter is very desirable, but is required only in special circumstances.

You need access via a modem to other, external computer resources. You need whatever measurement or monitoring devices are required to detect, measure, and process data used by the AI system.

It is desirable to connect the computer systems that make up individual work stations via a network so the computer systems can share resources such as printers, spooler, and plotters. Several types of networks are available. Just be sure that everything can be hooked up with minimal difficulty. You should be able to connect every device in a network without doing many push-ups (rewiring, setting switches, altering software, and so on).

General Hardware Considerations

Let's put these recommendations together to form an ideal AI system. An ideal AI system has a combination of hardware like the system shown in Figure 6.2.

The term *ideal* relates to having a full-blown development environment for AI. A *development environment* is a system that contains hardware and software used to create AI systems. Contrast this with an *applications environment,* which is a combination of hardware and software used to solve real-life problems. For example, the expert system named R1, which configures computer systems, was created within a development environment. Once R1 was developed, smaller applications environments were used to configure computer systems. An AI system used for development can also be used for applications, but the reverse situation seldom obtains.

When several devices are available that could perform adequately, use these criteria to select components of your system:

- Small is better than big.
- Fast is better than slow.
- Compatible is better than make-it-work.

- Quality is better than shoddy.
- Expensive is better than economical.

Each computer system, exclusive of shared resources, should fit into a work-station space. If you need more than one work station, it is better in most cases to have several computers on a network than to have several terminals hooked up to one big computer, although there are exceptions. When you must process immense amounts of data and several people must use a few terminals to access the computer, one big computer can work very well.

The work-station concept is relatively new because a work station usually has a desktop or personal computer. This type of computer was developed last, after minicomputers and mainframes, in the current evolution of computers. The network concept is newer yet. To some people, new is good because it implies reliability. You must decide this one. The prevailing trend, in the evolving AI market, is to produce AI work stations that can be integrated with other systems.

Against this background, here is an illustration of a characteristic artificial intelligence development environment. Be aware that you need software to run the hardware. The characteristic software for a development environment is shown in the next section, *Software Requirements and Alternatives*.

Study the work-station environment. While it shows the major components, you have alternatives for installing them. For example, we show a physical spooler. A spooler is a device or mechanism that temporarily stores files while the files await their turn to be printed. The spooler need not be a physical device. It can be a program embedded in the software that runs the network.

Let's digress a moment to look at networks. Look for these situations when you examine possibilities for installing a network:

- Components in the network can be separated according to your physical environment, but there are always limitations. For example, a network might allow two work stations to be separated by up to 60 meters. If your work stations are 100 meters apart, you must alter the environment, devise some means of "mailing" information, or not use a network.
- A network might not allow access via a modem, or other transmission vehicle, to external computers, and you need access to outside resources at both the work station and the controller nodes in the network. In particular, you may need to download foreign languages from an external computer to your work stations. Some networks do not allow this, others do.
- A network might provide up to 16 nodes (attached work stations or peripherals), and your people require 21 nodes.
- A network might provide addresses for up to four attached peripherals, and your people require attachment of 12 peripheral devices.

Go back and examine the discrepancies in each situation. We included these situations to

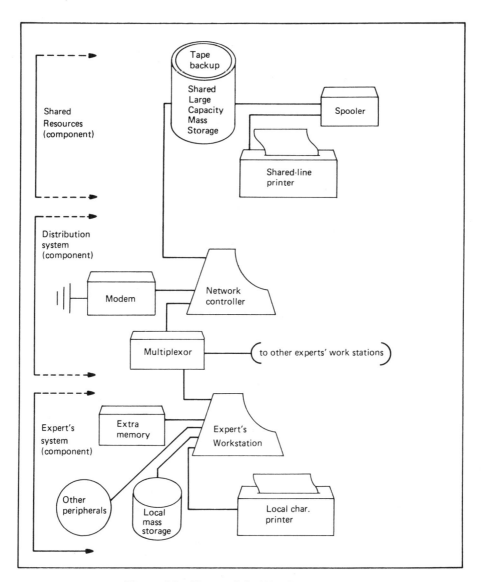

Figure 6.2 Characteristic AI hardware system.

illustrate the relationship between knowing what your system must do and finding a system that does it. This is exacting work. You do not find the answers in the generalities expressed by sales reps. This is extremely important.

If you study the features of computer systems offered by several companies who market AI systems, the hardware will seem remarkably similar. For example, most companies offer the Ethernet network. Your task is not to determine that a company offers Ethernet or not. Your task is to determine how the company offers Ethernet and whether

Ethernet is the best network for your situation. A particular company might have a different, but superior, network for an AI system. This possibility will increase as smaller start-up companies enter the AI market and as subsidiary companies make networks for computers produced by large companies. The AI system in Figure 6.2 is nominal. Here are the major relationships:

- In the degree that you need focused applications, you can scale down the AI system, perhaps even reaching a point where a small, single work station is sufficient.
- In the degree that you need diversified development of tools and applications, you can either increase the size of your network or obtain more powerful computers.

The system we illustrated costs about $100,000. It is more difficult to price large systems because the number of options increases geometrically. In a small system you choose peripherals from a few hundred options. In a large system you choose peripherals from several thousand options. It becomes exceedingly difficult to make the right choices as the size of the system increases.

In fact, this problem became so acute that human experts at DEC could not provide adequate solutions. Consequently, an expert system called R1 was developed specifically to configure large DEC computer systems. Then R1 was generalized to configure several types of large computer systems.

SOFTWARE REQUIREMENTS AND ALTERNATIVES

An AI system contains an assortment of software. Shopping for a system, you will find immense variety in implementation of software. If you use established criteria to guide your shopping, you'll be amazed by the number of times a particular software package will have almost every feature you need, but will lack some crucial feature.

More than in selecting hardware, you'll probably compromise your selection of software. Within some limits, this is not serious because you can change the way you perform tasks. When you examine software, note these types of things:

- **Software Category:** Programs fit into loose categories according to their function. Thus, programs are tools, utiltities, drivers, applications, and so on. By knowing the category, you can keep track of what is what.
- **Software Version:** Programs also come in versions. The version denotes the program's lineage, so to speak. For example, IntelliCorp introduced an AI development tool named *KEE* in 1984. Later, in version 2.0, *KEE* was expanded to classes and assertions, as well as ordinary programming procedures. In most cases, a higher release number indicates a newer, more advanced version of a program.
- **Software scope:** The scope of particular software packages varies immensely. For example, some packages just do text editing. Another ostensibly similar package might provide text editing and record keeping. This occurs most often with lan-

guages and operating systems. Sometimes an operating system and a language are distinct entities. The language runs on top of the operating system. In other cases, the operating system and the language are one integrated environment.

Lets look at the major software components.

Operating Systems

You have choices. Some expert systems are written entirely in Lisp. In this situation, the kernel (core program that runs the computer system), the operating system (a program that executes commands, formats discs, stores files, and so on), and all tools and applications are one giant set of programs. While this has been done, it is not necessary to write an entire AI system in Lisp.

Most AI systems employ layers of software in which, collectively, you find these things:

- Microcode of some type runs the microprocessor. This code interacts with the microprocessor and the kernel of an operating system.
- An operating system provides a link between the microprocessor programs and the commands and functions used by a human to run the computer system. The operating system also supports execution of assorted tools and applications programs. Some operating systems provide many tools, languages, and applications programs directly.
- Lisp runs on top of the kernel or core of the operating system. Some dialects of Lisp can interact with the operating system in assorted ways. This includes calling operating system commands, file-handling routines, or foreign languages. This can also include providing customization of any number of features.
- Myriad applications and tools can run on top of Lisp. This will include most expert systems and programs that allow you to create expert systems.

You can see that the stack of programs running above the processor level can become very high. This is why you should ensure that the performance of software in each layer is optimized to execute rapidly. If the programs in any layer degrade performance, the entire software system slows down.

Because most people have layers of software, UNIX is a popular operating system. You get an instant reaction when you tell people you intend to use UNIX as your operating system. UNIX was created by Bell Laboratories and has been extended substantially by many people. While UNIX is called an operating system by most people, it is really a programming environment as much as anything else.

Whatever you call it, UNIX is preferred by some people and despised by others. There are many versions of UNIX. The differences between versions are significant. Some versions have been stripped down so they fit into small, personal computers.

In general, a version of UNIX contains these features:

- **A Kernel:** The kernel is a core program that interacts with the computer, provides essential commands, and supports the assortment of programs provided within the total UNIX environment.

- **Editors:** After you log onto UNIX, you can invoke one of several editors and create text. **Vi** and **ed** are UNIX editors. A text formatter called **troff** lets you create nicely formatted hard copy of text files.

- **Data Communications:** Programs such as **aterm, mail,** and **send** provide assorted communications.

- **Language Processing/Compiling:** In the UNIX operating system, you can use an editor to write a C, FORTRAN, or Pascal programs, and then use **cc, fc,** or **pc,** respectively, to compile the program.

- **File Control/Manipulation:** Commands such as **mkdir** (makes a directory), **rm** (remove files), and **cp** (copy, link, or move files) let you handle files.

- **System Administration and Maintenance:** Numerous commands are available for installing commands, terminating processes, building special files, and initializing disks.

- **System Intrinsics:** In general, intrinsics are commands that let you invoke or alter basic processes. As examples, **chdir** lets you change a directory; **exec** lets you execute a file; **mount** lets you mount a file system; and **stty** lets you set terminal options.

Besides these major features, UNIX provides libraries and utilities. A library is a set of programs of a particular type. A utility is a program that performs a specific, routine task such as formatting a disc, backing up a file, or altering the directory of a disc. Most versions of UNIX also include subroutines, on-line documentation, and I/O routines.

We focused on features of UNIX because it is a popular operating system and because it illustrates how an operating system can supplement a dialect of Lisp by adding useful commands, functions, and programs. We also focused on UNIX because it illustrates how an operating system fits into a layered approach to building a software system that accommodates the capabilities of its hardware system.

It is not necessary to use UNIX for AI systems. In the daily use of a computer, it is easy to forget that the computer system consists of hardware and software. Several very adequate operating systems are available for use in an AI system, and any operating system you investigate will have an assortment of features. For example, at the level of small personal computers that have limited AI software, the MS DOS 2.0 operating system or the Pascal environment is often used.

We mentioned that many people do not like the UNIX operating system. Perhaps you fit into this group. This should not be a problem, because other operating systems are available. For example, several AI experts like the OPS5 system, a rule language developed at Carnegie-Mellon University that is tailored to the AI environment. At this writing, OPS5 was the most popular AI programming environment. OPS5 illustrates a principle that may appeal to you, namely that it is often better to use efficient algorithmic procedures to create AI software than to use pure AI techniques and Lisp. At present, many people want software that uses procedures to facilitate programming.

Still other people like operating systems that were created for particular computers or that have specific features. For example, at Edinburgh University in Great Britain, a language called POP-2 was developed as an alternative to Lisp. Before long, POP-2 was extended at Sussex University and thereby turned into an integrated programming environment. That is, it became its own operating system, language, editor, debugger, and so on.

As you read more about the development of AI, you will encounter this situation often because each expert in AI has opinions about what should be done. We discussed UNIX because, in the transfer of AI from the laboratory to the world at large, many people have become familiar with UNIX. It is, in some circles, the people's choice, a choice that can be hotly debated. We also mentioned UNIX because most companies that market AI systems market UNIX as a basis for running the software.

You will hear about several types of operating systems as you shop for an AI system. Look beneath the surface and determine exactly what features are available. Your task, the proverbial trick, if you please, is to select an operating system that does not degrade overall software performance and that supplements features provided by Lisp and related AI software within your particular hardware system.

Lisp

Tools and applications programs for AI systems are written in Lisp in the United States because Lisp lets you process symbolic information (nonnumerical information) as easily as numerical information. The list-processing capability of Lisp is unparalleled. With Lisp you can write programs that efficiently and effectively process data that consist of sentences, paragraphs, and rules.

It's probably heresy to say this, but it is not mandatory that AI programs be written in Lisp. You could write AI programs in BASIC, Pascal, or FORTRAN, but it is much more difficult to do so when you want to develop very powerful programs and use the power that recursion adds to processing symbolic information. We referenced Lisp to the United States because many people use Prolog in Japan and Europe.

The system you purchase will not have Lisp per se. Lisp is a computer language, but it is also generic. You will actually have some dialect of Lisp. Let's see what this entails.

Dialects of Lisp

You need an industrial-strength dialect of Lisp to use the power of AI. Having used this term for some time, here is the definition of an industrial-strength Lisp.

The core of your Lisp dialect should contain a rich assortment of powerful functions. You would expect this, but what is a powerful set of functions? The number of functions in a dialect of Lisp varies from about 200 to about 10,000. The average is about 500. The number of functions is not terribly important because Lisp functions can be defined and added to the language. The power of the functions lies in how they provide access to enhancement features. As you read brochures, check to see if the the advertised dialect of Lisp provides or accommodates these types of features:

- **Large Virtual Address Space:** A large virtual address space lets you run programs that exceed the size of your system's absolute memory. The definition of ''large'' varies in accordance with your needs. A 32-megabyte virtual address space is adequate for most work-station systems. A large AI system might need a 128-megabyte virtual space.

- **Efficient Memory Management:** Memory management is dynamic in Lisp. That is, memory is managed as a program executes. Unlike most conventional languages, memory is not allocated and fixed before a program executes. This is not bad, as such. It just means that the implementation of garbage collection, cache memory, streaming, and so on should promote efficiency. This becomes very technical. You don't need to understand the details, but you should ensure that memory management accommodates your needs. Compared with some languages, Lisp is rather slow. Slow is a relative concept, however, and the cost of increasing execution speed goes up geometrically.

- **Foreign Language Calls:** Many excellent programs are written in FORTRAN, C, Pascal, and other languages. If your dialect of Lisp can make foreign language calls, you can integrate these foreign programs with your Lisp programs. This can save programming time or speed up program execution.

- **Extensive I/O:** Input/output situations vary from checking a device to see if a bit is high or low to complex satellite communications. Lisp dialects vary a great deal in whether and how they handle certain types of I/O. For example, a robotics system needs a full range of I/O capabilities for transferring bits, bytes, characters, codes, numbers, vectors, and arrays.

- **Object-Oriented-Programming:** This method of programming lets you create objects and manipulate them efficiently. For example, an object can inherit characteristics from other objects. This increases programmer efficiency by preventing repetitious specification of details.

- **Packages:** This feature lets you integrate programs written by assorted people and access common data without encountering conflicts between the routines written by the assorted programmers. That is, packages help prevent conflicts that could occur when a program calls a routine and there are several routines that have the same name.

You'll read about other features. The point is this: Check which features are available and relate them to your needs. The advanced features can significantly increase programmer or system efficiency.

AI System Interfaces

The interfaces to an AI system fit into several categories and have several labels. Let's start below the level of an AI system and work up.

- Small, simple computer systems have an operating system and fundamental set of commands in ROM (Read Only Memory). That is, the program that operates the system and lets you issue commands is in the computer in a chip in permanent memory that you cannot change. You turn on the computer and the operating system "comes up," ready to use. A displayed prompt such as a dash, rectangle, or special character indicates that you can enter and execute available commands. This capability to enter commands is the interface to the system. In most cases, this capability is limited to doing fundamental things. For example, you might RUN a program, SAVE a file, or FORMAT a disk.

- More complex, but still simple, computer systems add a language system to the operating system. The language system contains a computer language such as BASIC, an editor that lets you write programs, and an interpreter that lets you execute (run) programs. The language system may be in ROM, but more often the language system is loaded into the computer's memory from a disk. The editor is an interface to the system and there are lots of editors. Graphics and text editors are the most common types.

- The complex computer systems used for AI use several types of software. One type is a special program that provides a human interface to the AI system. The human interface programs let you move around in an AI system and execute fundamental commands. A human interface lets you access and use editors, file managers, operating systems, text processors, terminal emulators, and such. The human interface lets you coordinate the operation of the entire AI system.
The original human interfaces for AI systems were developed in the early 1960s, shortly after McCarthy invented Lisp. These human interfaces provided an editor for writing programs, an interpreter for evaluating Lisp programs, and an assortment of commands for saving files and such. Soon after Lisp was invented, the EMACS editor was created. It became the prototype human interface for AI systems, but just as many dialects of Lisp were developed, many versions of EMACS were developed. The EMACS human interface, and derivatives such as ZMACS and NMODE, have two principle features:

- The human interface "comes up" in insert mode. This means you can write and edit textual documents or Lisp programs.

- You can execute any of about 500 commands, depending on your version or derivative of EMACS. When you are in insert mode, and at prescribed times when you are in other modes, you can execute a command. Commands can be executed in several ways. Here are the most common:

   a. Hold down the CONTROL key and press a letter.

   b. Hold down the CONTROL key, press the letter X, and type an appropriate entry.

   c. Hold down the CONTROL key and press a letter, then hold down the CONTROL key again and press a different letter.

   d. Press the META key and press a letter.

   e. Press the META key, press the letter X, and type an appropriate entry.

   f. Hold down the CONTROL key, press the META key, and press a letter.

   g. Hold down the CONTROL key, press the META key, and type an appropriate response.

As you might suspect, you must memorize the possibilities at a fundamental level, but many derivatives of EMACS provide alternate means of executing commands (e.g., a mouse or softkeys).

In addition to executing commands, you can be in any of several modes: Text Mode lets you enter text; Lisp Mode lets you write and interpret Lisp programs; Browse Mode lets you examine assorted files.

The assortment of commands lets you move around in the AI system environment. For example, when you are in Browse Mode, certain commands let you move around the AI system and examine files in assorted directories.

As you can see, human interfaces such as EMACS are powerful, but they are extremely difficult to use when you must memorize everything you do. Imagine the combinations of commands you can issue via combinations of CONTROL, META, and letter-key presses.

The use of CONTROL and META commands in EMACS type interfaces was dictated by limitations in computer technology in the 1960s. At the time, the CONTROL and META keys provided an effective way to differentiate between typing the letter *A* in a memo when you were in inset mode and issuing the command that was linked to the letter *A*. When the CONTROL key was held down or when the META key was pressed, insert mode was interrupted, and pressing a letter key issued a command.

This was an effective technique then, but it is an outmoded technique now. Today, other technology is available, but the AI community has not yet adequately used the technology to develop advanced human interfaces. Let's look at this, because it relates to your purchase of an AI system.

The pioneers of AI wanted to create dialects of Lisp and use Lisp to develop tools and applications programs. They did not want to develop human interfaces per se. Programmers seldom want to develop any software below their focused level, nor do they usually have the time to do so.

Programmers—Lisp experts, in our case—are expert computer users. They either use an interface with little difficulty or they adjust to using an available interface. In most cases, programmers are directed, in company projects, to create a new language (a new dialect of Lisp), a new tool, or a new application program. They use available human interfaces and modify them as required. If they make any modifications, they are modifying old code; they are not creating new code.

We mention this because many end users like a product, but are dismayed by the haphazard and cryptic manner in which the product works.

Programmers do not develop a new human interface and then use the interface to create the new language, tool, or application. Actually, it is seldom possible to do this. You cannot have an interface written in a language you are developing. Later, after the language, tool, or application is developed and released as a product, a programmer could go back and create an excellent human interface for using the language, tool, or application. But this is not often done.

The implication of this, during the years that AI was nurtured in university labs and think tanks, was that the AI community of experts learned to live with EMACS-type human interfaces in spite of using memorized commands and procedures. Some of them even grew to like EMACS. Today, they will argue its merit long into the night.

The implication is this: People do not like a human interface that requires excessive memorization of commands. Today, people like user-friendly human interfaces. This fact led to utilization of these things:

- Menus display available program options.
- Prompts are written in English instead of cryptic programmer terms.
- Softkey labels are displayed on a screen in highlighted positions that correspond to the placement of softkeys on a keyboard.
- A mouse or knob is used to select program options. An arrowlike cursor indicates the mouse or knob location on the screen. The cursor is moved to an icon, a window, a command, or a menu option, and then a button or return key is pressed.

The degree to which and the manner in which you find newer, user-friendly features in the human interface for an AI system will vary. Recently, developers of AI systems have not done away with the EMACS-type human interfaces, but they have added a window management system to the human interface, which lets you use a mouse, dedicated keys, or function softkeys to execute the commands previous users had to memorize.

This is an interesting development because it illustrates the weight of tradition, even in a field as new as AI. It also illustrates how developers have accommodated the wishes of new users and placated the established AI community. In the future, expect to see new and powerful human interface that have no basis in EMACS or other antiquated interfaces.

Today, expect to find a spectrum of human interfaces. Some will be a straightforward EMACS type editor. Some will be adaptations. A few will be new or will be an adaptation of some other old interface. For example, we recently used a human interface in which you could use EMACS CONTROL and META key commands directly (if you knew them), or you could use function softkeys (the corresponding softkey label was displayed on the screen), or you could use a mouse in conjunction with icons displayed in a special window. That is covering all the current bases!

Whatever, the human interface for your personal AI system should be powerful and friendly. The terms *powerful* and *friendly* have several dimensions. In concept, you should be able to access and use the total AI system. That's the powerful part. You should be able to use the system without pressing a lot of keys, typing a lot of commands, or looking up a lot of information. That's the friendly part. Let's look at this more closely.

There should be a visible display of any command that can be executed from your current position within the total AI system. The visible display can be an icon, a softkey label, or a menu. The point is this: What you can do should be displayed. You should never have to execute a blind command; that is, execute a command you had to memorize.

Available commands should let you move horizontally across the human interface, accessing available features, and should let you interact vertically with the operating system, Lisp, and other software that sits on top of Lisp. This other software includes all tools and applications software. That is, you should be able to jump to any part of the total system, and then move vertically or horizontally within that part with ease. It should not be necessary to execute long sequences of commands.

The keyboard should have dedicated Lisp function keys. It should not be necessary to memorize and use ⌈ CONTROL ⌋ commands, but you should expect to examine documentation to see how a command works. It is unreasonable to expect a totally pushbutton AI system to be very powerful. Expect to conceptualize how commands, functions, and macros work. By the way, at a fundamental level, a macro is a feature of a computer system where pressing one key, or taking an equivalent action, executes a series of actions. Within Lisp, the term *macro* has a more technical meaning.

Getting back to the keyboard, suppose you have just written a Lisp program and wish to execute the program. It should not be necessary to execute a CONTROL-META-D to go to the beginning of the program, and then execute a CONTROL-META-E to execute the program. There should be a dedicated key labeled EXECUTE that you press after you type the last right parenthesis to run the program.

The interface should have windows that let you see Lisp programs, results of evaluated programs, and information about the programs on the screen at the same time. Another window should display your location in the system. Another window should continuously display and update functions and commands you can use. A Help window should be available at all times, and it should be possible to obtain help by pressing a dedicated key labeled HELP.

When you are not using Lisp, and instead are using a tool or application, the window system should provide uncluttered working windows. The working windows should let you do whatever the program does (e.g., edit text, format a page of printed text, back up files on a hard disk drive, place graphics figures in a document, print a report).

Each working window should include a highlighted subwindow that displays the status of the window and displays your options for working within the window. For example, suppose you browse through the files in a directory. The highlighted status window should display the directory path that indicates where you are. In particular, if you are in the JONES directory in the USERS directory in the SYSTEM directory, the display might read:

/SYSTEMS/USERS/JONES . . . scanning files in directory

The menu part of the highlighted subwindow should display a menu of available options. Again referring to the file browser example, the menu of options might include:

Browse Create Delete Translate Edit Quit

This way, you always know where you are in the system and what you can do.

Here is the principle: If the menus and prompts are cryptic, and if you have to press or hold down several keys to make the system work, then the human interface is not friendly and you will have to memorize specific information to use the system.

Figure 6.3 is an illustration of an ideal human interface. Be aware that the contents of the windows would change as you use the system. Notice these things: The window system for the human interface is not busy; the arrangement of the windows is suited to how people are trained to read information; and the use of a cursor and highlighting makes it easy to find the active window.

In short, your human interface to the AI system should contain a broad horizontal base of capabilities and should integrate vertically with other software in the system. The point is this: Do not saddle yourself or your domain and knowledge experts with a weak human interface. The human interface is your means of accessing the entire system. It needs to be powerful, state-of-the-art software. Unfortunately, few state-of-the-art interfaces are available. Examine this area very carefully and in great detail. You should ask more questions about the human interface than about any other part of the AI system software.

Using Foreign Languages

Much knowledge has been stored in computers via programs written in languages such as C, FORTRAN, and Pascal. The language simply named C is used to write many operating systems. For example, UNIX is written in C.

It is desirable for your dialect of Lisp to call these foreign languages and use them. This way you have access to existing files which contain information.

Not all AI systems let you call foreign languages. When you can call them, the procedures vary. The procedure is not important provided you can effectively use foreign language routines within your AI system.

Having discussed the software components, here is a generic illustration of how they fit together (Figure 6.4). Be aware that your particular software system might lack certain components or be structured differently. Let's examine the components and their relationships.

The arrows indicate potential interaction. For example, a single-ended arrow leads from the processor instruction set to the operating system, but it does not return because you cannot often interact directly with processor microcode from the operating system. On the other hand, a double-ended arrow connects the human interface and the operating system because you can move freely between the two. For example, in the operating system, you could execute a command that would load the human interface. In the human interface a QUIT command would let you return to the operating system. In the human

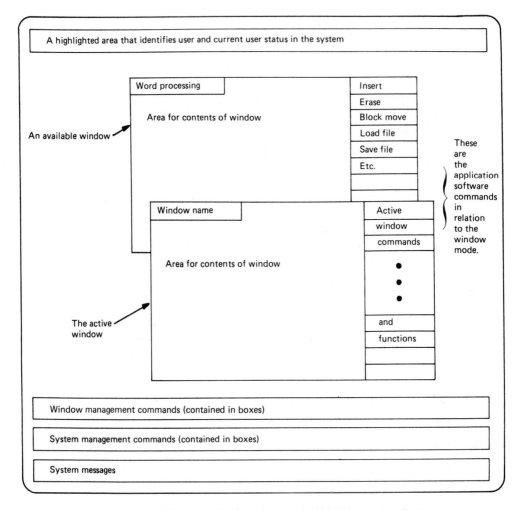

Figure 6.3 Sample screen of ideal human interface.

interface you could load and use Lisp, an application program, or a systems development program, which would let you create applications programs, development tools, or in rare cases, both.

Notice that from any point above the human interface, you can use the human interface to view On-line documentation. Many schemes are used to let you get Help. This is just one possibility.

Notice also that in the area around Lisp and the human interface, the arrows suggest much interaction between types of software. Depending on your system, this can range from a simple turnkey system that climbs from the microcode to an application to a complete freedom to move around from one software type to another. For example, assume

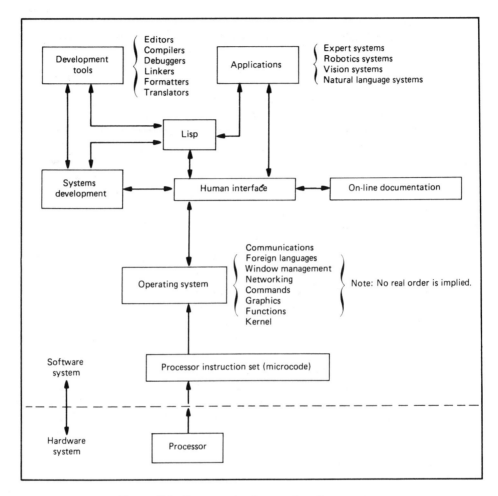

Figure 6.4 Components of a generic software system.

you are in the human interface. You could move to Lisp to gain its features and then move to the systems development program. In this program you could create an application program; then you could move to the development tools software and use the compiler to translate your application into a computer code that executes rapidly. Then you could store the compiled application in the applications software and use it as required. Wow!

In interviewing several knowledge engineers, we found these more or less sequential work patterns:

1. A programmer acquires an AI system. The hardware is installed. This means that all the devices are hooked up and switches are set. The operating system is loaded and the process of configuring all the software in the system begins. To do the

configuration, the programmer makes extensive use of operating system commands, intrinsics, subroutines, and libraries. Such things as networks, communications, window management, and graphics are configured. Then the human interface, Lisp, and other software are placed in mass storage and configured. Tapes are the usual initial source of the software you purchased.

2. After downing some coffee, a programmer brings up the operating system, loads the human interface and Lisp. Then the programmer calls an editor from the development tools software and creates an application program (e.g., an expert system). At assorted times, after things appear to be working, the programmer leaves the editor and calls a compiler to change the application program into compiled code. Then the application program is executed. Usually it does not work, so the programmer uses a debugger to see what's wrong. This cycle goes on until the application program works.

3. At this point, an application has been created, so the programmer returns to the human interface and stores the application in the applications software, where the program can then be sold as a product or used as required.

As you can see, the patterns of work can become very complex. This complexity, or potential complexity, creates your need for an excellent human interface, an industrial-strength Lisp, and powerful development tools.

The complexity also accounts for why people want effective systems development software. It is easier for people, including programmers, to use this software to create applications than to always write them from scratch in Lisp. An analogous situation is that of using a graphics editor to draw and plot a pie chart or using a language such as BASIC to create and plot the chart. Most people can use a graphics editor, but most people cannot write programs. This same phenomenon accounts for why some people prefer Prolog over Lisp to do AI work. The principle is this: To the extent that your people can use development software via procedures to create applications programs, your people do not need to be Lisp experts; they just need to be knowledgeable about what they develop.

By now you should realize that choosing appropriate software for your AI system can become very complex. It can also be quite simple. You should also realize that you must effect a match between your hardware and your software. An AI system does not work effectively when the hardware and software are not matched. For example, you would not use a small application program on a large minicomputer unless you had the minicomputer and were leveraging it. Nor would you use powerful tools programs on a microcomputer. Let's see how to effect a match by looking at software and types of AI systems.

Be aware that we are talking about an entire AI system from scratch. In reality, you will probably already have bits and pieces of hardware and software that must be consolidated into an AI system. For example, your company might already have a large minicomputer and you might need a small applications program. Then, of course, you would purchase the applications program and use it on the minicomputer.

TYPES OF AI SYSTEMS AND SOFTWARE

AI systems range in size. Some systems are small hardware-software systems that have a simple operating system (e.g., MS DOS 2.0), a microcomputer-size hardware system, and a focused application program that solves specific problems. Exceedingly complex hardware-software systems lie at the other end of the spectrum. We have talked about hardware and software, but we have not said much about how they are related or classified.

You have more options for using an AI system when you have a large computer, several operating systems and human interfaces, a powerful dialect of Lisp, and many tools such as compilers, debuggers, formatters, terminal emulators, and translators. This type of AI system is powerful, but it is expensive and very difficult to use. Most of the pioneers of AI worked to develop this type of system.

Today, many people are interested in smaller, simpler, less complicated AI systems that either solve specific problems directly or can be programmed to solve specific problems. If you investigate this type of AI system, you move away from large systems that have myriad tools and move toward systems that use application programs.

Using application programs, you work less with operating systems, dialects of Lisp, or tools. An applications program lets you solve problems by doing most of the work for you. That is, an applications program automatically performs most of the tasks you could perform, but do not wish to perform, at the operating system, Lisp dialect, or tools levels. Applications programs run on top of your operating system and Lisp. Let's see how an applications program might be created.

AI experts have written programs, usually in Lisp, that use objects or frames to help you model and store knowledge within a well-defined subject area. There are distinctions between objects and frames, which we will discuss later.

To continue, a well-defined subject area can be any block of knowledge that can be classified as being distinct from other areas of knowledge. For example, early expert systems were developed to diagnose blood disorders, configure computers, and operate a steam plant. It was more difficult to develop expert systems that could edit novels people wrote or translate an article written in English into Spanish. Editing and translating are arts as much as they are sciences or specific bodies of knowledge. AI is suited to sciences. It is not yet suited to arts, but AI experts are making excellent progress.

Getting back to the objects and frames, as you learned earlier, an object is a thing and all the operations you can perform on it. You can have a great deal of knowledge about the objects within any particular identifiable subject area.

Modeling the knowledge in a defined subject area is the major initial step in creating an AI application. People can argue for years about how to model a body of knowledge correctly, but once some decisions are reached, a model can be developed. The objects in the model can be analyzed and the operations you can perform on each object can be determined. Then an AI application can be created that uses the objects and performs the operations. That is, an object-oriented AI application can be created. Within this type of applications software, you can describe, define, access, and update an object.

If you use a frame-oriented AI system instead of an object-oriented AI system, you still begin with modeling the knowledge within a defined subject area. Then you create a frame, or template, which lets you enter data that represents each element in a body of knowledge. The data for a given frame is much like the data in a record in a data base, but there are important distinctions.

In a data base, you do not want any transfer of information between records. For example, you would not want 40 different people to inherit the Social Security number of a master record. Each record must have a distinct name, Social Security number, and address in a data base. In a frame-oriented AI system, it is desirable for frames to inherit data from other frames. Just how this occurs can become very technical. You should inquire about particulars when you examine a frame-oriented AI system.

Here is our point: If you can get an object-oriented or frame-oriented AI application that lets you create programs to solve your specific problems, or if you can get a system that can be customized to solve your specific problems, then give the system careful, deliberate consideration. In this same vein, it is often possible to use an existing application or have your knowledge engineer and domain expert modify an existing application so that it solves your particular problems, especially when the software used objects or frames as a basis for handling data. The objects or frames often make it cost effective for you to modify an AI application rather than develop a new AI application.

This short discussion covered much ground. Let's consolidate your major options:

- You can buy applications that work directly to solve problems. Your people need subject knowledge, but do not need much knowledge about Lisp.
- You can obtain rather generic applications that incorporate objects or frames, which can be modified to suit your needs. Your people need subject knowledge and some knowledge about Lisp.
- You can use special software in which procedural algorithms are used to supply parameters related to some problem. Then the special software, in effect, creates an application program. Your people need subject knowledge and must learn how to work through the procedures.
- You can use object- or frame-oriented programming to develop applications rather efficiently, but you'll need to go through all the development steps. Your people need subject knowledge and considerable knowledge about Lisp.
- You can use pure Lisp to create just about any program you like, from an operating system to an application.

While there are many variations, you'll find the entry point for selecting software in one of these categories.

Whether you focus on development or applications, look for intergration and compatibility when you examine software. All the software must work together. This is the key feature. Your programmers should not have to write many programs that link software you have purchased, although "many" cannot be easily defined. It is often necessary to write programs called drivers which interface assorted devices. It is also often necessary to modify a few lines of a program so the program uses one feature or another. If a sales rep mentions some modifications and your programmers complain bitterly, then the modifications are probably excessive.

The human interface should be designed so you can easily move around the entire software environment. The human interface should not require excessive memorization of CONTROL, META, or ESCAPE commands. Softkey functions, menus selection, and labeled keys should be used for execution of commands. Having a mouse is fashionable, but not necessary.

In examining AI systems, you will find two major types: turnkey systems and components systems:

- **Turnkey Systems** more or less run themselves. *Turnkey,* literally refers to a jailer, a keeper of the keys. In computerese, it refers to software systems that start up automatically and then guide a user via menus and input prompts.

  Turnkey systems work in rather exact and limited ways. That is, the turnkey system "keeps the keys" with regard to what you can do and how you do it. In general, turnkey software packages run small AI systems. For example, a computer system that contains a Motorola 68000-generation processor, a 12-inch monitor, one megabyte of memory, a 20-megabyte disk drive, and a dot-matrix character printer is a small system.

- **Components Systems** do not run themselves. Instead, a user employs a set of tools (editor, dialect of Lisp, compiler, debugger, operating system) to create a customized AI system. Components systems are much more complex than turnkey systems. Users of components systems must be domain experts (know a subject area). You may need to employ a knowledge engineer (an AI expert). In general, each software package is a component of a large AI systems. At present, a minicomputer with a high-speed 32-bit processor, two or three monitors, 5–10 megabytes of memory, several disk drives with up to two gigabytes of mass storage, and a dot-matrix line printer is a large system.

Between the extremes of large and small, AI systems vary. In principle, software developers either (1) create a turnkey system that does a certain thing very well in an extremely user-friendly manner, or (2) they create a components system that provides a maximum number of tools on the smallest possible computer system. But there are so many variations of these themes that it can be difficult to make distinctions.

In this realm, beware of advertised claims. Quite frankly, a marketer who tells you that a $15,000 stand-alone system does the same things as a $100,000 networked system is lying. In the same vein, a marketer who tells you that a turnkey system, which has a thin user manual, does everything that you can do with a components system, which has several thick manuals, is also lying.

In the overall scheme of developing software for AI systems, the major factor that limits progress is the rate at which a program for an AI system becomes too complex for humans to deal with the program. In selecting software, finding the compromise between obtaining powerful software and determining the ability of your people to use the software for its intended purposes is the major factor in how well your total AI system will help you solve specific problems.

No person we know writes a significant program that runs properly and serves its intended purpose the first time it is executed. After a program is written, programmers can spend days, or months, finding bugs that cause a program to malfunction. As a program becomes complex, and AI programs can be incredibly complex, the problem of finding a bug increases geometrically. You do not want to give your people an impossible task, and you do not want to saddle your people with inadequate software.

The AI system we will discuss was being developed during 1984. It had potential, but it was not actually working. Here is an example of putting together an actual AI system that illustrates what we have been discussing:

1. **The Need:** Build a land vehicle that drives on a road without a human operator. This focuses the problem. The major areas of AI are vision, motion, and electronic control of a vehicle (a bastardized robotics).

2. **Consultation:** After many discussions between AI experts and assorted engineers, models for determining what constitutes recognizing and staying of a road are conceptualized. It was determined that the vehicle should examine the short-range, intermediate-range, and long-range dimensions of road navigation.

3. **Options and Decisions:** Given the general models, assumptions, and conceptualizations for how the vehicle should navigate a road, engineers and mathematicians determine how to implement an AI system that can drive the vehicle. They examine these things:
   a. Direct ranging via laser or light sensor.
   b. Corridors of free space.
   c. Dead-reckoning subsystems.
   d. Domain-specific knowledge related to ground topography, 3-D road models, straightness and parallelness, and discrimination of road against a background.
   e. Anticipating road changes.
   f. An assortment of other factors such as perceiving and avoiding obstacles and navigation or road networks.

4. **Developing a Prototype System:** This is an interesting part of the total task because both general types of AI systems are needed. The prototype system and much simulation was operated by a small, specialized, turnkey system housed in the vehicle. Many people who obtain AI systems will need this combination.

5. **Testing the vehicle:** This part of the project was just getting underway as we went to press.

We used this example because it illustrates an application of AI that is on the leading edge of what people were doing in 1984–85. For more information, examine the ''*Computer Vision*'' section of the proceedings from the IEEE-sponsored and AAAI-supported *First Conference on Artificial Intelligence Applications*.

The First Conference on Artificial Intelligence Applications, IEEE Computer Society, P.O. Box 80452, Worldway Postal Center, Los Angeles, CA 90080 (December 1984). ISBN 0-8186-0624-X (paper)

The paper, contained in the above-cited proceedings, from which we obtained information, is:

ROSENFELD, AZRIEL, LARRY DAVIS, AND ALLEN WAXMAN. *"Vision for Autonomous Navigation,"* Center for Automation Research, University of Maryland, College Park, MD 20742.

In short, as we have said many times, analyze your needs, shop around, and buy an adequate system. Do not be misled by claims. Get down the the nuts-and-bolts level of what a system can or cannot do.

The next chapter discusses ways to climb the learning curve once you have a functioning AI system. In particular, you find out how expert systems can learn from their mistakes, thereby gaining new knowledge and improved efficiency.

CLIMBING THE LEARNING CURVE

After a conventional application program is placed in service, it is essentially left alone save for an occasional bug fix or minor revision. The program is said to have entered the *maintenance phase* of its development.

Artificial intelligence applications, on the other hand, are continuously evaluated, updated, revised, debugged, and enhanced throughout their lifetimes. Once the initial implementation is in place, the real work begins, and the program is said to have entered the *evolutionary phase* of development.

This calls attention to a significant point of departure of AI programs from conventional programs: Conventional programs are maintained; AI programs are evolved.

Artificial intelligence systems require evolution because knowledge and intelligence are not static entities. We cannot declare that on a certain date we know everything there is to know about a particular domain, for tomorrow there will be new discoveries, new theories, and new situations to deal with. Yesterday's knowledge will become obsolete.

Learning is an essential part of intelligence. A computer that can learn is more autonomous and efficient that one that cannot. Accuracy and performance will increase automatically with time. The computer will become "wiser" and more "experienced" as it ages.

Computer learning is certainly a noble goal, but like so many areas in artificial intelligence, research is still in its infancy. In this chapter we will briefly survey some of the thrusts in this field, indicating what is possible today and what is likely tomorrow.

METHODS OF LEARNING

Learning by Being Programmed

Learning by being programmed is the way most all computers acquire knowledge today. With this method, a human being gathers the knowledge, designs computer representations for it, codes it in a programming language such as Lisp, loads it into the computer's memory, debugs it, updates it, modifies it, and so on.

The only intelligence in this scheme is exhibited by the human being. The computer is totally passive. Obviously, this is the method that AI is trying to obsolete. Let's move on to human methods of learning.

Learning by Being Taught

Learning by being taught involves two players, a teacher and a student. In artificial intelligence applications, the student is the computer. The teacher may be a human expert or a book, videotape, or audio cassette on the subject of interest.

With this method, the teacher presents the information to the student; but unlike learning by being programmed, the student is responsible for assimilating the information into his own knowledge base.

Much research is being conducted into this area, but major road blocks are impeding progress. The most critical is the lack of an adequate interface between the student and the teacher. Computer vision and natural language processing are not yet sufficiently developed to allow human beings and computers to communicate easily. As in all teaching situations, no learning can take place until the student and the teacher are on the same wavelength.

Assuming that the teacher and the student can communicate, the next aspect of the teaching situation that must be simulated is *student feedback*. The successful student is not passive; he must ask the teacher to clarify points he does not understand. Thus part of learning is knowing what questions to ask.

Ideally, the computer would become its own knowledge engineer. The computer would conduct its own interview with the domain expert, assimilating the knowledge and calling the expert back for further clarification if inconsistencies are detected. Certain existing expert systems include an interviewing feature to extract relevant information from the user, but such systems are oriented toward problem solving in an existing domain rather than information gathering in a new domain.

Along these same lines, the computer/knowledge engineer would also have to integrate incoming knowledge into the knowledge base. This involves defining objects, assigning attribute values, setting up classes and relationships, creating rules—in short, the computer would have to translate raw information into the appropriate knowledge representation in the knowledge base. Since a general theory of knowledge representation has not yet been established in the AI community, computers are not likely to assume this function in the near future.

Learning From Experience

Learning from experience is a completely unassisted method of knowledge acquisition. It is a continuous process in which existing knowledge is checked against reality for validity and efficiency. When discrepancies or opportunities for improvement are found, the necessary adjustments are made to the knowledge base.

A simple but essential requirement of learning by experience is the ability to remember past experiences. Computers, as a rule, don't do this. They process whatever data they are given, return their results, and move on to the next task.

One easy way to store experiences in an AI application is to keep a record of the number of times the rule has been successfully used. Successful use is defined as the number of times the rule has been invoked, *minus* the number of times the rule has led to a dead end and backtracking has occurred. This information can be used to decide which rule to select when confronted with several candidates who otherwise appear equally good. The rationale is that if one rule is used successfully more often than another, try the more successful rule first.

Another good technique would be to attach probabilities to rules that indicate the likelihood of a rule's success in a given situation. The probability could be computed from the frequency of successful use; however, computers have no understanding of what a situation is. A "situation object" was not included in our representation scheme in Chapter 3.

One proposed method for representing stereotyped situations is called a *frame*. A frame is similar to an object definition, but contains much more information. A frame may include:

- All objects in the situation.
- All relations defined between the objects.
- All rules in effect during the situation.
- Instructions for how to proceed if something unexpected happens.
- Instructions for using the frame.

If frames could be included in the knowledge base, then situations could be identified by their attributes, just as objects can. Every time a situation arises, the system notes which rules are invoked to solve the problem and maintains probabilities for success. The probabilities are used to recommend a course of action when an identical or similar situation is encountered later.

Feedback is another essential component if learning by experience is to succeed. The adage, "People learn from their mistakes," applies to intelligent computer systems also. When a computer reaches an incorrect conclusion, it needs to know where and why its reasoning process failed. Then when the situation arises again, the same mistake will not be repeated.

Correcting errors in judgment usually involves adding new rules to the knowledge base, or deleting or modifying existing rules. It is likely that this will have to be done by the domain expert and knowledge engineer, since the system that made the error probably cannot troubleshoot itself.

Learning by Discovery

Learning by discovery is the highest form of learning and the most difficult to simulate on a computer. It has only been successful in extremely regular and well-defined domains. For example, one expert system successfully uses this method to discover mathematical concepts from a set of primitive axioms. It can do this because the domain of mathematics is extremely systematic.

Learning by discovery involves combining known facts together in previously untried ways to come up with new facts. Often the jump from old facts to new conclusions required *insight*, which is not a well understood area of human cognition.

Learning by discovery often collects facts from several subject areas. General world knowledge is also a major factor. Because AI systems are currently incapable of acquiring broad-based knowledge and general problem-solving skills, it's unlikely that major breakthroughs in this area will materialize any time soon.

AI AND YOU

ORIENTATION

You are now familiar with the fundamental concepts of Lisp and AI. Perhaps you have reached some of these conclusions:

- AI can make the world a better place in which to live and can enable people to achieve an elevated level of humanity.
- AI is for screwballs who live in ivory-towered universities; it should remain there.
- AI is a dangerous concept, especially if it is used by the military-industrial complex to control the lives of common people.
- AI is the most potentially useful problem-solving tool ever invented. It could help people achieve unparalleled growth in problem-solving capability and thereby enable them to explore new areas of thinking.

We suspect you have formulated some strong opinion by now about the potential for AI to help people. Continuing in this vein, if you are like most people, your attitude is either very positive, very negative, or very passive. People are seldom partly positive, negative, or neutral about computers or about AI. Perhaps an anecdote can illustrate this.

We were showing computer products at a show in a large shopping mall in 1983. A woman and a teenager walked by. The woman did not look at us, but the teenager, obviously very interested, stopped and wanted to examine our running demonstration. The woman jerked the teenager's arm and said, "Get away from those computers! We're never getting a computer as long as you live under my roof!'' It was clear that we were observing two different attitudes toward computers. This is common, and the next paragraph discusses our point with regard to AI.

The stage is set for people to use AI. As far as the people of the world are concerned, your personal attitude is unimportant. At an individual level, your attitude is important because it dictates how you contribute to the AI movement.

You can decide to accept or reject the AI movement. The short-term future of AI will be determined largely by the degree to which people accept the potential of AI and purchase and use AI systems that still need much development. The jury is still out on this matter. Some of the great countermovements in history were started by people who refused to support an activity other people thought was important at the time. At present, it appears that the use and development of AI will depend most on the industrial-military-information complex. No level of government is currently inclined to fund university research, especially research that does not have immediate and obvious utility. Actually, most universities face lean years and stringent accountability. We'll see what happens.

AI, TECHNOLOGY, AND THE TIMES

The technology for doing AI is available. Memory is less expensive. Processors are faster and more diversified. Sufficient mass storage capacity is available. Software, while still limited, is much better than it was. New technology is being created at a fast rate.

Several companies produce AI products, and many other companies are beginning to introduce AI products. The tiny ripple created by people who brought up R1 on a DEC computer is becoming a giant wave. Symbolics, Xerox, Lisp Machine, Apollo, Sun, Tektronix, DEC, and IBM introduced AI systems in 1984 or earlier. It is a flood-tide situation much like the one in which microcomputers flooded the market from 1978 to 1983. Like the microcomputer situation, the hardware is more developed than the software. It will be relatively easy to select an adequate hardware system that can evolve over several years. Examine the software much more carefully. Try to get software that functions adequately at purchase time and can be easily upgraded over several years.

The social climate is ripe for accepting AI because the people of the world face enormous problems, and many people believe AI can help them solve those problems. We are talking here about people in agencies, corporations, and governments who have the resources to wield enormous power. They want solutions to problems and are willing to examine the possibilities for AI to help them obtain those solutions. That is, they are willing to support the development of AI, to a degree, in the hope of creating means to solve their problems, but that attitude will not last long unless they are successful. These people are supporting continuation of research that was originally done in universities, but unlike a university atmosphere, where research can usually be done just to obtain knowledge, these people lack long-term patience because other people in the entities they direct expect results.

The attitude just mentioned obtains because the people with power and resources regard AI as a potentially powerful tool. They do not regard AI as an entity to be nurtured and developed for its own sake. The lives of powerful people are driven and guided by a complex of ego gratification, power plays, role modeling, and perceived conflict. Within this environment, many of them currently believe that using rather primitive AI systems now, on the premise that the AI systems will rapidly evolve into more powerful machines, will make them front runners in an area that has immense potential. Many of the people who developed AI in the first place do not like this situation. Some of them feel betrayed because they do think of AI as something to be nurtured. Others do not want to lose control of a computer system they feel is not yet ready to be used. Still others are unsure and apprehensive about what will happen to the development of AI. But whether intellectuals like it or not, the situation no longer exists in which a few people can develop AI in universities or think tanks.

In the series of processes that led to the development of the original AI systems, it took centuries or decades to develop new technology. Today it takes only months or years. In this vein, you'll probably witness an exponential decrease in the amount of time required to create increasingly complex AI systems. You'll get to witness more development of technology than anyone ever imagined, however exciting or frightening that development might be. The use of AI systems for more and more applications at faster and faster rates will force people to deal with enormous political, ethical, social, and moral problems.

Signs of these problems are already showing up in courtrooms, in union-management contracts, in the retraining and relocating of blue-collar workers, and in the matrix of available jobs. For example, in the federal arena, the Food and Drug Administration (FDA) became very interested in the computer software used in expert systems when they found out that expert systems were used to diagnose illness, prescribe drugs, and suggest treatments for diseases.

FDA officials conducted an investigation in 1984 and, based on that investigation, said that they plan to regulate the development and use of ''intelligent'' software, among other things. One of the other things the FDA plans to do is define an intelligent system and define when an intelligent system provides a service. You are aware, of course, that definitions are everything when it comes to guiding federal actions.

PEOPLE, PSYCHOLOGY, AND AI

Each new movement initiated by people during recorded history has been shaped by many factors. The dynamics that shaped previous movements will shape the AI movement, but there will, of course, be unique wrinkles. In the AI movement, factors such as technology, economics, and politics are important, mostly in how they facilitate or constrain processes. But however these factors might impact processes, the psychological factors most influence the direction and significance of the movement. As more and more people learn about and use AI, they will develop the attitudes and orientations that will eventually determine what happens to the AI movement. We will discuss several potential outcomes later in the chapter.

In the next several sections, our discussion is food for thought; we have not provided any answers. We are not aware that anyone has dealt effectively with the potential of AI to create more problems than it solves, nor are we aware of much research into how AI fits into the total scheme of people's affairs.

So far, writers have focused on the what and how of AI and AI systems. We do not deny the importance of this surface-level reporting. People need to be informed. But we believe it is equally important to examine the why of AI. We believe people should think, consciously, about what AI is, what it could do, and whether the people of the world would be better off with it or without it. We want people to be acutely aware that a psychology of AI will develop and will accompany the AI movement. That psychology will have a powerful effect on the movement. Is it possible that within the current information age, people will be able to impact the psychology that develops more than they did in the past? The outcome should be interesting.

PEOPLE, PROBLEMS, AND AI

In their search for paradise, people have always had problems. The industrial revolution was a milestone that made it possible for many people to transcend working for physical existence. People finally reached a level where they could enjoy pleasure. People enjoyed the fruit provided by the industrial revolution during the quiet 1950s via big houses, big cars, travel, and barbecues. People educated their children to the highest level ever achieved by a society. The ''ever upward'' outlook enabled some people to conceptualize AI. The science fiction movies reflected this outlook.

The educated children grew up and instead of becoming exemplary conformers, they raised questions because they saw the injustice and inequity that prevailed in American society. America's young people sought change in the way Americans functioned, and they were successful. America's first well-educated generation created the turbulent 1960s. They made people at every level aware of and concerned about events that were outside the real scope of their lives. People got involved, and they changed the world. AI prospered because government agencies and private foundations provided liberal grants for research and equipment.

The 1970s was a depressing decade; some call it the Down Decade. Americans did poorly in wars, foreign affairs, schools, and factories. People discovered that being involved took a lot of time and effort. They discovered that ''the system'' could usually outlast them. The response of government to the protests of the 1960s was to develop more definitions, regulations, policies, and laws than have ever existed in any government. In the 1970s, government reports were measured in thousands of pages. According to evaluations, government-sponsored projects were ineffectual. Elected officials turned their attention to other matters. The torrent of money available for research became a trickle.

Unable to solve America's or the world's problems, people sought quieter, more localized environments in which they could cope successfully with situations and problems. This trend continued into the 1980s. To illustrate this withdrawal, recent surveys show that secondary school and university students have little awareness of world affairs and are not interested in things that lie outside the personal scope of their lives. John Naisbitt's *Megatrends* contains an excellent description of how Americans are responding to the current national situation.

Our point in briefly discussing the last four decades is this: The search for paradise is a drive, not a project or a goal. The search has never been systematic. The discrepancies between existing conditions and perceived needs fuel an ongoing search. Within any movement, people have identified certain undesirable conditions and have then attempted to alter or eliminate them, emerging with a new set of conditions. What happens, however, is that new, but totally unforeseen, conditions arise and become end products of the movement. Here is a pair of anticipated and unanticipated outcomes:

- People entered the 1960s knowing that injustice and inequities prevailed. They protested. Government and other agencies responded via grants for examination of everything from the sex life of the tsetse fly to the nature of minimal brain dysfunction. AI benefited from this generosity. Researchers invented the systems people are buying today. This was anticipated.
- People entered the 1960s hoping to establish conditions in which all Americans could become vitally involved in decision-making processes. They attempted to create strategies for getting people involved, but surveys show that today's young people, who will experience the AI movement, are mostly concerned with surface-level aspects of living. This was totally unanticipated. Today's students were supposed to become the world's premier citizens. Instead, they became self-centered and self-serving people who live moment to moment.

This is interesting because most predictors indicate that the AI movement, which is supposed to give people powerful problem-solving tools, will actually create millions of low-level service jobs and a few high-level, high-tech jobs. Oddly enough, the upcoming generation might be ideally suited to the predicted outcomes.

Whatever happens, the people will justify their actions, as they always do. It is a natural trait. For example, people do not just go to war. They go to war in the name of God, or to free oppressed people.

People need a cause for what they do. People become uneasy when they do not have a cause, and look for things to believe in. For example, Americans were floundering a bit before the 1984 Olympics were held in Los Angeles. The boycotts and assorted problems had an adverse effect on preparations for the event. Then, due to the absence of stellar performers from certain countries, the American athletes did very well. Millions of Americans rallied around the athletes. Gold-medal winners such as Mary Lou Retton became instant heroines; Edwin Moses became the example of dedication and perseverance. Even winners of bronze medals in events such as men's gymnastics, where Americans had never done well, were celebrated.

It was having a cause that drove people to invent the wheel, devise ways to use fire, harness electricity, and split the atom. At a surface level, there was the challenge to do these things; the "because it's there" syndrome. At a higher level, the drivers in society invent new things to help other people live the good life.

For many years, people did not question the long-range value of a product. Nylon stockings and tractors were accepted immediately. It took longer for people to accept automobiles. Blacksmiths thought the automobile would fail. Races between horses and cars were held. The horse usually won, but the marketers of cars prevailed. You know what happened to blacksmiths.

Our point in discussing products is this: When automobiles were introduced, there was no discussion of availability of gasoline, lead poisoning, pollution, or terrible working conditions for roughnecks (people who work on oil rigs). That discussion never occurred, although it should have.

Today it is vital for people to discuss the consequences of doing this or that. People have elevated themselves to a state in which individuals, agencies, and corporations should not introduce a product based on new technology without first discussing how the product will change others' lives. This discussion should extend beyond marketing strategies and profit motives and incorporate the philosophical dimensions of what a product can do within the prevailing scheme for what the world should be like.

People should raise and answer questions related, for example, to consequences that accrue from using AI, manipulating genetics, and creating bionic people. At present, people do not have these discussions. We have attended the introduction of several AI computer systems, and the question of what the system can do to people is never raised. We are often dismayed by the calm manner in which a high-technology company invents a computer system that runs a robot that puts 70,000 people out of work or, at best, forces them to relocate and retrain themselves for other employment.

Read on. We have attempted to provoke your thinking.

THE ROAD TO AI AND PSYCHOLOGY

Few people give conscious thought each day to how previous generations struggled to develop civilization to its current state. Most people think about these things when they sit around campfires or when they are personally affected by milestone events (the dropping of an atomic bomb or going off to war).

People easily forget lessons learned from history, partly because history is dull and totally vicarious. For example, in the 1940s secondary students read about the plague, a disease that killed half the population of Europe, with complete indifference. They were truly shocked when the atomic bomb was dropped on the Japanese. Today, students read about the dropping of the atomic bomb with complete indifference. A rally in 1984 at a San Francisco high school to commemorate the bombing of Nagasaki drew only 47 people; not even the Japanese students attended.

Our point in mentioning a psychology of history is that people have arrived at the threshold of using AI systems by engaging in a long, difficult struggle to create what they believed was a better means of living. Sometimes people struggled against the elements (floods, earthquakes, tidal waves, drought, and such). Sometimes they struggled to overthrow ideological or social systems (tribalism, Feudalism, socialism, and capitalism, for example). Sometimes they struggled to create better products (spears, wheels, printing presses, or automobiles, among many). Whatever the arena, people have struggled toward what they believed was a better way of living, however nebulous the overall concept might be, and they have not thought much about where they were going, except in the present. If an improvement was immediately beneficial, people accepted it. People have seldom created five-year plans; there are no overall 200-year plans. Corporations usually have quarterly plans, yearly plans at best. The lumber industry has 150-year plans for the cutting of trees.

People did not need a psychology of paradise when they were scattered and close to nature. They need one now. People can now live at a metaphysical level. They can create bionic people, use AI, kill each other with push-botton weapons, and live in electronically monitored environments. They need a psychology of the what, who, how, when, where, and why of pursuing paradise. They need to know what paradise would be like if they reached it. People need to know how they would function if they got to paradise. People have reached a point where they cannot viably go on without first deciding where they are going.

If you are reading this book, you must surely have asked by now, Why does anyone need AI, Lisp, or expert systems? We began this book by looking at the scientific milestones that led to AI. Then we examined Lisp, AI, expert systems, and AI systems in general. This chapter focuses on AI and you, so let's examine some social aspects of inventing and using AI.

THE SOCIAL TRAIL TO AI

Archeologists tell us that people began as hunters and gatherers. Theologians tell us the same thing, but they use very different vehicles and means. Whatever the source of your descriptions, early people had the capacity to wish for things and translate those wishes into products (tools, weapons, clothes).

Overall, they worked hard to devise better ways to obtain food, water, and shelter. It was no accident that they learned to appreciate and want a superior cave, spear, or club. While you can debate the heredity vs. environment learning theories, people learned to want things. Historians remind us that from the dawn of written records until the 1960s, few people questioned the value of materialism. Today, many people question its value.

The invention of agriculture cast people into a more routine way of performing daily tasks. People did not punch a time clock, but they did work long hours at routine tasks. But most people did not question the value of the work ethic during this time. Today many people question the value of the work ethic.

The gradual development of complex machines and the gradual mechanization of work helped people provide necessities; these changes gave people more time to improve society. People reached a point where they did not devote every waking hour to survival. They had time to invent schools, complex religions, politics, representative government, and other constructs of modern civilization. People had time to conduct talk shows on television.

But few people doubted the value of work, the regulation of one's time, or the value of a collective society during these times. There was little need to process information; life proceeded at a slow pace; travel was restricted; communication was mostly just local gossip; a person could count on spending a lifetime in one career.

Wholesale industrialization increased worker productivity and gave people more leisure time, but most people lived in the slow lane. It's no accident that many people embraced the "good old boy" life-style.

We mention these things to establish a setting, not to provide a history lesson. History suggests that people came to value many things that are now of questionable value, as an inevitable consequence of their struggle to overcome natural forces in their lives. Today many people question these values. Something must have happened to cause so many people to forsake values in a few years that were developed over centuries. Let's look into this.

THE NEW SOCIAL TRAIL TO AI

Today, people have largely overcome the natural forces that drove them to invent and use products that enhanced their lives in a material sense. People have gone beyond the exploration of most natural frontiers. The natural frontiers have been conquered. The highest mountains have been climed. The bottom of the ocean has been probed. The world has been circumnavigated by a single person in an open boat. The atom has been split. People go regularly into shallow space. Some probes are examining the immediate deep space.

People no longer photograph natural phenomena; they produce motion pictures of entirely hypothetical creatures and phenomena. People explore space, an activity not related to survival; they develop high-speed communications via satellite and other devices, activities that are not related to survival; they extend life beyond the natural levels of living. People have developed enough military capability to destroy the people of the world hundreds of times over with unnatural weapons far removed from the spears and clubs that caused people to meet face to face. People have reached a metalevel of existence in the last few years.

High technology in general, and computers in particular, have effected enormous change in how people conduct their lives. But the most significant change is this: People are transcending an existence grounded in things and achieving an existence grounded in images. Today, people give immense attention to electronic representations of things.

- Children do not play marbles with friends, they play video games.
- People do not get news via gossip from friends; they get news from television personalities.
- People are not humans applying for a loan at a bank; they are files in a data base. A negative balance causes a computer to "eat" their plastic cards.

The pace of this is too much for some people. They have reacted against this trend by creating assorted countercultures:

- Millions of people have forsaken technology and returned to the land. They have returned to a life where they use simple, real tools to create simple, real goods. The barter system is alive and well again.
- Some people function within a technological society, but they regularly use drugs to escape it. They can give many reasons for taking drugs, but the bottom line is that they need to escape their technological society and move into a world that is temporarily without pain.
- Other millions of people have not just forsaken technology, they have forsaken living and just drift from day to day—unemployed, unmotivated, and uninspired.

Along the new social trail to AI, people transcended most of the things their ancestors thought comprised paradise. Along the new social trail, people reached a metalevel of existence and never slowed down enough to really appreciate what they had. For example, when the microcomputer movement started in 1978, people who attended shows as COMDEX in Los Vegas, Nevada, were amazed at what the small computers could do. In 1984, a mere seven years later, people were bored.

The microcomputer is an incredible machine. A few of them can perform low-level AI tasks. How could people be bored? The answer, of course, is that people are still driven to attain new levels of existence without taking time to determine what they are trying to achieve and without taking time to appreciate what they have. People are accepting AI without first answering questions related to what it will do and why they need it. They are only asking questions about how, where, and when.

WE HAVE AI. WHAT NOW?

The people who invented AI and developed AI systems effectively hid their work from the public for about 30 to 40 years. Writing this book, we asked people who work in assorted capacities to describe AI. Most of them did not know what AI is, let alone what it does. Many people thought AI meant "artificial insemination." More formal surveys have produced similar findings.

We point this out for two reasons: (1) relatively few people control the destiny of AI; and (2) relatively many people do not know how AI will affect them. Will the people who control the future of AI, like the elite minorities of the past, plunge millions of people into a movement with relatively little personal accountability? You are aware, of course, that powerful executives have contracts that guarantee their personal success and fortunes even when the companies they direct fail. Whether the pro-AI minority will be accountable is moot. More on this later.

Our research has convinced us that AI has immense potential to change every one's lives. Its potential is not limited to helping a few specialists solve peculiar problems.

While AI is ideally suited to solving exceedingly complex problems, it is also ideally suited to performing intelligent searches and sorts that are designed to find suspicious people according to criteria established by a special interest group. We cannot overstate the importance of his. Without pointing a finger, it is fascinating that the prototype AI systems being created by some entities use demographic information and specialized rules, stored in a knowledge base, to identify suspicious people according to self-serving criteria. More on this later.

AI is emerging at a time when people are able to function at metaphysical levels. Today, as AI begins to shape people's lives, the people who control the destinies of the masses deal with images, not with things. Has it occurred to you that nowadays people talk about the image of the President, they do not talk about the President; people use statistics to talk about the advantage of contained nuclear war, they do not talk about the killing of people; people talk about the marvel of the information age, they do not talk about why they need to process so much information; people talk about ultrafast 32-bit processors, they do not talk about why they need ultrafast processors? Has it occurred to you that robots are making cars; people are not making cars? These things should occur to you because dealing with images instead of things, dealing with statistics instead of people, and dealing with information instead of principles have created more problems for people than any phenomena in recorded history. The perceived problems are a consequence of living at a metalevel.

Today, people are possessed by problems. They wonder why children take drugs and commit suicide, wonder why schools cannot educate children, and worry about what will happen to the space movement. Talk shows, soap operas, and other media pour out a continual stream of unresolved problems. People are possessed by problems without being able to solve any one significant problem: education, poverty, drug abuse, war, drought, crime. The beat goes on.

People ought to be getting somewhere, but they appear to be unable to appreciate what they have or to determine where they are going. People have worked for centuries to achieve a level of material and leisure existence they believed would be satisfying. For some reason, the satisfaction has not been what people thought it would be.

Now, people live in an age of high technology, which includes AI, but they are not sure about what to do with the technology in the long term. Writers tell people that the industrial age is over; the information age is upon them. This is fascinating, because the geometric progression in the passing of ages is getting steep. For example, take a moment to think about the dates associated with the Stone Age, Bronze Age, Iron Age, Agriculture Age, Industrial Age, and Information Age. Interesting! Will the AI Age last about two years? How many ages could we pass through by the year 2000?

People read books like Naisbitt's *Megatrends* and Toffler's Third Wave to perceive the future, but they do not take time to examine the present and then delineate the effect of using expert systems, robots, communications systems, or other accoutrements of the computer-information age. There is a high probability that people will plunge into AI without ever stopping to smell the roses.

However you perceive the current world scene, it seems that AI, collectively, could help people solve certain problems, provided the experts know how to solve the problems and know how to use the solutions. But this time, it seems equally clear that AI should not be used to shape the lives of millions of people just because it's there. This time it seems clear that people need to define why they are using AI; they also need to define what versions of paradise they hope to obtain by using it. People need to determine whether they want to move in the directions implied by the nature of AI. People need to sit down and define, in advance, a direction for their lives. It will be interesting to see if they do so. At present there is little evidence that they will, although some AI experts did express some concerns about this at the 1984 AAAI National Convention.

In the past, most development of high technology occurred because of the "it was there" syndrome. People could have existed for many generations with very little high technology, but they had the ability to engineer new products, so they did. With the high-tech products, musicians play louder music, writers process more words, and news commentators develop their acting careers.

Few people would suggest a shutdown of all the high-technology factories. They believe the beat must go on. Jobs, sales, profits, and vested interests are at stake. The problem with this orientation is that continual development of new products occurs as a result of pure accretion.

It is no accident that at the end of a project, managers ask engineers what they can do next. Nobody ever suggests shutting down a factory, laying off people, and not making more advanced high technology available to people, for obvious reasons; the economy would suffer or collapse entirely. We're stuck with our present concept of the economy because the people who promoted capitalism never took time to examine the long-range effects of establishing it as the way to manage an economy. One can make similar cases for socialism, communism, and other "isms."

In the same vein, the creators of Lisp developed it because they were tired of playing with numbers. They saw a huge stack of symbolic information just dying to be processed. Since they worked in a safe university environment that promoted inquiry and research, they invented Lisp so they could process the lists of words and sentences. Once Lisp was developed, it was used to study gaming strategy. Once gaming strategies were developed, the newly discovered concepts and principles were used to examine intelligence in general. Now, several years later, you can read about AI and purchase an expert system.

Within the next several years, you will be using AI systems. What will they do? What will they cause? People do not agree, partly because most people have no concept of the cyclic evolution of products, an evolution in which: (1) the development of products, (2) the use of resources, (3) the use of products, and (4) the reclamation of products are cycled back into loops designed to maintain a planned style of living and a balanced ecosystem. The standard evolution of products follows linear paths with much branching that creates a dendritic pattern. Some of the paths end and others continue as bases for an ever-increasing number of products. There is little, if any, cycling in the evolution of products. The increases in the number and type of specialty shops illustrates this linear and dendritic evolution of products. It does not seem likely that people will balance themselves within their ecosystem. People are still preoccupied with the linear and dendritic upward and onward pursuit of paradise.

Whatever might happen, people have AI and AI systems, and they will probably create myriad AI products. Here are some pairs of opinion about what could or should happen as the use of AI systems becomes commonplace:

1. AI systems are not really very different from other technologies used for automation and increased productivity. They are really quite trivial.

1. AI has given birth to a new class of machines, machines that can perform tasks that require reasoning, judgment, and intelligence that could previously only be performed by humans. AI can do, or will be able to do, anything people can do.

2. Automation via AI systems will create massive unemployment, especially among highly trained people, and will at the same time create many unskilled jobs such as kitchen helpers and fast-food workers. Automation will create massive relocation problems.

2. Automation, by its nature, increases productivity. Increased productivity always creates more jobs. There is never any shortage of work; there is only a lack of distribution of wealth. Distribute the wealth of productivity and you create a need for goods and services.

3. The *law of comparative advantage* holds that people and machines can be fully employed, regardless of their relative productivity, because labor can be employed in its productive areas; capital can be employed in its productive areas.

3. The *law of comparative advantage* does not account for essential issues: that labor can be employed in equilibrium with capital at a living wage, and that wages will not drop as capital creates increase machine productivity.

4. There will always be a demand for large amounts of labor if demand is potentially infinite, and demand is potentially infinite at this time.

4. AI systems will create increases in the exponent of productivity, an exponent that is already exponential. Such a superexponential increase will quickly overtake demand, even if it is currently infinite.

5. It is not desirable for a society to increase consumption, either in goods or services, just to keep employment high.

5. The goal of the free-market, competitive economy is to create ways to increase consumption of both goods and services.

This stating of opposites could go on ad infinitum. The point of our discussion is that you need to consider many viewpoints, filter out your orientations, and set your course of action. We have attempted to establish a setting in which you think about *why* you use AI as carefully as you think about *how* to use it.

We suggest you acknowledge that many people do things to become famous, to have an impact on society, or to pass time away with no concern for consequences. You should acknowledge these motivations and then not succumb to their rationales. We believe that if you use AI or expert systems to solve previously unsolvable problems, you must also acknowledge the entire spectrum of consequences that obtain from solving the problems.

The literature about AI usually contains descriptions of AI or AI systems, with liberal doses of opinion. Here's an example of opinion. In *The AI Magazine* (Summer 1984, Vol. 5, no, 2), Nils Nilsson states that:

> Placing obstacles in the path of either using or abetting technology might be called a "Luddite approach" to the economic problem of unemployment. This approach is unfair to humanity because it condems us to continue toiling when toil is unnecessary.

Later in his article, Nilsson states that the approach is unfair, that slowing down technology would worsen conditions in a country, and that foreign competitors would soon outrace the country and leave its people unemployed and in poverty.

We do not patently disagree with this, but we do wish to make a point. Nilsson might have meant a country like the United States, and he might have been thinking about a complex, industrialized economy. Actually, there are many countries that function quite well without AI, without technology, and with near-total continuous employment. These countries have done these things for years, and there is no indication that their people are unhappy or suffer excessive hardship. Actually, these countries could probably exist for many generations with fewer problems than Americans face in one generation. Our point is this: You have a responsibility to examine what you read both in the overall context and what AI systems can do and in the narrow context of why you need an AI system. Then you are responsible for seeing that AI is used for beneficial purposes that transcend your self-serving purposes.

Lets explore some dimensions of accountability.

WHO IS ACCOUNTABLE IN AI?

Imagine this scenario. You are an executive who has purchased an expert system that diagnoses liver ailments. You hired medical and Lisp experts who created this expert system. They fed all known information into a computer, together with many rules for analyzing symptoms of liver ailments. Apparently the system worked better than was expected, but the first three patients, who were treated on the basis of recommendations made by the expert system, died. Can the domain or Lisp expert be sued? Can you be sued? Can the expert system be sued?

We consulted legal experts who told us that, within certain limits, anyone can be sued. The major question is: Can they make a case? The legal experts told us that the expert system could not be sued, but you, the medical experts, and the Lisp programmer could be sued! The legal experts also told us that there are few precedents for dealing with recommendations made by computer programs; it is a new area. Consequently, the reaction of a jury could not be easily predicted.

This scenario is interesting, or frightening, and it certainly relates to accountability, but it is not our primary focus. Accountability has a more encompassing scope in our minds. Let's go a bit further.

Recall that we discussed how an expert system could learn. If your system has this capability, and if several knowledge experts feed all existing knowledge about an area into a computer, and if the expert system acquires new knowledge as it functions, then have the experts made themselves obsolete? Are they no longer in control or needed? Science fiction writers have often described futuristic computers that took over, so to speak. Will this really happen? What would people do if it did?

Our first dimension of accountability is this: We believe the capabilities of AI systems could reach undesirable levels; consequently, we suggest that systems should be designed so they process knowledge and make recommendations, but people should determine what to do with the recommendations. We suggest that expert systems should learn in the sense that they apply their learning to making more reliable recommendations, but that is it. We suggest that the creators and users of expert systems in particular and AI in general are accountable for seeing that this happens.

Going further, the highest level of accountability is twofold: (1) an application of technology must solve a problem; and (2) an application must not create additional problems. People have not previously been accountable at this level. In our consultation with legal experts, we discovered that development, progress, profit, jobs, and exploitation have ranked far above accountability, as we view it:

- The atomic bomb was developed and dropped on a nation of people with little regard for the problems it created: the arms race, radiation contamination, and the threat of nuclear war.
- Medical researchers have discovered ways to eliminate diseases and thereby make people live longer with no regard for problems created by a disproportionately large senior citizen population.
- Chemists have created pesticides and related products to increase farm productivity with no regard for problems created by waste materials and related contamination.

This list could become very long, but it illustrates the need for people to determine how accountability is applied to artificial intelligence.

Here are some questions concerning the use of AI:

- Is a company that creates robots which build cars, thereby putting 350,000 people out of work, accountable for relocating and retraining the displaced people?
- Is an agency that creates an expert system which educates the children of America accountable for giving the children the freedom of curricular choice offered by human teachers?
- Is an extension of the federal government that creates and uses an expert system which monitors the growth and development of children and their subsequent recruitment into athletics accountable for letting the athletes choose the way in which they participate?

These systems, and many others, either exist or have been proposed without any of the accountability we suggest. We suggest that if the proponents of AI systems are not accountable as implied, systems will create more problems than they solve.

WHAT OBSTACLES SHAPE THE USE OF AI?

We have discussed the nature of AI, Lisp, and AI systems. Then we discussed how people acquired AI; we mentioned several moral and ethical implications of using AI. We used this sequence because we feel you should examine the ''why'' and ''whether'' dimensions of AI before you examine the practical dimensions. We hope you consider the ethical and moral questions, but we are aware that day-to-day realities will force you to solve an ongoing series of practical problems.

The exigencies of acquiring and using an AI system fall into the following categories:

- **Acceptance:** The metalevel at which people function today enables them to treat anything with disdain. For example, the nomination of a female vice-presidential candidate, surely a historic event, was dismissed as tokenism by many people. To acquire an AI system, you must sell your board of directors, managers, or colleagues on the idea. AI is very threatening to many people. You will encounter resistance in direct proportion to how using AI threatens the people who decide to buy or not buy a system. Your rationale must contain a full consideration of human orientations (profit, job retention or realignment, AI system productivity). You can expect prolonged, stiff resistance to acquiring a system from diverse groups.

- **Knowledge:** Categorization and utilization of knowledge is extremely difficult. Expect people to disagree, often to the point of being ludicrous, about these things: domains of knowledge, classifications of knowledge, propositional rules, and problem-solving strategies. Humans function comfortably with innuendos, judgments, rumors, and such. Computers do not. Unfortunately, an AI system of any type performs in accordance with the validity of the knowledge and rules it uses. Your experts will argue about this for some time.

- **Reliability:** Humans know that humans make mistakes. Humans also forgive humans, sometimes to astounding degrees. For example, humans often excuse and rationalize the behavior of criminals who commit beastly acts. But humans do not forgive machines. To be accepted, an AI system must function with far greater reliability than a set of experts. This means you must often develop an AI system up front at great expense before you benefit from using the system. The development period can last several years.

- **Cost:** Marketing people and microcomputer aficionados claim you can buy AI systems for a few thousand dollars. Yes, you can buy them, but the systems do not solve significant problems. They let you mess around with a few situations. True AI systems require ultrafast microprocessors, immense amounts of memory, immense mass storage capability, complex operating systems, and sophisticated programs. If your domain of knowledge is small and well defined, you can buy AI systems for somewhere between $50,000 and $100,000 (an oil exploration procedure covered by about 200 rules). A moderate system for a well-defined area that has about 500 to 1000 rules will cost between $100,000 and $500,000. Beyond this, you can spend several million dollars for a comprehensive system—for example, a system to analyze U.S. criminal proceedings trials.

- **Development:** Having acquired a system and a set of experts to use it, the development of an AI system is exceedingly complex. The knowledge and Lisp experts can, at times, look like fumbling, bumbling intellectuals who are wasting your time and money. Do not be misled by appearances. You pay for much thinking, arguing, debating, and such. A step forward can be preceded by apparent steps backward. Gradually, the system will begin to work. Developing an AI system can tax your patience and endurance, especially in the areas of robotics, vision, movement, voice recognition, and natural languages.

- **Management:** Few people have ever managed AI systems. It is a new area. You can develop PERT charts, but you will need to revise them often. You will think, on many occasions, that you are managing ooze. To manage an AI system, you must create order from diverse complexity, coordinate people who are not used to regimentation, and function at a level of excellence that people have never before achieved. You must achieve efficient management without stifling the creativity of experts.

Yes, the practical dimensions are staggering. But the existence of AI systems implies that the practical dimensions can be handled. Your major overall problem will be to establish and achieve firm objectives in an arena that has been dominated by hazy, experimental, and evolving objectives. From 1960 to 1980, AI systems were developed in an atmosphere of "opensure" (let's see what we can do). You will have to change that and achieve an atmosphere of closure (develop and use a well-defined system within a project environment).

WHAT ARE THE MAJOR LIMITATIONS IN AI?

While the concept of AI has been around for many years, AI systems have only recently become available because of technological advancements and cost reductions in several areas. Memory is much less expensive, processors are much faster, and mass storage is much larger. The factors that currently limit the development of more powerful systems fall into four categories:

- **Software:** Not enough powerful software is available. Some powerful dialects of Lisp are available, but it is easier to develop an AI system when you have a complete Lisp environment which includes an expert system that lets you develop AI systems. In particular, more tools are needed.

- **AI Methodology:** There is a lack of AI methods and techniques. The AI field rewards pure thinking, innovation, and hacking; it does not reward globalization or organization of research. That is, the inventors of AI methodology pursue whatever interests them. There is an extreme need for research into and publication of articles about specific methods for creating AI systems efficiently and effectively. The experts should not be regimented, but they should become more organized.
- **Shortage of Trained Knowledge Engineers:** Universities are not producing an adequate number of them. Several companies are closing the gap, among them Hewlett-Packard, the Xerox Research Center at Palo Alto, IBM in Palo Alto, and Digital Equipment Corporation. The continued development of AI provides an excellent opportunity for universities, industries, and governments to cooperate.
- **Processors:** The ability of AI systems to process knowledge, in its broadest sense, must increase dramatically. This means that processors must become more complex and much faster. Parallel processing methods must be developed and then improved.

With adequate resources from industry and government, enough people can be induced to study AI and subsequently overcome these limitations.

Given the recent exodus of university people to industry, both the degree to which and the manner in which these limitations are removed may rest with private enterprise and dedicated agencies. The military complex is becoming more involved at this time. There is a high probability that if you are an executive who intends to develop an AI system, you could directly influence the future development of AI systems.

CAN AI BENEFIT PEOPLE?

We believe AI can help people reach an elevated level of living, but we have many reservations. In previous sections we provided information, described situations, and offered suggestions. The suggestions did not tell you what to do. Instead, they elevated the scope and level of your awareness and made you think carefully about the why of AI as well as the who, what, where, when, and how.

You are the who in AI. AI experts, working in universities, will create systems much as university professors have created systems for over 400 years, but you are the one who can bring AI to the people. You bear an awesome responsibility, because AI has the potential to change the way people function more than anything else in recorded history:

- AI systems could be used to process all trails and administer sentences. Think about what that could do to our legal system.
- AI systems could replace every worker in the world who performs a routine assembly-line function. Think about the implications for employment, leisure time, and personal human fulfillment.

- AI systems could be used to teach people and to impart more knowledge in less time than any set of teachers. Think about how it could revolutionize education.
- AI systems could monitor the health conditions of all Americans and make personal recommendations for how each person should function at points along a lifetime. Think about the implications for the medical profession, personal fulfillment, social orientations, and life-styles.
- AI systems could measure data, discover relationships, and make recommendations for myriad phenomena (weather, ocean currents, climate). Could we replace weather forecasts, or get them right?
- AI systems can accept knowledge from any definable area, apply rules to processing the knowledge, and make recommendations. Think about this. Could the systems replace virtually every consultant in the world? Could the systems learn to have compassion and wisdom? Is this a part of intelligence, artificial or otherwise?

AI systems can do other things, but if you consider how many people would be impacted by the things we listed, you will discover that AI would affect nearly everyone.

We have barely scratched the surface. Actally, this book is a primer. But from reading it, you know about AI, know how to acquire and set up a system, know what AI can do, and are aware of responsibilities. If you are interested in learning more, consider doing these things:

- Read all the articles you can find. Soon you will become familiar with the basic concepts, experts, involved companies, and major issues. There are major issues that stem primarily from the fact that AI is emerging; it is not established. You will encounter supporters, detractors, and speculators. Read about all points of view with a calm, open mind.
- Read some more advanced discussions of AI. Push yourself up the learning curve. You can deal with the pros and cons of AI better as you acquire more information about it. Appendix C contains a list of sources.
- Go to a conference on AI. It is a bit difficult to learn when and where they are held. A call to the marketing departments of some major comapanies (Hewlett-Packard, IBM, Xerox), or to some major universities (Stanford, M.I.T., Carnegie-Mellon) should put you on track. Also, write to the organizations listed in Appendix C.

You should investigate possibilities for about a year. Be aware at all times of the features you require in an AI system, and focus your analysis of available systems according to these needs. Then go over your data, select a system, and begin the process of developing your particular AI system. It is especially important for you to view your entry into AI as but one of several steps in an evolving movement. The system or systems you obtain today will certainly evolve, and your expertise in an AI system will evolve and grow. Try to anticipate where you will be as well as where you are. In the scheme of things, you might consider this general sequence:

- At present, AI systems feature operating systems and languages (Lisp or Prolog). Therefore, people could acquire development systems and use them to develop many assorted tools. The tools (assorted software packages) could be marketed.
- Given more and better tools, people could rely less on operating systems and languages, and use the tools to develop applications of every type and size. The applications could be marketed.
- Beyond this, it is difficult to offer any suggestion whatever, because it is not possible to predict how people will use AI applications.

Within this sequence, the AI systems can decrease in size and complexity. The systems also move from being user-driven systems to being turnkey systems. Select your niche in the scheme of things and make your way.

May the force be with you!

NEXT-GENERATION SPECULATION

ORIENTATION

The next generation will be the fifth generation of computers. Previous generations used vacuum tubes, transistors, integrated circuits, and silicon chips (microprocessors). You are currently using computers that use fourth-generation technology.

In previous chapters we presented information and made a few comments about its significance. We tried to be objective, and we let you know when we were not being objective.

This chapter is different. This chapter discusses the future, the things that could happen, should happen, ought to happen, and ought not to happen. In this chapter, we have mixed emotion with presentation. We offer suggestions and make rash statements. We have tried to challenge you, stimulate you, perhaps even make you angry. We tried to motivate you to go beyond this book and acquire additional information. Enjoy!

Edward Faigenbaum and Pamela McCorduck wrote a book in 1983 entitled *The Fifth Generation,* published by Addison-Wesley, Inc. In the book, Feigenbaum and McCorduck discussed research underway in Japan that has these objectives:

- The fifth-generation computers will have ultrafast processors. Besides handling ordinary computation, distribution of data, and logical operations, the new processors will be able to reason using vast amounts of information.
- Information available to fifth-generation computers will be continually updated, reinterpreted, and adapted to fit evolving circumstances. But the most revolutionary

feature is this: The vast amount of information will be available *at any time* to users in *whatever form the user requires.*

- No special expertise will be required to use the fifth-generation computers. The users can specify needs much as they would ask a human for help. That is, the requests can be made via a natural language, not via programmed prompts and other typical computer entries.
- The fifth-generation computers will speak in conversational tones, show pictures, model concepts, and accept and transmit handwritten or keyboarded messages.
- The fifth-generation computers will be reliable and sufficiently inexpensive to be used in schools, offices, factories, and homes—anywhere someone needs access to information.

Sound impossible? We thought so, and after reading 10 pages of *The Fifth Generation,* we were skeptical. But then, people scoffed at the airplane, the atomic bomb, and the space shuttle.

After reading the book, we examined other information about the fifth generation of computers. Gradually, we discovered there is little basis for believing the Japanese will not succeed. Some Americans believe the Japanese are using the wrong language, Prolog. Others believe the technology for what they propose is not available or has not been adequately tested. You'll read a potpourri of opinion about what the Japanese will or will not do and whether they will succeed. The opinions are interesting, but are not the heart of the fifth-generation concept. The heart of the fifth-generation concept is this: whatever your inclination might be, the Japanese plan to corner and market the use of the world's knowledge.

The Japanese reckon that the manufacture of automobiles will decline and that, in its place, they will sell knowledge itself to the world. They will also sell products and services that are knowledge intensive. The Japanese plan to do this worldwide by the 1990s. They plan to exhibit prototype systems by 1987. In short, the Japanese have projected what our view of paradise will be and they plan to market it.

Sounds like Buck Rogers? It *is* Buck Rogers, and the Japanese are almost there!

Meanwhile, people in the rest of the world are doing very little to be ready for the knowledge explosion, despite research which shows that people have elevated themselves above the industrial age and have entered the information age. By the way, to get information about the information age, read John Naisbitt's book, *Megatrends.*

In the rest of this chapter we'll discuss what the United States is doing and how the fifth generation might impact our lives.

THE U. S. ORIENTATION AND A DIRECTION

Several years ago, Henry Steele Commager, a distinguished American historian, discussed the nature of Americans in a book he called *The American Mind.* Commager talked about the basic nature of Americans: hypocritically optimistic, inclined to talk about problems while not solving them, and justified in doing anything that is American. The latter characteristic is perfectly recursive. According to Commager, in the United States, if something is justified, it's American; if something is American, it's justfied. How perfect! If you are doing something illegal, cite the precursors that justify your actions. If you want to do something, cite the thing being done as the rationale for doing it.

Many of Commager's views were criticized by other historians, but over the years, Commager appears to have been correct more often than incorrect. Here are some highlights.

Americans have always thought that some things are dangerous and other things are not dangerous. Americans ignore nondangerous things and protect themselves against dangerous things, but they protect themselves at a surface level until something drastic happens. Then they overreact and respond to challenges with vigor.

Coupled with this, Americans employ concepts such as manifest destiny and slogans such as "Remember the Alamo" to guide their actions, but they seldom have a long-range plan for anything. Instead, Americans collect short-range evidence about this or that and blunder along reacting to this or that situation in terms of immediate expediencies.

Even the collection of evidence is guided by immediate expediencies. For example, Michael Dertouzos, director of the Laboratory of Computer Science at M.I.T., lamented America's lack of planning when he stated, at the 1984 Annual Conference for the Association of Computing Machinery, "We must [in AI] get off the moon-shot mentality. The moon shot dealt with a mature technology and every step was well known. The only objective was doing it well, but here [in AI] we're still exploring. We must stop and turn over stones—look them over, evaluate, and choose." A bit later, Dertouzos stated, "To me, fifth generation means long-term research, 10 to 15 years." As you'll see, Americans are true to form; they are doing very little. For more details, read:

SULLIVAN, KATHLEEN. Long-term Research Key to Quest for Next Generation,'' *Computerworld* (October 22, 1984), 30.

Given these tendencies, let's examine how Americans are dealing with the development of fifth-generation computers in Japan.

Actually, Americans are doing very little to respond to the Japanese effort to develop powerful AI systems. Their response has been extremely indifferent to, even ignorant of, challenges to their predominance in computers. Americans are, as usual, willing to let matters take care of themselves. The United States has no plans for developing fifth-generation computers except in the degree to which individual companies undertake or have undertaken an AI project.

The orientation is entirely predictable. In the 1930s, when Japan bought steel from the United States and built a mighty army, Americans did not bat an eye. After all, Japan was no threat. What could Japan do? Well, some older people remember World War II. Today's children have no knowledge of the significance of December 7, 1941.

On the other hand, in the 1950s, when the Russians launched Sputnik, Americans were exceedingly distressed and launched an all-out effort to put a man in space and to bolster the school cirricula in mathematics and science.

As for how to use AI, Americans are right on target; they have no plan whatsoever. Recent political administrators have been preoccupied with the military complex and traditional American values. At present, AI products suffer from an identity crisis. People have little knowledge about AI or about what can be done with AI systems. Few resources are available for research.

Like they have so often behaved in the past, Americans are tinkering with whatever interests them at the moment. Exercise is in. The environment is out. An advisory position in the Environmental Protection Agency is a "nothingburger." Dieting is chic. Going to college is boring. National defense is important. The space shuttle is cute. Hunting and trapping are deplorable. We must save the whales.

Will AI receive the same type of surface attention? The 1984 Olympics motivated Americans to commit more money to swimming and gymnastics lessons for their four-year-old children than has been spent for research in AI in 10 years.

People in the AI community are distressed by the tendency of Americans to tinker with things and ideas at a surface level on a short-range basis. Experts fear that a small group of Americans will market expert systems in the name of AI, hoping more to get rich instantly than to promote AI and use it wisely for a long period of time.

AI is already a broad field. The term encompasses several areas: gaming strategies, natural languages, knowledge systems (expert systems), vision systems, voice recognition systems, knowledge representation and reasoning, and intelligent robots. AI experts fear that this situation will remain stagnant until something happens to coalesce activity.

People who use AI should realize that progress needs to be made along several fronts: getting fresh, bright people into the field; conducting ongoing research; and utilizing advancements to create useful products. Most experts have reasonable expectations for what should be done. They know that AI cannot remain in the laboratory forever, serving their particular interests. They also know that current hardware and software must be used to solve significant problems while research is conducted to discover significant breakthroughs. The experts know this, but as has so often been the case, Americans do not know this.

At present, no American vendor offers products across the AI spectrum, nor is any vendor likely to do so. There is no national center for the exploration of AI applications. The Pentagon is involved in AI work, but it focuses on military applications. There is no congressional investigation of the potential of AI systems. There is no coordinated effort among universities to train AI graduates. There is little subsidization of people who want to study AI. Americans are staying in a "we'll react to a situation if something comes up" mode, their usual stance.

The stance we have described is typical and predictable. In each preceding chapter we indicated that AI systems have arrived on the national scene and that most Americans are not ready to use them. The American people embrace life-styles provided by high technology. They readily listen to loud music, watch colorful displays, and entertain themselves at home. It was easy for Americans to accept and live in the metalevel of existence provided by high technology. They accepted heart transplants, genetic engineering, and modifications of their hormones. They readily drifted toward an era in which they need information on a grand scale.

But now that Americans have drifted into an information age, they have not done much to determine how to handle information and use it to solve their problems. Americans need to come to grips with information and the implications of using AI to manipulate it. They need to fund the AI movement and deal with it intelligently, or they should not get mixed up with it at all.

Unfortunately, Americans have reached a plateau where they do not know which concepts are most important. They do not have a significant direction or plan for their lives. Americans have not done much to define the future. Lacking these things, the fact that Americans are looking back into their past and attempting to restore established, traditional values is predictable. In 1984 the sale of memorabilia was a multibillion-dollar industry, everything from old Coke bottles to restored Model T's.

Unlike the 1700s, when Americans felt it was necessary to break ties with England; unlike the 1800s, when they believed it was necessary to conquer the frontier; and unlike the 1900s, when they thought it was necessary to build the greatest industry in history, Americans have reached a stage where they are uncertain about what to do. But the Japanese have decided what to do. They believe that people around the world will attempt to use knowledge to reach unheard-of mental heights. The Japanese believe people will engage in "knowledging" for its own sake as people attempt to reach paradise, or should we say as people have always attempted to reach paradise. The Japanese might not be correct, but they do have a direction. Americans are waiting, as usual, until they face a crisis. They will probably do something, but the something is not known at this time.

Some Americans are concerned about the overall situation. Mostly, they come from the AI community, large computer companies, and the military complex. People who work in these areas have pointed out, mostly to small audiences, that the United States must respond to the Japanese challenge. Their rationales include these factors:

- The modeling of the mind depends on availability of knowledge about the mind. Whoever commands the most knowledge can make the most significant advances in understanding how humans think. Whoever learns first how this occurs will have an immense advantage over other people in areas such as marketing, education, and national defense.
- People who can solve problems faster and better than other people have an advantage in every arena of living: politics, sports, work, leisure, and so on.
- People have arrived at a threshold at which they have the means to develop nonhumans that perform human functions. Whoever commands the nonhumans has an advantage in determining who survives on earth.
- National defense is linked to how well weapons respond intelligently to threats to peace. Intelligent weapons require AI systems.

We have no quarrel with these rationales. Instead, we suggest that you examine them and determine their merit to you personally.

We suggest that people, by their very nature, will pursue every avenue available to them. We suggest that in the near future, you can expect to see androids, humanlike automatons, and huge robots. You will be able to access, from your home, most of the world's knowledge. Just as President Wilson said, "The business of America is business," we suggest you will hear a future President say, "The business of American is knowledge." We suggest that whatever your disposition, people will compete for survival as the world becomes more crowded, and that the people who command the best knowledge and problem-solving techniques will survive. Consequently, we suggest that you have an obligation to ensure that AI systems are used for the common good of all people.

We know that many people will believe this is a naive orientation, but we suggest that AI systems have the potential to elevate people to a level where such things as war, crime, poverty, and ignorance disappear. We also believe that if AI systems are not used to achieve these goals, people will compete with each other with ever more sophisticated and assorted systems until they reach levels described so often by science fiction writers, levels in which life has no purpose other than to exist.

SOME U. S. FIFTH-GENERATION PROPOSALS

Americans have not been at ease, as a nation, to undertake something for the common good of the people. We have, however, undertaken projects in the name of national defense.

When the Russians launched Sputnik, Americans responded immediately with several projects. The NDEA fellowship programs (National Defense Education Act) provided scholarships for people to get advanced degrees in science areas. NASA (National Aeronautics and Space Administration) was orgainzed and given the job of putting a man in space as soon as possible. In true form, these programs were eliminated or reduced once the threat to our security was eased.

Now, as the Japanese mount their effort to corner the market on knowledge, Americans have made these proposals:

- The United States should create a **National Center for Knowledge Technology.** The center would become a repository for knowledge about technology in general and AI systems in particular. The center would store the knowledge and make it available to companies that develop AI systems.
- The United States should commission IBM, since it is the largest computer company, to build AI systems that would compete with those envisioned by the Japanese.
- The United States should develop an agency, similar to NASA, that would marshal available resources and build AI systems that would compete with those envisioned by the Japanese.
- The United States should create a center that would coordinate AI projects undertaken within corporations. The center would provide a liaison between corporations and function as an advisory group to ensure that all dimensions of research in AI are explored. Appropriate projects would be funded during early, high-risk stages of research.

- The United States should complete a pilot project designed to examine the feasibility of creating AI systems of the type envisioned by the Japanese. Then future actions could reflect conclusions drawn from the pilot project. This way, huge amounts of money would not be wasted.

These are the major proposals. As yet, no proposal has been accepted. Most have not been seriously considered. Collectively, they have merit.

Each specific proposal would face stiff opposition. Those that suggest cooperation between corporations are at odds with antitrust laws and the general philosophy that corporations compete with each other. Other proposals suggest giving information to all that a few seek to protect. Still others suggest giving knowledge to one corporation that every corporation ought to share. The best proposal will be one that maximizes the capability of the United States to develop AI systems and make them available to all people for the common good of all.

We suggest that the proposals should be examined and that some actions should be taken. To quote Feigenbaum and McCorduck, "What faces us, if you like, is the Louisiana Purchase in the manifest destiny of computing."

At present, faint glimmers of hope emanate from a few corporations that have AI projects underway and from a few universities that have remained committed to research in AI. A few products are available, but no products are available that have fifth-dimension capabilities.

AI: BOON OR BOONDOGGLE?

You are reading this book at a perilous time. It is a time of promise, but it is also possible that people are building towers of Babel.

On one hand, the founders of AI have tried to bring AI to fruition for 25 years. That is a short period of time in the scheme of things, but it is a long time in a person's life, especially in an area that demands such high levels of cognition. Discouragement has often followed encouragement. The experts know that most of their progress was due to advancements in technology and to lowering the cost of computer memory rather than to breakthroughs in understanding human intelligence. They know that the artificial part is real; the intelligent part is often something else.

By 1980, many experts became skeptical. Some were very disappointed to find AI working its way into the common marketplace. Your reading outside this book will let you see this.

On the other hand, people have a right to use major concepts to help them solve problems. AI is a major concept, at least as important as fire, the wheel, systems, and integrated circuits. People certainly have a variety of problems. We hope these two things occur:

- The experts in AI will not become cynical or otherwise inclined to leave the field. They have contributed much. There is more to do. The movement of AI from the laboratory to the marketplace should create myriad situations in which experts could identify new areas of research and potential benefit.

- The people will not expect too much too soon. The people will not treat AI as a panacea and will realize, instead, that they must realistically determine how to use AI and adjust success criteria accordingly.

If these two orientations come together, the success derived from moving AI from the laboratory to the market could be spectacular because evidence generated in the market could be a stimulus for research in the laboratory. A mutual oscillation could be created where advancements are created in the laboratories and moved into the market, and the use of advancements in the market could provide evidence that motivates new research. For example, starting from a different basis, the Japanese decided to focus attention on creating intelligent systems as part of the fifth-generation movement. That movement is expected to last several years before the Japanese market actual products. But the Japanese are using advancements beyond the laboratory during the development period to provide feedback that guides research.

In the past, Americans have organized movements when they perceived the need to do so. The space movement was a recent example, which was catalyzed when the Russians launched Sputnik. Although American and Japanese cultures are not the same, perhaps the use of AI beyond the laboratories can provide an adequate stimulus, a stimulus that causes us to use our talent and resources to ensure that AI benefits all people.

We believe this could be done, but we also believe that research belongs in the laboratory and development of products belongs in the market in the United States. This dual function has worked in the past. Doing research in industry (we refer to real research) has not worked well in the past.

The book we mentioned above, *The AI Business,* contains an excellent article by Marvin Minsky called *The Problems and the Promise* that addresses many of our concerns. Here is a potpourri of Minsky's ideas. As there are several quotes and collections of quotes, read them and get the flavor of what he says:[1]

- "It is my impression that American industry does not understand the way ideas develop or how they have to be nurtured in order not to fall behind in the long run."
- "It is very important in AI to pick good problems to work on. But look carefully, at the applications systems: they are wonderful, they save money, and they solve problems. But are they intelligent."
- "You rarely see an adult with the attention span of a child. . . . My point is that there is very little research going on right now. . . . The general principles of most expert systems are close to specifications published . . . over ten years ago. . . . If we do not encourage people to work on simple matters [in research], we are going to lose out, and our software will come from Japan."

[1] Marvin Minsky, "The Problems and the Promise." *The AI Business,* Patrick H. Winston and Karen A. Prendergast, eds. (MA: MIT Press, 1984). Reprinted with permission.

- "Many of my students do not do projects . . . because we cannot afford to buy enough . . . equipment per person that is needed to pursue basic research at full speed and with high morale."
- "None of the artificial-intelligence groups in industry is doing really basic research. . . . In general they are not working on the kinds of things that ten years from now could produce a new wave of intelligent systems, just as the current wave of expert systems comes from the basic research done in the mid-1960s."
- "There is a language, called PROLOG, that is becoming popular. . . . The Japanese have decided to use . . . PROLOG. . . . I think the Japanese will program in PROLOG for two or three years, write some very sophisticated programs, and then give up and go back to LISP. But even after a three-year waste of time, they will be ten or fifteen years ahead of Americans who are still trying to get industrial people to use languages like PASCAL."
- "The key feature of LISP is that you can either compile things or leave them in their source-code form. . . . A modern language is one that can talk about itself as well as other things."
- "Let me return to the people problem. . . . There is no place I can send him [a good student] other than a university, and the universities have stopped expanding on the whole. . . . There is no place a good student can work for five or ten years on a really hard problem the way all those Einsteins and Pasteurs did when they faced a hard problem."
- "The United States is in a state of remilitarization. . . . I complained that there then was a plan to build one hundred B1 bombers. As Carl Sagan said . . . one day, maybe we can make do with ninety-nine. Just one of those machines that cost $1 billion would probably pay for ten years of basic research."

Notice the overall messages. AI was developed in the research laboratory, and in time several advancements were made that were used to build expert systems. Those systems are appearing in the market, but the basis for continued research is disappearing because Americans are not vitally concerned with the potential of AI over the long run. Again, Americans appear to be concerned with the present and preserving the past.

There is a paradox in our overall discussion of AI that we wish to leave with you as food for thought.

Since people organized themselves and decided to develop a better way of life, that development has always been aimed at creating less dependency on the whims of nature, more creature comfort, and more leisure time. Gradually, people reached a point where they could discuss whether an experience was meaningful and whether they were personally fulfilled, instead of running from a saber-toothed tiger, a very meaningful experience that allowed no time for discussion of the merit of running. This means people had reached two points: (1) they could conduct life at a metaphysical level, and (2) the pace of change accelerated in the options people had for living.

In early times, when the pace of living was slow, it was not necessary for people to prepare for or carefully guide the future. One could expect to row a Roman ship for a lifetime, however short that lifetime might be. But today, when the pace of living and change is very rapid, it appears to be extremely desirable to define what the future should be like and take steps to determine the future, instead of just waiting for it to happen. For example, given the rate at which change occurs today, a parent cannot determine many tangible dimensions of the world in which their children will live. Just fifty years ago, many children expected to run the family business for generations.

Is it possible that the rate of change has become excessive and that people should use AI and other tools to slow down the haphazard determination of the future and make things a bit more stable? Is it possible that the pell-mell rush to find paradise has created so much confusion that people cannot focus on anything long enough for it to bear fruit? Is it possible that people need to initiate discussion of the meaning of "meaningful" and use tools and models for intelligent behavior that could emerge from AI?

May the force be with all of you.

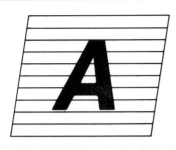

AI GLOSSARY

INTRODUCTION

This glossary is for AI nonexperts who want information about terminology while they read books or articles, attend shows or conferences, and examine product brochures.

Each definition is correct in a generic and general sense. Many definitions are not totally correct in a technical sense. There are three major reasons for this:

- The experts who created AI had diverse backgrounds. They were mathematicians, logicians, psychologists, physicists, and so on. The evolution of terms in AI reflected their diverse backgrounds. Some concepts have several labels; others are defined differently, depending on the context in which they are used.
- The definitions of some terms change in technical ways according to the complexity of the context in which they are used.
- The companies that market AI products have conventions for dealing with files, writing programs, configuring software, and installing hardware. Their conventions and marketing strategies can constrain the definition of terms.

GLOSSARY TERMS

A

ABEL: An expert system for diagnosing electrolytic disorders, developed at M.I.T.

Advanced Memory Allocation: In some computer languages, space in memory is allocated for variables in the program before the program is executed. Some languages require declaration of all variables used by the program at the beginning of the program. Contrast advanced memory allocation with the dynamic memory allocation used in Lisp, the primary language of AI. The differences in allocation of memory for variables constitute a major distinction between a symbol-manipulation language and a conventional language. Other major differences relate to recursion and symbolic computation.

AI: An acronym for artificial intelligence.

Algorithm: A specific, step-by-step procedure used to solve a specific problem. For example, certain differential equations can be solved by using the substitution-by-parts algorithm. The term *algorithm* is used in many contexts, but it always refers to a procedure for performing a task.

Antecedent: In logic, the first part of an *if . . . then* statement is the antecedent; the second part is the consequence. In the statement,

if the temperature falls below 70 degrees, *then* turn on the furnace.

the part about the temperature is the antecedent; the part about the furnace is the consequence. This type of logic is used to develop rules for many AI systems.

Application: In software, a program that helps a person perform a practical task. People performed these tasks before the computer became a useful tool. The idea is that an application program lets a human perform a task in a more efficient, cost-effective, or accurate manner. Thus, with a human operator, spreadsheets do numerical analyses; word processors write and edit documents; data bases facilitate record keeping; and general ledgers do accounting. Application programs usually employ windows, menus, prompts, and commands to help people work efficiently. Contrast application program with languages, utilities, and tools, which are used to write application programs.

Architecture: The term has several contexts. It can be a framework or structure used to organize and relate problem-solving activity, especially problem solving done with expert systems. It can be the principles of knowledge engineering that determine the framework or structure for an expert system. In another context, architecture refers to the particular design features of a hardware system.

ART: An expert system for building systems, developed by Inference Corporation.

Artificial Intelligence: An area of computer science that uses models of human reasoning to solve problems. The problems have enough elements of uncertainty to preclude use of specific algorithms.

Artificial Vision: A branch of AI in which engineers create software that lets devices recognize shapes and respond differentially, depending on the perceived shapes. Robots and some military weapons use artificial vision to detect entities.

Assumption: Two contexts: a plausible statement within a theory that has not been verified, or a self-evident definition whose truth is accepted within a system.

Atom: In Lisp, a fundamental, singular element that cannot be decomposed. For example, in the list (3 blind mice), 3, BLIND, and MICE are atoms; they are unique entities that cannot be divided into other, related structures.

Automatic Programming: In software, a specialized program that, given a sufficient knowledge base, does these things: explains actions taken by the system; accepts knowledge from a user and rewrites a program to incorporate the new knowledge; and remembers actions taken by the system and rewrites a program to incorporate the actions. To a degree, automatic programming lets a program learn from its actions or use input to alter its actions. Automatic programmers, a term applied to automatic programs, are used to write expert systems. An expert gives the program a domain model and domain principles (knowledge) and the automatic programmer writes an expert system for the specified domain.

B

Backward Chaining: A procedure used in expert systems in which goals are achieved recursively. That is, a system first enumerates the antecedents for achieving a goal, and then it establishes the antecedents themselves as goals. In backward-chaining, a user supplies a goal for an expert system to achieve and the system finds appropriate antecedents.

Backtracking: In expert systems, a procedure used during a search in which the expert system guesses solutions to a problem and either: (1) outputs the guess if it is a solution, or (2) if the guess is not a solution, backtracks to a previous point in the procedure and makes another guess.

Belief: Two meanings: (1) a hypothesis, and (2) an accepted confidence in a certain orientation.

BETA: Battlefield exploitation and target acquisition, an experimental system developed by TRW Corporation, Defense Systems Division.

Binary Program Space (BPS): A segment of a computer's memory, just above the Lisp microkernel, that contains compiled code for functions and programs used during execution of Lisp programs. Binary program space overlaps the heap to include the static heap.

Bit: The smallest element in a digital circuit. The binary digit 1 represents a high electrical state. The binary digit 0 represents a low electrical state. The idea of a bit is the basis for translating electrical states into binary numbers which themselves can be translated into data, a computer language program, or a natural language statement.

Bit-mapped Display: A video system that employs bits of read/write memory to represent dots (pixels) on a screen. Setting a bit results in illuminating the bit's corresponding pixel. A typical bit-mapped display might use one million bits, arranged in a 1000 by 1000 matrix, with certain bits illuminated, to display text or graphics. By refreshing (resetting) the bit map periodically, the text or graphics can be changed. The video system is often a monitor, interface card, a designated part of memory, and special ROM-based programs.

Bound Variable: In Lisp, an atom that appears in a function's parameter list is a bound variable. Any atom that is not bound is free or unbound. See **Dynamic Scoping, Lexical Scoping, Global Variables,** and **Local Variables** to get a more complete idea.

Buffer: A distinct set of bytes in a computer's RAM memory that is used for temporary storage of a file, a potential file, or a part thereof. AI files are often very large. It is usually easier to work with a file when it is divided into parts and the parts are stored in buffers. In another context, files are stored in buffers while they await being sent to a printer because a printer cannot work as fast as a computer. Without the buffers, the computer would overwhelm the printer.

Bus: The complex of circuits that transmit bits, bytes, or words among the processor and other devices in a hardware installation.

Byte: A contiguous set of eight bits treated as a unit. The pattern of the eight bits can represent characters, numbers, flags, and so on in accordance with accepted conventions for creating software code. For example, in American Standard Code for Information Interchange (ASCII), a byte that contains the binary digits 01001011 represents the letter K because the binary digits translate into $64+8+2+1$, which is 75, the ASCII code for K.

C

Calculus: To most people, a subject in mathematics. In AI, a calculus of something is a method of analyzing, using special symbols. For example, an expert in AI might talk about a calculus of beliefs. This is equivalent to having a method of analyzing beliefs, presumably for the purpose of establishing a usable set of them.

Canned explanations: In software, a fixed, displayed message that explains an action taken by a computer system. Error messages are canned explanations that inform people about system failures or incorrect entries. In expert systems, canned explanations explain solutions to problems. Canned explanations are not efficient because a programmer must anticipate every conceivable explanation for every conceivable solution.

Certainty: A measure of confidence in a proposition, hypothesis, or rule in an expert system.

Closure: Closure is attained in Lisp when an environment is attached to a function definition. Unlike some computer languages, closure in Lisp varies, depending on the type of variables used in a function. Lexical-free variables are closed at definition time. Dynamic-free variables are closed at evaluation time.

Common Lisp: A powerful dialect of Lisp, probably destined to become the Lisp of the future. Common Lisp is touted by many as the merging industrial-strength Lisp, which can be used as a basis for a development environment.

Compiler: A program that translates source files (programs written in a language such as Lisp) into object or object-code files (machine-language files that can be given to a processor for execution).

Computer System: A combination of hardware, firmware, and software that functions collectively to perform required computing tasks.

Concept: A class of things, phenomena, or schemas that has an assigned label and definition that other people recognize. Any particular thing, phenomenon, or schema can be classified as belonging or not belonging to a concept. Computers, electricity, and democracy are concepts whose members are things, phenomena, and schemas, respectively.

Configuration: (1) a process of setting up software so that it runs on a particular hardware installation, and (2) the particular settings that allow software to run on a hardware installation. For example, software for a hardware installation that has two monitors could be configured to output automatically to one monitor and output to the other monitor on user intervention and designation. Like installation, configuration is usually a one-time process.

Consequence: See **Antecedent.**

CONS Node or CONS Cell: In Lisp, a data structure that contains two fields. Each field holds a pointer to another Lisp data object. The data object can be an atom, another CONS node, or another Lisp object. This is a major concept because CONS nodes are highly related to Lisp concepts such as dynamic memory allocation, variable binding, dynamic scoping, and garbage collecting.

Control: A procedure that determines the order of problem-solving activities done by an expert system.

Control Key: A key on a keyboard that is held down while another key is pressed to give the other key a different function.

Crysalis: An expert system for analysis of data related to protein crystallography, developed at Stanford University.

Customizable: A computer language or other software is customizable when a user can alter a feature and thereby suit the feature to a particular situation. Most dialects of Lisp and most software written in Lisp are customizable. Customizing software is not the same as configuring software. In configuration, software is adjusted so it runs on a particular hardware installation. In customization, software features are fundamentally altered and might or might not run on a particular hardware installation.

D

Data File: In software, a file that contains data (numbers, words, names, sentences). Contrast with **Program File.**

Data Object: In Lisp, a data object is an object such as an atom, list, or function which itself is data in a data structure for another object.

Data Structure: In Lisp, in a generic sense, everything can be data that has some structure. The data structure for a CONS node is determined by two cells called car and cdr, which contain pointers. The data structure for an atom is given by its property list. In general, a data structure is determined by how an object in Lisp arranges the parts that comprise it. For example, the data structure of the Lisp object called a symbol is determined by the contents of a symbol's property list, print name, and package cell. This is important in AI because the data structures in a program can change dynamically during program execution. The computer system's memory determines the collective size and number of data structures the system can support. See **Property List, Object,** and **Package Cell** to get a more complete picture.

Debugger: A tool or utility program that helps a person find errors in a program. Debuggers work in many ways, depending on how they were implemented. A debugger is useful in a development environment, but not in an applications environment. For example, a person who purchased a turnkey application program would not need a debugger.

Dependency: A relationship between the antecedents and consequents that is produced by applying an inferential rule. Dependencies indicate the manner in which decisions are derived from previous decisions or data.

Development Environment: A reference to a computer system (hardware, firmware, and software) that is specifically designed to help a person write applications software. Characteristic software in a development environment includes an operating system, a human interface, a powerful editor, and perhaps an automatic programmer. Contrast with **Programming Environment.**

Disk Drive: A hardware device that contains or accepts a disk that is used for storage of files. A disk contains a medium that can be magnetized, and thereby can contain information. Flexible disk drives and hard disk drives are popular types. AI systems require hard disk drives because such drives have a much greater storage capacity and because they work much faster. Flexible disk drives can be used to store assorted small programs. Capacities of most flexible disks range from 100 to 800 K-bytes. Capacities of most hard disks range from 10 to 400 M-bytes. Tape drives, which were popular in the 1970s, are still used on some large systems. Many hard disk drives have a tape backup capability. With this capability, a person can duplicate the files on the hard disk and keep the backup files in a safe place.

Drivers: In software, drivers are special programs that interface external devices with the operating system of a computer. Drivers provide communications between the computer and keyboards, monitors, disk drives, printers, plotters, and other external devices. Drivers are often written in machine language.

Dynamic-free Variables: In Lisp, in the context of calling a function, the value of a dynamic-free variable is not necessarily found in one environment. A dynamic-free variable can have a value within several environments; that is, the variable can be bound within several environments. See **Lexical-free Variable** to get a more complete idea.

Dynamic Linking: In Lisp, values are linked with variables when a function is called, not when a function is defined.

Dynamic Memory Allocation: In Lisp, memory management is completely automatic and occurs during run time (the time when a program executes). This means that values are assigned (bound) to variables when a program is executed, not before a program is executed. It also means that values for a variable are not retained. Different values can be assigned each time a variable is used and the space allocated to unused variables can be reclaimed for new allocation during program execution via a process called garbage collection.

Dynamic Scoping: In Lisp, free variables are dynamically scoped when they are bound when a function is called. Contrast with **Lexical Scoping.**

E

EDD: An expert data base designer, a Prolog-based expert system developed by Silogic Incorporated.

EMACS: An editor (a human interface) that is widely accepted and used within the Lisp/AI community. It is available in several forms in popular AI systems.

Environment; in Computer Systems: An environment is the total of the hardware installation and the software configuration that makes up a computer system, usually in the context of looking at how to perform tasks effectively within a defined area. For example, a total development environment for expert systems would contain all the hardware and software needed to create expert system programs, but would not contain turnkey expert systems per se.

Environment: In Lisp, an environment is the domain, or domains, in which a function can use variables. This covers some ground: A set of variables and bound values is an environment; a set of bindings is an environment; and an atom that is bound to an object is found in an environment. The idea is that when a function is called, a domain exists that determines which variables used by the function are bound. This concept relates to free variables, global variables, local variables, and scoping.

Execution Stack: In a language, a segment of memory that contains values of variables. The values can be pulled from the stack or pushed onto the stack, according to how the language is implemented, during execution of a program or a call to a function.

Execution-driven Reasoning: A procedure that uses current data and decisions to build hypotheses about pending, unobserved events. The procedure also allocates resources to activities that confirm and monitor the expected events.

Expert System: A computer system that, by way of emulation, performs tasks which require use of specialized human skill and knowledge. It is usally assumed that the computer system performs a task at least as well as a human expert on a cost-effective basis.

Expertise: A set of capabilities that can be demonstrated only by a human expert. Expertise includes knowledge, skills, and metacognition that enable a human to function economically at a high level. The metacognition is usually the most important component of expertise. It is also the part of expertise that AI systems try to emulate via heuristics.

Explanation: A description of the desirability of something, based on the presentation of goals, laws, and heuristic rules.

Extensible: In a computer language or in some software, extensible means that the existing features of the language or software can be used to add new, and integrated, features to the language or software. Integrated means the features are available in the same ways as the original features, and can themselves be used to further extend the language or software. Lisp is an extensible computer language. The NMODE and EMACS editors are examples of extensible software.

F

Fact: A statement or datum that is an accepted representation of something.

File: A set of bytes that forms an entity. For example, a block of data, a program, or a module can be a file. In most cases, the type of file is determined by how the file is stored magnetically, how the file is represented, or how the file is used. For example, a file might be stored in an ASCII or a binary format. As another example, a file might be a program or a block of data.

Firmware: A program permanently stored in read-only memory (ROM) that performs a specific task. The microcode that operates a processor, the programs that operate monitors or keyboards, and the programs that boot (bring up) a computer system are usually firmware. Contrast with software.

Flag: In firmware or software, a bit that triggers one action when set to 1 and triggers a different action when set to 0. For example, a monitor might display black on white when a flag is set to 1 or display white on black when a flag is set to 0.

Flavor: In Lisp software, flavors relate to objects and methods which, collectively, provide object-oriented programming. To operate on an instance (an instance variable) of an object, a flavor contains the messages that are passed to the object. The messages in the flavor determine the method that performs an operation. A flavor can make it easier to develop applications programs. For example, the windows used in applications programs can be created by flavors of objects. Since the class called windows is an object, and since a particular window is an instance variable of the object, a particular window can be altered by changing its flavor, a relatively easy task. While this is complex, the nonexpert should know that the flavors, methods, and objects provided within object-oriented programming are powerful vehicles for developing software. Also see **Method, Object,** and **Object-oriented Programming.**

Font: A set of type of a particular size and face. A face is the style and proportion of a symbol (a character). Size is given by points: 8 point, 10 point, 12 point, and so on. Sans serif and helvetica are popular fonts.

Font Editor: In software, a font editor lets a person alter the font used to display text or print files.

Form: In Lisp, a form is another name for a program. All Lisp forms are lists in which the first element is a function and the remaining elements are arguments. See **Function** to get a more complete description. Also see **Program.**

Forward-Chaining: A procedure used in expert systems that produces decisions recursively by affirming consequences that are associated with an inferential rule with given antecedents. A human interface program lets a user enter the antecedents. The inference engine (another program) uses the antecedents and an inferential rule to return the consequences. For example, a user might enter symptoms of an illness and the system would return an explanation of the illness and prescribe a treatment. Contrast with **Backward Chaining.**

Frame: In Lisp software, a frame can be used to represent knowledge via instances, property lists, schemas, units, or records, depending on how a frame is set up. The advantage in using frames is that attributes of an entity in one frame can be inherited from an entity in another frame. Frame-based and object-oriented programming is a fundamental part of AI, especially in expert systems. Frames appear in two major contexts. In an application program, a user employs a frame to input data about a situation. In a development environment, a programmer used frames to create rules and such for an expert system. The frames help the programmer create a system efficiently.

FranzLisp: A popular dialect of Lisp, developed at the University of California.

Free Variable: In Lisp, in the context of calling a function, a free variable is an atom that is not found in a function's parameter list. In other words, an atom whose value is accessed or changed, but which is not a parameter of the function, is a free variable with regard to the function. Contrast with **Bound Variables.**

Function: In Lisp, the function is a major part of a program. Here are the basics:

- A left parenthesis indicates the beginning of a list, which can be a program under certain circumstances.
- If the first element of a list is a function, the list is a program. Otherwise, it is just a list.
- In a program, the function uses the remaining elements of the list as arguments. The arguments themselves can be atoms, lists, or other functions.
- The function uses its arguments in accordance with how the function is defined and how the arguments work. Finally, the function returns a value. A function can produce certain useful side effects.
- A right parenthesis that matches the original left parenthesis ends the program.

For example, in the program:

    (plus 2 3)

the (plus 2 3) is a list whose function is plus. The 2 and 3 are the arguments of the function. When the function is called, the values of the arguments are added and the function returns the value, 5, which is an atom. Here is the distinction. In the list (red white blue), the red, white, and blue are elements of a list. If red was previously defined to be a function, then the list is a program with white and blue as the arguments for red. The function red would return a value according to how it was defined.

Function Call or Calling a Function: In Lisp, a program can step outside itself and have a function perform tasks according to how the function is defined. This is calling a function. The called function returns a value, which can then be used by the program. For example, a program that searches through a data base to find people in a certain occupation might call a function that alphabetizes the people's names before the program prints their names.

G

Garbage Collection or Garbage Collecting: In Lisp, a process that removes unnecessary bindings, refreshes pointers, and reallocates memory. After garbage collection, reclaimed memory is available for binding variables. Some garbage collectors work in two phases. First, the garbage collector runs through memory and marks the CONS cells which have values, properties, or function definitions for atoms. Second, the garbage collector passes through memory again and notes unmarked cells. The unmarked cells are reclaimed. That is, they are returned to a free storage area in memory.

GEM: The interface for the management system used in Steamer, an expert tutorial system that teaches one how to operate a steam plant, developed by Bolt, Beranek, and Newman, Inc.

Gigabytes or G-byte: The number of bytes given by 2 raised to the 30th power. This is 1,073,741,824 bytes, or 1.073741824 billion bytes. The storage capacity of large AI systems reaches the G-byte level.

Global Variable: In Lisp, a global variable is bound at the top level so that its scope is as wide as is allowed. Global variables are bound all the time. For example, the program

```
(setq count 10)
```

binds the value of the atom **10** to the variable **count** and makes **count** a global variable. Contrast with **Local Variables.**

H

Hardware: The physical devices such as a processor, monitor, and disk drive in a computer system.

Hardware Installation: In a computer system, hardware installation is the process of connecting the computer and all peripheral devices so that all devices in the system can be used. This includes inserting interface cards, connecting cables, setting switches, and soldering cable wires to connectors. In AI systems, this process can become very complex and often requires help from an expert.

Heap: In Lisp, the heap is a segment of memory in which data structures of Lisp objects are stored. Some dialects of Lisp have a static heap and a dynamic heap. The static heap lies inside binary program space, where its contents are not subjected to garbage collection. The dynamic heap is subject to garbage collection, a process that reclaims space periodically. For example, interned symbols go into binary program space (the static heap) to keep them from being moved during garbage collection.

Heuristics and Heuristic Rules: A heuristic rule is a method for performing a task in accordance with tips, hunches, often-used strategies, or metacognitions. While heuristics (the use of heuristic rules) does not guarantee success, it usually enhances the probability of success many fold. A heuristic rule is different from a recipe, which prescribes an exact procedure. For example, people use heuristic rules when they employ apparently unrelated intuition, hunches, and strategies to solve an unfamiliar problem. Heuristics comes from the black box dimension of psychology.

I

Implementation: The process of creating a computer language, and the particular manner in which a computer language works. For example, one implementation of Lisp might use a compiler in a certain way; another implementation might not have a compiler at all.

Inference Engine: In software, especially in expert systems, a program that determines how rules and other knowledge in a knowledge base are selected and used to solve problems. See also **Rules Interpreter.**

Inference Rule: An association between antecedent conditions and consequent beliefs that enables the consequent beliefs to be deducted from antecedent conditions. The term is used with forward and backward chaining in expert systems.

Installation: The process of connecting the hardware in a computer system, and the particular hardware that makes up a computer system. For example, one installation could be a processor, keyboard, monitor, and disk drive.

Instance Variable: In object-oriented programming, an instance variable is a particular object from an object class that will be operated on according to a method determined by a flavor.

Interactive Multiprocessing Environment: A term often used in brochures that market AI products. In this context, the environment is a set of software that can be readily accessed and used; multiprocessing means the computer system can do several tasks at the same time (e.g., print graphics while a user writes a program); and interactive means the user can make entries during execution of a program which alters the manner in which the program executes.

Interface: In hardware, an interface is a card or a device that allows transfer of data between the computer and peripherals. In software, an interface is a program, often called the human interface, which employs prompts, menus, typed entries, and commands to let a person use a total software environment. A human interface often incorprates an editor or can be used with an editor. See **Environment** to get a larger picture.

InterLisp: A major dialect of Lisp that is especially suited to development of large Lisp programs of the type used in applications software. InterLisp was developed by Bolt, Beranek, and Newman in Cambridge, Massachusetts, and by Xerox at the Palo Alto Research Center in California. Compare with **MacLisp.**

Intern or Interned: In Lisp, a symbol is interned in a package when it is accessible in the package and is owned by the package or by another package from which it can be accessed. This means that, given a print name for a symbol, the Lisp reader can find the symbol in a package when it is interned, and cannot find the symbol in a package when it is uninterned. An uninterned symbol can be used, but it is not available from any package.

Interpreter: In software, a program that translates program statements in a source file into an equivalent set of machine language statements that are sent to a processor for immediate execution. The steps required to interpret a program vary among Lisp dialects.

- Usually, a person uses an editor to write a program (a form).
- Once written, the program is submitted to the Lisp reader. The reader translates the program into machine language code, which is given to a preprocessor.
- The preprocessor translates the machine code into micro code, which is submitted to the processor.
- The processor executes the program.

This is the overall procedure for executing a program that is interpreted. Contrast **Interpreter** with **Compiler.**

Invoke: The process of calling a function or executing a program. For example, invoking a program is equivalent to loading a program into memory and executing the program.

IPE: Intelligent Program Editor, an expert system that analyzes software, developed by Advanced Information and Decision Systems, Inc.

K

KEE: A tool for assembling knowledge bases for expert systems developed by Intelligentics Incorporated.

Kilobyte or K-byte: The number of bytes given by 2 raised to the 10th power. This is $2\times2\times2\times2\times2\times2\times2\times2\times2\times2$ or 1024 bytes.

Knowledge: A collection of facts, assumptions, beliefs, theories, and heuristic rules. It is difficult to AI to adequately classify all the elements of knowledge. Facts are explicit agreements like: water boils at $100°$, but you must also recall several essential assumptions (e.g., Celsius, sea level, pure water, etc.). On the other hand, heuristics are strategies for best guessing that help people solve problems.

Knowledge Acquisition: A process in which knowledge is obtained, especially from human experts.

Knowledge Base: The specific collection of knowledge used by a computer system, especially an expert system. The knowledge can be facts, assumptions, beliefs, or heuristic rules.

Knowledge-based System: See **Expert System** and **Inference Engine.**

Knowledge Engineer: A human who has expertise in building artificial intelligence systems, especially in building expert systems.

Knowledge Source: The entire set of knowledge for a defined domain, especially a subject area. There are some gray areas in the definition that include: (1) the experts who supply the knowledge; (2) the codification that makes knowledge applicable to an expert system; and (3) the degree to which knowledge is relevant to a specific problem.

L

Language: In software, a language is a set of defined words and symbols and the operations that can be performed with them. In particular, Lisp is a computer language that uses atoms, lists, and functions as the principal basis for writing programs. Contrast with **Natural Language.**

Learning: A process in which acquisition of some type of behavior results in a person's or system's being able to function better than was possible before the learning occurred. Learning occurs when, as a consequence of a learning process, a person or system can perform a task with increased competency. The competency can vary, but it usually relates to efficiency, completeness, or complexity. For example, learning how to use several additional Lisp functions, a programmer might write more efficient code.

Learning Process: A series of steps in which a person performs tasks designed to enable him or her to acquire ability to perform higher-level tasks. For example, upon reading definitions, working through examples, and discussing options for using functions, a person might acquire ability to write Lisp programs.

Lexical-free Variables: In Lisp, the value of a lexical-free variable is found in one environment, and is not found in several environments.

Lexical Scoping: In Lisp, free variables are lexically scoped when they are closed at definition time (the time a variable is used in a function). Contrast with **Dynamic Scoping.**

Lexicon: The morphemes of a language (the most fundamental linguistic parts that cannot be subdivided), or the words used within a subject area.

Libraries: In software, a collection of routines which, when loaded into memory, add features to the primary software being used. Libraries are available for most languages.

Lisp: A computer language that is often used for development of artificial intelligence software because of the ease with which it processes lists and does recursion. John McCarthy got the idea for Lisp in 1956, began implementation in 1958, and completed implementation in 1962. The first implementation was named Lisp 1.5, often called McCarthy Lisp.

Lisp Object: In general, a Lisp object is a data structure that can be any of several things: a number, vector, symbol, list, function, or macro, depending mostly on its representation in memory (its internal representation).

Lisp Printer: See **Lisp Reader.**

Lisp Program (Form): A Lisp program is a list that contains a function and can contain other functions, atoms, or lists as arguments. A form is another name for a program. For example, in the program:

(plus 2 3)

the plus is a function and the 2 and 3 are arguments that happen to be atoms. See **Function** for additional information.

Lisp Reader: In Lisp input/output, the Lisp reader is related to the Lisp printer, to objects, and to the print names of objects as follows:

- Print names are the printed representation of objects, which are data structures stored in memory. The Lisp printer accepts a Lisp object and sends the characters of its print name into a stream, which can be output (e.g., displayed on a screen).
- The Lisp reader accepts a stream of characters (a print name) as input, interprets the characters as the representation of an object, builds the object in memory, and returns the object, ostensibly so that you know the process is completed.

Lisp Symbol: A Lisp symbol is a data object that has three apparent components: (1) a property list that provides a symbol with modifiable, named components; (2) a name that is used to identify the symbol (printname); and (3) a package cell that is a data structure used to locate a symbol, given its name.

List: In Lisp, a list is a collection of elements within parentheses. The elements can be any of several things: atoms, functions, or other lists. For example, the list (car '(red white blue)) contains the function CAR, and the list, (red white blue), where red, white, and blue are atoms. The ' is shorthand for *quote,* a function that causes Lisp to treat the following atom or list as an entity. Without the quote, Lisp treats the entity as a program whose first element, red, is a function with arguments white and blue. Lisp also has a function named *list,* which accepts two lists as arguments and returns them as elements of a list.

Local Area Network(LAN): A combination of hardware and software that directs the use of resources by linked computer systems. How the computer systems are linked and how they share resources is the network. The Shared Resource Manager (SRM) is a local area network. The "local area" is a relative concept related to the allowable distance between the host and a device. The allowable distance is usually 50 to 100 meters. Almost any device can be in a network. Some local-area networks have a modem connected to the host computer system. The modem lets the host computer communicate with remote computers or with remote networks.

Local Variable: In Lisp, calling a function narrows the scope of function's variables. When the scope of a value of a variable is limited to the code that gets evaluated during a call to a function, the variable is a local variable. Otherwise, it is a global variable. Local variables have no corresponding data structures, packages, or property lists. Instead, they are placed in the execution stack during execution of a function and disappear when the function returns a value.

M

Machine Language: In software or firmware, a technical and low-level language in which code is represented as a series of grouped 1s and 0s (binary digits). Machine language is called the ''native'' language of a processor because machine language code can be executed without conversion by a processor. Programmers often use mnemonics such as JMP, BRK, and RTN to represent the groups of 1s and 0s. Programs that use these mnemonics are assembly-language programs that must be assembled (translated into machine language) before they can be executed.

MacLisp: A major dialect of Lisp that was implemented at M.I.T. Since it was implemented, MacLisp has often been used to develop fundamental computer software: kernels, compilers, tools, and such. Compare MacLisp with InterLisp, which was developed by Bolt, Beranek, and Newman in Cambridge, Massachusetts, and Xerox at the Palo Alto Research Center.

Macro: In software, a macro is generally a function which, when called, executes several related tasks without user intervention. For example, a macro function might bring up a software package, load drivers for peripheral devices, and set up a host of default conditions (e.g., load all the directories required by a certain user). In Lisp, some forms make macro calls instead of executing directly. In these cases, a macro is a function from a form to another form or forms that computes a new form, which is evaluated. That is, the original form is expanded into a new form, which is evaluated. This is consistent with the general idea of a macro, a function that executes several related tasks.

Market Philosophy: In AI, the prevailing market philosophy has three major characteristics. One, AI technology is applied to unusual problems to provide cost-effective solutions that are not available via conventional computing. Two, AI is an evolutionary, not revolutionary, technology which has a high rate of change, but which does not make existing computer systems obsolete. Three, AI methodology can be integrated with existing means of solving problems and thereby help people solve problems over a broader range of situations.

Megabyte or M-byte: The number of bytes given by 2 raised to the 20th power. One M-byte is 1,048,576 bytes, or 1.048576 million bytes. One byte is usually equivalent to one alphanumeric character. The memory of most AI systems reaches the megabyte level.

Meta: A prefix that can imply several things. It can be: (1) a key that gives other keys certain functions in editors; (2) a denotation that an affixed term has a higher meaning; or (3) a denotation that an affixed term has a different meaning.

Metacognition: People who have expertise have metacognition, a knowing about complex things without being totally aware of how or why they know something. For example, an expert in magnetics knows the concepts and principles of magnetics and also, in rather intangible ways, knows how magnetics works and how to use it.

Metaknowledge: Knowledge about knowledge. At a fundamental level, metaknowledge is knowledge about what one knows. For example, when a person is asked to recall a phone number, the person may or may not be able to recall the number, but the person always knows whether he can recall the number. Knowing the number is knowledge. Knowing whether the number is known or not known is metaknowledge, quite a different thing. Continuing in this vein, if a person cannot recall a number (knowledge) and knows this (metaknowledge), but the person knows a strategy for recalling the number, the strategy is heuristic. Knowledge, metaknowledge, and heuristics are highly related bases for development of AI systems.

Metarule: A rule that tells how rules should be used.

Method: In object-oriented programming, a method is the particular manner in which an operation is performed on an instance (an instance variable) of an object of a particular flavor. See **Flavor** and **Object** to get a related picture.

Micon: An expert system for designing single-board computers, developed at Carnegie-Mellon University.

Mouse: A hand-operated peripheral that lets a person move a displayed pointer to a desired location on a screen display and press a button. When the button is pressed, the computer performs the task implied by the location of the cursor. For example, given a menu that displays several functions, positioning the pointer on a certain function and pressing the button probably calls the designated function.

Multi-mode: A descriptor of programs that can function in different modes. For example, the NMODE editor can function in text-mode, which lets a user do word processing, or in Lisp-mode, which lets a user write, edit, debug, and interpret Lisp programs. Other modes, such as browse-mode, are available.

Multitasking: Multitasking refers to a hardware installation and an operating system configuration that lets a user perform two or more tasks at the same time.

Multiuser: In computer systems, a hardware installation and operating system configuration that lets more than one person use the resources of the system at the same apparent time.

N

Natural Language: A conventional method of communicating at a symbolic level. English is a natural language. Contrast natural language with **Language.**

Natural Language Understanding and Translation: A branch of AI in which experts develop software that lets a user interact with a computer system via spoken or written statements. Translation software converts a natural language statement into an equivalent statement in another natural language—for example, English into German.

NOAH: An expert system for planning robotics projects, developed by SRI International.

O

Objects: In AI software, an object is a fundamental but complex concept that occurs in several contexts. In one context, many people refer to atoms, lists, functions, macros, and even programs as data objects or objects that can be used in a Lisp program. In a more specific context, people refer to objects used in object-oriented programming. In this context, objects relate to methods and flavors. A particular object in a class of objects is called an instance of the object. That is, the particular objects in an object (a class) are called instance variables. It is possible to perform operations on the instance variables in an object (a class of things). A method for an operation is the instructions for an operation on instances of an object. A flavor is the specifics that constitute a method. Within a program, the objects can be hierarchial so that an object can inherit instance variables and related methods and flavors from another object. That is, an object can inherit from a super-object and can also, via methods and flavors, add to or change what gets inherited. Read the definitions for **Object, Flavor, Method, Inheritance,** and **Object-oriented Programming** in concert to get the overall concept of object-oriented programming.

Object File or Object-Code File: In software, a file produced by a compiler or an assembler which contains machine-executable statements. Contrast object file with **Source File** or **Source-code File.**

Operating System: An operating system provides an interface between the processor and the programs that perform useful tasks. Characteristic useful tasks include creating directories, saving files, creating windows, sending electronic mail, and initializing discs. The assortment of programs that run on top of an operating system includes languages, tools, applications, utilities, and libraries. UNIX and OPS5 are popular operating systems in AI.

OPS: A combination language, operating system, and software package that is suited to the development of expert systems. OPS was developed at Carnegie-Mellon University specifically for developing expert systems and was used to develop R1, one of the first successful expert systems. Several versions are available. OPS5 is popular, especially on minicomputer systems.

P

Package and Package Cell: In Lisp, a package is a data structure that determines the mapping from print names (strings) to Lisp symbols. Thus, a package is one means of ensuring that entities used by Lisp are uniquely named, thus avoiding name collisions. Only one package is active at one time during execution of a program, but it is possible to refer to symbols in other packages. A package cell, in a symbol's data structure, contains the entry that points to the package that owns the symbol.

Paradigm: A model in the general sense. In AI, a paradigm is context dependent. For example, in an expert system, a pardigm is the design of the expert system. This includes all elements of the software that constitutes the expert system: operating system, knowledge base, inference engine, strategy, user interface, and such. The paradigm is very specific, including, for example, the format for stating rules in the knowledge base and the rationale for using, discarding, or updating a rule.

Parallel Processing: In hardware and microcode firmware, the partitioning of a complex computation into related subcomputations and having two or more processors simultaneously perform the subcomputations so that an overall solution can be produced.

Parameter: In a computer language, a parameter is a variable or constant that appears in an expression or a function to restrict the specific form of the expression or function. In Lisp, the parameters of functions are highly related to concepts such as scoping and binding.

Personal Development System: In AI, a personal development system is a small, "stand-alone" computer system in relation to mainframe systems or networked work-station systems. A personal development system usually has about 1 M-bytes of memory, up to 20 M-bytes of mass storage, a mouse, a keyboard, a monitor, and a limited software environment (mostly a dialect of Lisp and related tools). Most people use a personal system to write specialized AI software, often small turnkey applications. Within a complete AI facility, a personal development system is ideal for prototyping a substantial AI system, especially during the edit, interpret, and debug cycles.

Pointer: In software, a number that indicates the location in memory of an object. For example, in the first CONS cell for a list, the car of the cell is a pointer to the first object in the list, and the cdr of the cell is a pointer to the second object in the list.

Portable Standard Lisp (PSL): A dialect of Lisp developed at the University of Utah.

Print Name: In relation to Lisp symbols, a print name is the literal string name of the symbol.

Program Execution: In general, program execution causes a computer system to perform tasks. In Lisp, a program is a list whose initial element is a function and subsequent elements are arguments. Thus, program execution in Lisp is equivalent to calling a function. When Lisp programs are interpreted, both data and functions have the same structure. Thus, a program can produce a function as a data structure, submit the structure to the interpreter's reader and preprocessor, and then automatically execute the resulting code. It is these aspects of program execution that make Lisp an ideal language for AI because they provide recursion and extensibility within a programming environment.

Program File: In software, a file that is a program, as opposed to being just data. The program is written in some computer language. Thus, the file contains computer language statements which themselves consist of key words, commands, variables, functions, or operations. Contrast program file with **Data File.**

Programming Environment: A reference to a computer system (hardware, firmware, and software) that is specifically designed to help a person write programs. Characteristic software in a programming environment includes an operating system, a language, an editor, an interpreter, a compiler, and a debugger. Contrast a programming environment with a development environment.

Prolog: In software, Prolog is a specialized language that provides certain logic programming features. The programming features emulate many of the procedures used in predicate calculus. Prolog is suited to theorem proving. Experts debate whether Prolog is better than Lisp for creating software for AI. At present, Prolog is widely used in Japan and European countries and Lisp is widely used in the United States. In particular, the fifth-generation computers being developed in Japan use Prolog. A. Colmerauer and P. Proussel developed Prolog in 1973 at the University of Marseille AI Laboratory. Later, AI experts at the University of Edinburgh in Great Britain added several logic programming features.

Property: In Lisp, an entry in a property list. Collectively, properties describe an object. A property can be a name, a definition, or a value of an object. A property can even be a significance of an object. See **Property List.**

Property List: In Lisp, a property list is associated with every Lisp symbol. A property list has zero or more entries, depending on the Lisp symbol and when it is used. See **Property.**

Prototyping: A process in the development of software in which a simple version of the software is written and tested. Bugs are removed and the testing process continues until it can be determined whether the software is feasible. When the software is feasible, the prototype is expanded so that it has an adequate interface and performs according to specifications.

PSI: An expert system that converts English language specifications into simple programs, developed by the Kestrel Institute.

PSL: See **Portable Standard Lisp.**

PSN: A procedural semantic network for a knowledge base using classes, objects, and relations, developed by the University of Toronto.

R

Read-eval-print Loop: In Lisp, the EVAL function, when called, effects a read-eval-print loop in which a form is given to an interpreter (the read part), the form is evaluated (the eval part), and a value is returned (the print part). The returned value is usually displayed. In some cases, evaluation of a form produces what are called side effects, actions taken by the system which are unrelated to the returned value.

Recursion: In software, a powerful concept in which an expression of some type is applied to itself to determine particular elements generated by the expression. In some recursions, some initial elements are assumed. Then an expression is applied to the assumed elements to obtain the next element. For example, in the Fibonacci sequence, the first two elements are 1, 1. The immediate successor, 2, is given by $1+1$. In general, succeeding elements, N, are given by $(N\text{-}1)+(N\text{-}2)$, so the sequence is $1,1,2,3,5,8,13, \ldots$ Most recursion requires specification of or accounting for an initial element or elements, whereupon succeeding elements are obtained by applying an expression to obtained elements. The factorial sequence is the classic example used by experts in AI.

REX: Regression expert, a frame-based expert system that does statistical analysis, developed by Bell Laboratories.

Robotics: A branch of AI in which engineers develop machines that perform physical tasks which were traditionally performed by humans. The machines, called robots, work in assembly lines, with complex weapons, and in hostile environments. In general, robots replace human workers when a task is repetitive, requires extraordinary strength, or requires precise, complex manipulation.

Rule: The means of associating elements of a pair in which one element contains an antecedent condition or conditions, and the other element contains a consequent proposition or propositions, within a deductive processes such as forward or backward chaining. A set of rules is a part of the knowledge base for an expert system.

Rule-based Program: Computer software that uses rules as its means of functioning.

Rule Interpreter: In software, especially in expert systems, a program that determines how rules in a knowledge base are applied to problem solving. The strategy, which determines how the rules are applied, determines the details concerning how rules are implemented. Forward chaining, backward chaining, and means-end strategies are popular.

S

Schema: An outline or diagrammatic representation of something, usually presented in a manner that shapes a person's thinking. In particular, a schema can be a mental construct that causes a person to view something in a certain way. In humans, schemas influence knowledge, metaknowledge, values, biases, ethics, and morals.

Scope or Scoping: In a program, scope refers to the extent to which a variable is bound (defined). For example, local variables are bound only within the code that gets executed during a function call. Global variables are bound in a larger context.

Semantics: A term related to the meaning, intention, or significance of a symbolic expression (statement). Contrast semantics with **Syntax,** an examination of the form of the expression, and with **Lexicon,** the set of terms used within a subject area or the morphemes of a language.

S-expression: In Lisp, an S-expression is a list; a list is an S-expression. They are fundamentally the same thing. S-expression is short for symbolic expression. An S-expression begins with a left parenthesis; contains functions, atoms, or sublists; and ends with a balancing right parenthesis. Spaces act as delimiters to separate atoms or sublists. Here are examples:

- (), the null list whose sybolic name is NIL and whose value is 0.
- (nancy sue janie), a list that contains atoms.

- (car (cdr '(a b c d))), a list that contains a function, car, acting on a sublist that contains a function, cdr, and another sublist, (a b c d). The ' is shorthand for the quote function. Spaces separate the atoms A, B, C, and D in the sublist.

Shell: In software, particularly UNIX, a program that runs on top of an operating system which helps a person use the operating system and provides an interface to higher-level programs such as tools and applications. UNIX operating systems have a Bourne-shell, a C-shell, or both.

Side Effect: In Lisp, called functions return a value. In some cases a function can also produce another action. For example, besides returning a value, a function might print a message on a terminal screen or change the value of a global variable. Depending on a programmer's intentions, the side effects of some functions can be more useful than the values they return.

Slot: See **Property** and **Property List.**

Smalltalk: A language and an environment for graphics and object-oriented programming, developed at Xerox PARC (Palo Alto Research Center).

Software: In a computer system, software is the programs that operate the hardware and, consequently, enable the system to perform useful computing tasks. It is usually assumed that software, in contrast to firmware, is stored on magnetic media such as a flexible disk, a hard disk, or a tape so it can be easily entered into a computer's random-access memory (RAM) and altered or executed. Major software categories include: microcode, drivers, operating systems, shells, languages, utilities, tools, and applications. The categories are not mutually exclusive.

Software Configuration: In a computer system, a software configuration is the exact manner in which generic software purchased from a vendor is set up so it runs properly on a hardware installation. During configuration, a person sets the code references to external devices, creates volumes in mass storage for subsequent storage of programs and data, specifies default conditions (e.g., inverse video prompts; blinking, boxlike cursor), and otherwise enables the software to function on a particular hardware installation. At a simple level, for example, a Lisp editor might be configured so it has two windows, does pretty printing, and sends program listings to a remote laser printer. In AI systems, the configuration process can be very complex and can require expert assistance.

Source File or Source-code File: In software, a file that contains a program. Contrast source file with **Object file.**

Specialist: A person who is an expert in a very narrow subject domain.

SRL: Scheme representation language, a program used for knowledge description, developed at Carnegie-Mellon University.

Standard Lisp: A dialect of Lisp in its own right, distinct from Common Lisp.

Swapping: A feature related to virtual memory. When a program is executing and when the processor attempts to execute a missing segment of code, virtual segments that are in memory but are not required are swapped for required virtual segments. The unnecessary segments are copied to files on the virtual memory device (usually a hard disk) and necessary segments are loaded into memory. The swapping takes time and slows down execution of a program, but it lets a very large program run in a moderate amount of memory.

Symbol: The name of a Lisp object. For example, an atom such as Joe B. Brown is a Lisp object, and Joe B. Brown is the symbol for the atom.

Syntax: The form or structure of a symbolic expression (statement). See also **Semantics** and **Lexicon.**

T

32-bit System: A reference to a computer system that has a processor which has 32-bit registers, a register being a distinct 32-bit sequence of locations that store electrical states (high or low), represented by 1s or 0s. Collectively, the contents of the registers are used to operate a computer.

Text Editor: In software, a tool or utility program that lets one write memos, reports, and assorted documents. In particular, a text editor is used to write source code for programs. In AI, EMACS-type editors are popular.

Time-shared Computer System: A multitasking and multiuser computer system whose resources can be accessed via remote terminals. Contrast this type of computer system with networked systems and personal development systems. The advantage of a time-shared system is that many users who have limited resources can use the many resources provided by a large computer system. The disadvantage is that the wait times between access times can interrupt work.

Tool Kit: In an environment, a set of programs used to create applications software. The exact nature of the programs varies from one system to another.

Tools: In software, tools are a collection of computer programs that, together with operating system and languages, help programmers develop other software, usually applications software. Editors, compilers, debuggers, linkers, and assemblers are tools software. Some people argue that tools programs are utility programs and that true tools are higher-level programs which help a programmer create applications programs. An example of the higher-level type is a program that accepts knowledge and rules and then writes an expert system program. To add to the confusion, some people claim that this latter type of program does automatic programming in the context that it provides an automatic programming tool.

Transparency: In expert systems, a term that generally means ''trust me.'' The basis for the term is complex, but it has these attributes: Human experts solve complex problems. People do not know if the experts are correct, but people generally trust the experts' judgment. People do not inherently trust machines, especially computer systems. For AI to work, people must trust the computer; that is, people must believe the computer provides correct solutions, solutions at least as good as those provided by human experts. This implies that an expert system must have transparency.

Turnkey System: In software, a program that boots itself and comes up in a format that lets a person perform tasks that enhance job performance in a particular area. Knowledge of programming is not required to use turnkey systems. For example, an engineer who designs parts might use a turnkey computer-aided-design system to speed up the rate at which parts can be designed and tested. Contrast a turnkey system with software such as a language which, within some limits, lets a person write any imaginable program. Applications programs are usually turnkey systems.

Type Declaration: In computer languages, type declaration is the assignment of identifiers to data constructs such as integers, real numbers, arrays, and strings. Lisp is a weakly typed language in which functions recognize the data objects used for arguments.

U

UNIX: In software, an operating system originally developed at Bell Laboratories. Over the years, many versions of UNIX have been developed. Today, UNIX is a collection of many programs (files) that provide commands, editors, file managers, formatters, and programming languages (e.g., C, Pascal, and FORTRAN). A kernel, which is the heart of any version of the UNIX operating system, handles fundamental operations. A shell surrounds the kernel to provide simplified access to UNIX capabilities. UNIX is a trademark of Bell Laboratories.

Utilities: In software, a collection of programs that perform useful but mundane tasks, such as backing up files, initializing disks, and changing the format of a file. For example, a person who transfers files between two different computer systems would probably use a utility program. As another example, most systems have a utility program that translates one type of file into another type.

V

Value Cell: In relation to a Lisp symbol, a value cell contains the value that is bound to the symbol.

Variable: In a program, a variable is a symbol that can assume a value during execution within the scope of the variable. For example, a variable, X, treated as an integer, can assume any of the values . . . , -2, -1, 0, 1, 2, . . .

Variable Binding: In Lisp, a variable is bound when a value for the variable is placed in the property list of the atom that represents the variable.

Virtual Addressing or Virtual Address Space: A reference to the maximum number of distinct locations (addresses) in the memory of a computer that can contain a distinct set of information. Beyond this number of locations, an address space must be partitioned (divided) into blocks, and the information in one space must be mapped onto a space in another device before more information can be placed in the space, or the information in the entire space must be mapped to another space before more information can be added to the space. See **Absolute Address Space** and **Virtual Memory** to get a more complete picture.

Virtual Memory: A complex feature of some computer systems in which the processor is able to use the computer's memory *and* mass storage to store an executing program. This is an extremely important feature in AI systems because programs are often too large to fit into main memory. With virtual memory, part of a program can be executed and, as required, the processor can obtain additional, necessary parts of a program from mass storage. Virtual memory works in concert with swapping and partitioning. Thus, the overall concept is that the computer's "virtual address space," is greater than the processor's "absolute address space." In AI, a system might have an absolute address space of 4 M-bytes and a virtual address space to 20 M-bytes or more.

VLSI design: A branch of AI in which engineers design very large scale integration computer chips. VLSI technology is a part of fourth-generation computing that has elements of fifth-generation technology.

W

Window: In relation to the software that operates a monitor or terminal, a window is a contiguous area for display of information, prompts, menus, and such. A window can be the same size as a screen. Thus, a screen might appear to have just one window. A window can be smaller than a screen; then several windows can be displayed. These windows often overlap and some procedure is used to pop a window to the surface. A window can be larger than a screen, thus displaying a portion of the window. One hears about pop up windows, scrollable windows, expandable windows, and such.

Word: In software, a contiguous set of bits, larger than a byte. Thirty-two bit processors use 32-bit words. A particular word might contain a pointer, two bytes, and a flag.

Z

ZetaLisp: A dialect of Lisp used by many people in the so called ''Eastern Lisp Community.'' ZetaLisp is a very large dialect of Lisp. More than 9000 compiled functions are available.

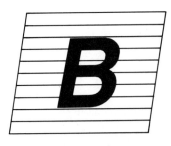

EXISTING EXPERT SYSTEMS

ORIENTATION

This appendix lists existing expert systems. It is not exhaustive; it is representative. A reference accompanies each item. To learn about a system, read the reference and then investigate at your discretion.

INTERNIST (Medicine)   INTERNIST uses information from 4000 internal medicine situations to diagnose problems related to 500 possible disease types. INTERNIST uses a taxonomy of disease types, together with rules, to link manifestations of a disease and provide explanations. INTERNIST was developed at the University of Pittsburgh by Pople and Myers.

POPLKE, H. E., JR., ET AL.   *DIALOG: A Model of Diagnostic Logic for Internal Medicine,* Proceedings of the Fourth International Joint Conference on Artificial Intelligence, September 1975, 848–855.

MACSYMA (Mathematics)   Development of MACSYMA began at M.I.T. in 1969. Now it represents more than 100 worker-years of programming effort and contains more than 300,000 lines of Lisp code. MACSYMA solves mathematical problems, especially problems such as integration and simultaneous solution of systems of equations that require excessive algebraic manipulation.
Many people at M.I.T. and external users have contributed libraries. Although the

program represents 100 worker-years of labor, MACSYMA is cost-effective because it is used daily in the United States, Canada, and Europe.

MYCIN (Medicine) MYCIN diagnoses bacterial infections and provides recommended antibiotic therapy. The program systematically applies rules that link patient data to infection hypotheses. MYCIN was developed at Stanford University by Shortliffe and several colleagues.

SHORTLIFFE, E. H. *Computer Based Medical Consultations: MYCIN.* New York: Elsevier, 1976.

GUIDON (Medicine) GUIDON uses the knowledge base for MYCIN about meningitis and bacteremia to teach facts and problem-solving strategies related to pulmonary function analysis.

CLANCEY, W. J., ET AL. *Intelligent Computer-Aided Instruction for Medical Diagnosis,* Proceedings of the 3rd Symposium on Computer Applications in Medical Care, 1979, 175–183.

PROSPECTOR (Geology) PROSPECTOR was developed for the U. S. Geological Survey and the National Science Foundation for mineral exploration by Duda and Gasching.

DUDA, R. O., ET AL. "Model Design in the Prospector Consultant System for Mineral Exploration." In *Expert Systems in the Microelectronic Age,* edited by D. Michie, 153–167. Edinburgh: Edinburgh University Press, 1982.

DENDRAL (Chemistry) DENDRAL generates structural representations of organic molecules from mass-spectrogram data, nuclear-magnetic-resonance data, and additional constraints supplied by the user. It is one of the first expert systems, dating back to 1965.

FEIGENBAUM, E. A., ET AL. *On Generality and Problem Solving: A Case Study Using the DENDRAL Program.* Machine Intelligence 6, edited by B. Meltzer and D. Mitchie, 165–190. New York: American Elsevier, 1971.

EL (Circuit analysis) EL performs steady-state analysis of resistor-diode-transistor circuits. It uses production rules to represent general electronic principles such as Ohm's Law. The assertions are facts about the circuit. The rule interpreter uses an antecedent reasoning system.

STALLMAN, R. M., AND G. J. SUSSMAN. "Forward Reasoning and Dependency-Directed Backtracking in a System for Computer Aided Circuit Analysis," *Artificial Intelligence* 9, 1977, 135–196.

AGE   AGE is an expert system used for building expert systems. It allows you to implement a broad spectrum of knowledge-based systems. AGE lets you develop forward- or backward-chaining systems.

Nii, H. P., and E. A. Feigenbaum. "Rule-Based Understanding of Signals." In *Pattern Directed Inference Systems*, edited by D. A. Waterman and F. Hayes-Roth, 483–501. New York: Academic Press, 1978.

You can read any of these articles to get a good idea about what an expert system is and how one works.

The list of expert systems is growing rapidly. You may, in reading books and articles, hear about these systems: MOLGEN (genetics), MECHO (mechanics), PECOS (programming), R1 (configuring computers), HASP (SU/X) (configuring computers), SOPHIE (electronics), TERESIAS (analysis), EMYCIN (analysis), and ROSIE (system building). This list is suggestive, it is not exhaustive. At the time we wrote this appendix, many new systems were appearing in the AI market.

The articles that describe expert systems are long, usually 20 pages or more. The titles suggest heavy content and technical reading. Do not be put off by this. Just be aware that you might need to climb a steep learning curve to understand expert systems, then take the plunge.

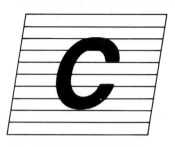

AI TRAINING AND INFORMATION

ORIENTATION

This appendix describes available training and information. If you are interested in AI, Lisp, or expert systems, and want to move up the learning curve, do these types of things:

- Determine the status of your situation in AI. Look for the who, how, what, where, and when in AI. By doing this, you identify and accommodate your place in the AI scene. For example, if you, as a vice-president, purchased an expert system and hired people to run the system, perhaps they need advanced training. On the other hand, if you, as a vice-president, decide which AI system to purchase, perhaps *you* need introductory training.
- Determine your current level of expertise in AI. For example, if you, as a knowledge expert, wish to attend a conference, ask the AAAI for information about the next conference. On the other hand, if you, as a student, wish to take some classes, read the section on training.

Focus on the nature of the training and information as you read this appendix. Much information suggests types of opportunities, but the actual information may not be current as you read this. For example, Claudia Mazzetti was the source of information for the AAAI as we wrote this appendix. She may not be the source now, but the address will likely be the same.

TRAINING

Training is available in several forms: formal courses, workshops, and tutorials. Select a form suited to the way you learn best:

- **Formal courses:** Several universities offer courses on Lisp and AI. M.I.T., Stanford, and Carnegie-Mellon have been the leaders in this area, but others are joining in: University of Texas, University of California, University of Pittsburgh, Rutgers University, Yale University, University of Maryland, University of Utah. Write to the registrar of a university you can attend and ask for information.

- **Workshops:** These are available from several sources: universities, organizations such as AAAI, corporations, and private businesses. Your problem is to learn where and when they are held. For example, "Commonsense Summer," was a summer-long workshop sponsored by the Center for the Study of Language and Information at Stanford University and by SRI International. The workshop focused on problems related to the consensus that intelligent behavior requires use of knowledge from the commonsense world. The workshop was suited to people who do research in knowledge representation, natural language, and vision. Workshops such as this are often sponsored by groups who focus on AI. Information about workshops is published in AI magazines, among other sources.

- **Tutorials:** These are available in many formats. For example, the AAAI provides tutorial sessions at each annual conference. Increasingly, hard-copy, on-line, and interactive tutorials are provided with an AI system. You can work through the tutorial material in one to five hours, in most cases. Firms that focus on instruction services provide custom tutorials for people, companies, or agencies under contract.

- **The EFDPMA:** The Education Foundation of the Data Processing Management Association offers courses on artificial intelligence and a course on fifth-generation languages. Write to: EFDPMA Conferences, P.O. Box 3608, Torrance, CA 90510.

Formal courses provide advanced training at the expense of rigid entrance requirements, high level prerequisites, and heavy course requirements, but you can effect quantum advances in knowledge and skill. Tutorials provide an easy, low-pressure environment in which you can experiment and proceed at your pace, but you may not acquire in-depth knowledge. Workshops are a mixed bag. They are beneficial when the content, the presenter's methods, and your inclinations merge into a happening. Otherwise, workshops are seldom helpful.

AI REFERENCES

References to AI materials and information are more readily available than in the past. Here are some sources of information that, collectively, can lead you to much information:

- *The Artificial Intelligence Report* is published monthly by Artificial Intelligence Publications, 95 First Street, Los Altos, CA 94022, Louis G. Robinson, Editor. This reference reports current, interesting developments within the AI community.
- *The AI Magazine* is published quarterly by the AAAI, 445 Burgess Drive, Menlo Park, CA 94025, 1 (415) 328-3123. Articles describe topics in AI, news, and conferences. Assorted reports about research, books, and new technology are included.
- *Artificial Intelligence* magazine is published by Elsevier Science Publishers B.V. (North-Holland), P.O. Box 1991, 1000 BZ Amsterdam, The Netherlands. The magazine is published in several languages for an international audience. Most recognized experts write for this magazine. The content is varied; the reading can be very heavy.
- *New Generation Computing* magazine is published in Japan by Ohmsha, Ltd., and is distributed in the United States by Springer-Verlag New York, Inc., Service Center Secaucus, 44 Hartz Way, Secaucus, NJ 07094. Articles describe the new fifth-generation topics. Some articles are general; others are very heavy.
- The University of Miami's Intelligent Computer Systems Research Institute publishes *The Applied Artificial Intelligence Reporter*. Write to: ICS Research Institute, P.O. Box 1308-EP, Fort Lee, NJ 07024.

CONFERENCES

Several organizations, universities, and corporations hold annual, regional, or topical conferences. Information about conferences is disseminated by word of mouth, brochures, flyers, journals, and magazines.

The American Association for Artificial Intelligence (AAAI) holds an annual conference that is a good source of information about the whole spectrum of AI. Details about the current annual conference appear in *AI Magazine*. Send inquiries to:

Claudia Mazzetti
American Association for Artificial Intelligence
445 Burgess Drive
Menlo Park, CA 94025

The International Joint Conferences on Artificial Intelligence (IJCAI) holds assorted conferences which are a forum for presentation of artificial intelligence research to an international audience. In particular, the IJCAI elicits long (5500 words) and short (2200 words) papers, which are included in the conference proceedings.

The following topics are emphasized in IJCAI conferences:

- **AI Architectures and Languages:** This topic deals with the hardware and software used in AI systems.

- **AI and Education:** This topic focuses on intelligent computer-aided instruction (CAI), but other connections between AI and education are examined (e.g., in what areas of education can AI best be used?)

- **Automated Reasoning:** This topic includes theorem proving, automatic programming, planning, search, problem solving, common sense, and qualitative reasoning.

- **Cognitive Modeling:** This topic is complex, and not currently well understood, but it focuses on understanding how the human mind works and creating AI models that emulate human mental capacities. For example, it is known that humans learn from experience. Having solved a problem once, humans use more effective methods the next time they solve a similar problem. AI systems should model this capacity.

- **Expert Systems:** This topic deals with the myriad ways computer systems are used to apply knowledge to the solution of problems.

- **Knowledge Representation:** Knowledge is used to solve problems, but few people are sure about the best ways to represent knowledge. This topic deals with the development of better schemes for making knowledge available for use in expert systems. At present, many systems use ''if . . . then'' statements to represent knowledge, but more powerful representations are being developed. The ''if . . . then'' statements are often called *situation . . . action* rules.

- **Learning and Knowledge Acquisition:** This topic focuses on heuristics and other dimensions of how humans behave so as to acquire knowledge.

- **Logic Programming:** Logic programming is an area within computer science that focuses, broadly, on programming as the assertion of declarative sentences and computation as the deduction of certain of their consequences. The general concept includes functional programming, for which the bases are the lambda calculus and combinatory logic. The purpose of logic programming is to help programmers plan efficient, logical computations. Computation in this sense is not limited to numbers and the traditional operations. For more detailed information, examine articles found in *The Journal of Logic Programming,* published quarterly by Elsevier Science Publishing, Inc., 52 Vanderbilt Ave., New York, NY 10017.

- **Natural Language:** This topic focuses on how humans use language and how those uses can be incorporated into AI. For example, one aspect of this is creating computer systems that act on any command a user issues (e.g., search through the Jones files), as opposed to current systems which act only on those commands they know (e.g., Edit <ENTER>/users/Jones.text).

- **Perception:** This topic examines visual, auditory, and tactile perception. For example, some people create AI systems that recognize spoken commands and act accordingly.

- **Philosophical Foundations:** This topic deals with philosophical bases for using AI systems.

- **Robotics:** This topic deals with the use of machines to perform tasks typically and traditionally performed by humans. For detailed information, examine articles in

The Journal of Robotic Systems, published quarterly by John Wiley & Sons, 605 Third Ave., New York, NY 10158.

- **Social, Economic, and Legal Implications:** This topic deals with the broad range of problems associated with the use of AI. At present, little has been done, but the future looks intriguing.

Most activity that occurs under the umbrella of AI falls into one or more of these categories.

ORGANIZATIONS, GROUPS, AND AGENCIES

The number of organizations, groups, and agencies connected with AI is increasing. Again, our list is representative, not exhaustive. Examine the list and contact appropriate entities, but be sure to use the list for extrapolation.

- **American Association for Artificial Intelligence:** The AAAI was founded in 1980 and now has over 6000 members. The AAAI sponsors an annual conference, publishes *The AI Magazine* and otherwise promotes AI. See the Conferences section for the address.
- **The Association for Computing Machinery:** The ACM has varied interests, one of which was to sponsor a conference in 1984 that focused on Lisp, the language of AI. The address is:

ACM
21 Congress Street
Salem, MA 01970

- **Bell Laboratories:** Bell Laboratories does not have just one single office or location. Several labs are scattered throughout the country. The collective Bell Labs do research in many areas. They recently became interested in AI and plan to develop a variety of products. In most cases, Bell Labs contribute to an area indirectly by releasing their developments to universities and industry.
- **Bolt Beranek and Newman, Inc.:** The BNN company illustrates another recent phenomenon in which a company is formed near a source of information and talent provided by prominent university research and cirricula. Based in Cambridge, Massachusetts, BNN capitalized on the resources for AI provided by M.I.T. Since 1965, BNN has developed several important AI products, including MENTOR, a language for Socratic CAI programs; BBN Lisp, later renamed Interlisp; Tenex (tm), the first demand-page operating system developed to support AI research; and several expert systems (SOPHIE, STEAMER, and KL-TWO). The address is:

Bolt Beranek and Newman, Inc.
10 Moulton Street

Cambridge, MA 02238
1 (617) 491-1850

- **Carnegie Group, Inc.:** The Carnegie Group illustrates a recent phenomenon in which university professors, who are prominent in AI, form corporations for the purpose of developing and marketing interactive knowledge-based systems and software tools. In most cases, they create components systems, as contrasted with turnkey systems, that use what are called *tools kits*. A tools kit consists of the usual programs: editors, compilers, debuggers, processors, translators, and so on. The address is:

Carnegie Group Inc.
Commerce Court at Station Square
Pittsburg, PA 15219
1 (412) 642-6900

- **Xerox Palo Alto Research Center:** PARC, as the Xerox research center is known, was founded in 1970 and illustrates an old phenomenon, supporting a think-tank environment in which superintellects examine problems in relatively free surroundings, applied to a new area. There are several think-tank centers around the country. The address is:

PARC
Stanford University Industrial Park
Palo Alto, CA 94301

- **TEKNOWLEDGE, Inc.:** TEKNOWLEDGE illustrates yet another recent phenonenon, in which a company is formed to focus on a particular dimension of AI—software, in this case. TEKNOWLEDGE wants to become known as the IBM of AI software. Started in 1981, the company creates custom expert systems for major corporations on a contract basis. Today the company has become more product-oriented, but continues to focus on expert system software, in contract to focusing on fundamental tools kits. The address is:

TEKNOWLEDGE
525 University Avenue
Palo Alto, CA 94301

- **The University of Texas Artificial Intelligence Center:** Here is yet another recent phenomenon, the U.S. Army Research Office funding a project designed to create an AI research facility in a world-class university not previously noted for AI research. The UT center was funded to the tune of $6.5 million. It is on the main campus in Austin, Texas.

The reader must understand that our list is representative. Many other entities do quality work in the AI field in many areas. Let our list suggest the types of work being done; conduct your own investigation—the list is growing rapidly. Basically, they are housed in corporations, universities, the military complex, and privately funded projects.

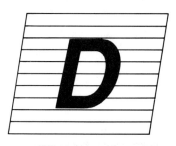

PRINCIPLE INFLUENCES
OF AI

AI began in the universities. Except for a few think-tank agencies, AI has been in the universities for its first 25 years. Now it is leaking out into the public.

It is presumptuous on our part to single out a few universities as contributing the most to the development of AI, but we need to mention some of the more prominent unversities to give you an overall picture of where AI was developed. Here are the universities that contributed much to the development of Lisp, AI, and applications of AI.

The big three universities are the Massachusetts Institute of Technology (M.I.T.), Stanford University, and Carnegie-Mellon University. These three universities did far more work in the AI field than others. Most of the experts you read or hear about came from these universities, worked at these universities, or had strong ties with them.

Many other major universities supported small AI projects or employed a professor who was interested in AI. As examples, the University of Utah developed Portable Standard Lisp. The University of Pittsburg developed some expert systems for diagnosis of medical problems. The University of Maryland researches the use of AI in small land vehicles. The University of Texas at Austin researches vision and motion. More universities are getting involved. We did not cite them because to cite one is to probably miss several.

The Pentagon contributed to AI research over the years. They used a dichotomized approach: development of weapons-control mechanisms and funding of university research projects.

Abroad, several universities contributed to AI. The University of Edingburgh often made significant contributions.

The primary development of Lisp, AI, and applications in AI occurred from 1958 to

1984. Then the mix of available developments, technology, and world conditions reached a point where AI was extended beyond the universities and think tanks into the industrial, military, and educational complex.

At present, the effects of this extension are not known, but speculation suggests these outcomes:

- More universities added AI programs to their cirruculum. The same universities will add AI centers and laboratories that will conduct research. For example, the University of Texas obtained a grant of several million dollars to add an AI center. Hopefully, these universities will create a stream of much-needed knowledge engineers.
- Several corporations formed a consortium designed to develop AI across a broad spectrum and disseminate information among members of the consortium.
- Many original AI experts, as they reach their fifties, sixties, and seventies, guided formulation of assorted groups that promote AI, sponsor AI classes and workshops, and conduct research. For example, several people from Carnegie-Mellon University formed the Carnegie Group.
- Xerox established a users group for people who purchased Xerox AI systems. Get information from your Xerox sales rep or call Dennis Dunn (1(818)315-2351). Monthly reports of activity are available in *The AI Dispatch,* published by Xerox, 250 North Halstead Street, P. O. Box 7018, Pasadena, CA 91109.
- The Xerox Palo Alto Research Center, known as PARC, hired Dr. John Seely Brown, a principle developer of expert systems, to guide their renewed emphasis on AI systems.

INDEX

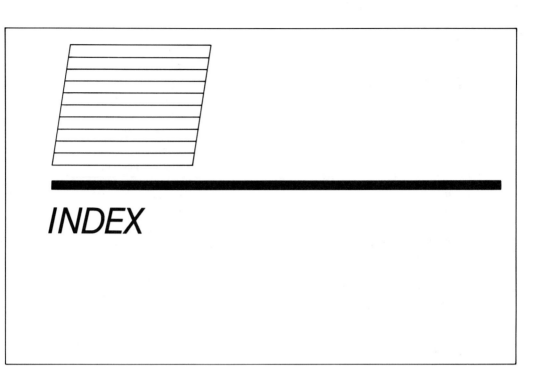

INDEX